A New Progressive Agenda
for Public Health
and the Environment

A New Progressive Agenda for Public Health and the Environment

*A Project of the Center
for Progressive Regulation*

August 2004

Edited by

Christopher H. Schroeder and Rena Steinzor

Carolina Academic Press
Durham, North Carolina

ISBN 1-59460-082-1
LCCN 2004114374

Carolina Academic Press
700 Kent Street
Durham, North Carolina 27701
Telephone (919) 489-7486
Fax (919) 493-5668
www.cap-press.com
Email: cap@cap-press.com

Printed in the United States of America
cover photo© photos.com

CONTENTS

PREFACE

This book represents the collective effort of many scholars associated with the Center for Progressive Regulation (CPR). It is fair to say that the perceived need in the progressive community for books like this one is the primary reason for CPR's existence. CPR is an organization of scholars established in 2002 to provoke public debate on how the government's authority and resources may best be used to advance the multiple social values that motivated the enactment of our nation's environmental, health, and safety laws. At the heart of CPR's mission are the dual convictions that an informed populace is essential to an effective and humane government and that government performs legitimate and essential functions when it serves as a forum for debate and action on social values. Government must act wisely, responsibly, and effectively, but it ought not to abandon these essential functions.

Like most collective efforts, this project required leaders who were willing to devote an added measure of time and effort to ensure that the resulting product flowed together as a coherent whole. CPR Board members Christopher Schroeder and Rena Steinzor, and CPR media consultant Matthew Freeman served as the primary editors for the project. They relied throughout the process on the research and editorial assistance of CPR's accomplished senior policy analyst Joanna Goger. Theresa Walker copy-edited the manuscript ably.

The work began with an exceedingly productive gathering of CPR scholars at Duke University in May 2003 under Chris Schroeder's able leadership. It continued throughout the following summer as individual scholars took responsibility for drafting chapters or parts of chapters for the book. The products of these individual efforts were collectively reviewed and debated at a gathering of the authors at Georgetown University in October 2003. Chris assembled the revisions that resulted from this meeting into a thematic whole, and Rena Steinzor edited the entire manuscript for coherence and consistency. In the meantime, Joanna Goger devoted many long hours to preparing the examples in the text boxes and refining the citations and references. Matthew Freeman provided the icing on the cake by making the manuscript more accessible to audiences who are not as steeped in the technical vernacular as the scholars.

In addition to Chris, Rena, Matthew and Joanna, I would like to thank the following CPR scholars who provided the essential analysis and ideas expressed in this book. Primary authors included Alyson Craig Flournoy, Robert L. Glicksman, Donald Thomas Hornstein, Douglas A. Kysar, Lisa Heinzerling, Thomas O. McGarity, Clifford Rechtschaffen, Sidney A. Shapiro, Robert R.M. Verchick, and David A. Wirth. Other contributing authors included Frank Ackerman, David M. Driesen, Sheila Foster, and Wendy E. Wagner. Introductions to all of the scholars are available on the CPR website at http//www.progressiveregulation.org.

Because this book is a collective effort, it goes without saying that every CPR scholar may not agree with every aspect of the analysis presented here, and not every scholar necessarily supports every prescription offered here. The book does represent a consensus of the CPR leadership, and it forms an essential foundation for future CPR efforts to bring progressive approaches to environmental, health, and safety regulation to the attention of policymakers and the public.

Finally, this book would not have been possible without the generous financial support of the Deer Creek Foundation, which took the initial leap of faith needed to bring CPR into existence and has provided continuing support to all of CPR's educational efforts. The Howard and Anne Gottlieb Foundation provided additional support for the publication of this book and the promotion of the progressive agenda contained therein. In these troubled times, it is institutions like the Deer Creek and Gottlieb foundations that in tangible ways project the optimism that is the essence of the progressive vision.

Thomas O. McGarity
President
Center for Progressive Regulation

A New Progressive Agenda for Public Health and the Environment

Chapter 1

Introduction

Three decades ago, Americans turned serious attention to preventing the harm that human enterprise does to our natural environment. The first problems we attacked were the most obvious ones: rivers and streams laden with pollution, grit in the air, and dump sites flooding basements with foul-smelling chemicals. We conquered many of these initial challenges only to confront a new set of more difficult problems.

The warning signs are in plain evidence: an epidemic of asthma among children, unacceptably high levels of mercury in the blood of women of childbearing age, lead in household water supplies, outbreaks of cryptosporidium and other pathogens in drinking water, lingering hazards from organic pesticides, and smog in all our major cities. Despite dramatic improvements in emissions controls, the government tells parents to keep their children inside on "Code Red" air pollution days, scientists tell us the planet is warming at an alarming rate, and runoff from hog farms and parking lots kills millions of fish.

These trends are no accident. Indeed, in the pursuit of a corporate-friendly business environment, the Bush Administration is working to reverse the steady march of environmental progress that has been made in the past few decades. It has opened wilderness lands to oil drilling and logging, given power plants a free ride on mercury pollution, walked away from international efforts to address global warming, refused to tighten emissions standards on automobiles, allowed outmoded power plants to operate indefinitely, dragged its feet on investigating pesticide hazards, permitted steady destruction of wetlands crucial to natural filtering of water, and turned a blind eye to the hazards of factory farming. Even this partial inventory of environmental and health problems should motivate us to redouble efforts to reduce the adverse consequences of human activity on the environment.

Saving the planet for our children and grandchildren has always been the inspiration for such efforts. But some of today's youth see a larger and darker picture. Asked by a National Public Radio interviewer to react to President George W. Bush's proposal for NASA to focus on returning humans to the moon and eventually traveling to Mars, schoolchildren visiting the Smith-sonian's National Air and Space Museum in Washington, D.C., responded fa-vorably because it would give humans somewhere to go "when the Earth dies." Imagine how much less confidence in the future children who live in poorer, more polluted countries must have.

If we are to remain optimistic about the future, indeed, if we are to have reason for confidence at all, we must approach environmental problems with a sense of urgency. But we do not. Instead, we often behave as if environ-mental degradation was merely a hypothetical problem. We counter scientific consensus about the scope of various hazards with cheap political posturing. We passively accept warnings that summer air is too polluted for the elderly and the very young to breathe without demanding to know who is responsi-ble. We fall prey to "greenwashing" advertising campaigns by industrial pol-luters. And we treat the manufacturers of toxic chemicals and other pollutants as if they have a constitutional right to pollute until government somehow manages to prove otherwise.

Policy debates increasingly are dominated by complaints that environmen-tal protection costs too much, that science has not demonstrated there is a problem worth addressing, that taking action to improve the environment threatens jobs and international competitiveness, and that profits will moti-vate businesses to protect the environment better than government could. In short, more than 30 years after many of the groundbreaking federal statutes that created bold programs to improve the quality of the environment and protect our health and safety, we seem to have lost the vision and the confi-dence vital to continuing such progress.

Nevertheless, this book starts from a place of confidence. It proposes a pro-gressive policy approach to controlling pollution and cleaning the environment and recommends concrete approaches to regulatory practice and decision-mak-ing. These recommendations are progressive because they are imbued with a forward-looking optimism about our collective ability to succeed, making the planet a healthier, safer place for people and nature. Government stands at the center of these progressive aspirations, reclaiming its rightful place as the guardian of the public interest in controlling unfettered industrialism.

The environmental movement that began in earnest three decades ago has looked primarily, but not exclusively, to government to translate concerns about environmental conditions into action. While all levels of government are thought responsible, to some degree or another, for responding to the call to action, the federal government has taken the lead. From the late 1960s to the mid-1970s, Congress enacted a wide range of federal statutes that protect public health and the environment, including the:

- National Environmental Policy Act;
- Clean Air Act Amendments;
- Occupational Safety and Health Act of 1970;
- Lead-Based Paint Poisoning Prevention Act;
- Federal Water Pollution Control Act Amendments;
- Noise Control Act;
- Coastal Zone Management Act;
- Consumer Product Safety Act of 1972;
- Federal Insecticide, Fungicide, and Rodenticide Act;
- Marine Protection, Research, and Sanctuaries Act;
- Endangered Species Act;
- Safe Drinking Water Act;
- Hazardous Materials Transport Act;
- Toxic Substances Control Act;
- Resources Conservation and Recovery Act of 1976; and
- The Surface Mining Conservation and Reclamation Act of 1977.

These statutes cover an enormous range of subject matter, and they each reflect political compromises in various ways. They also share three important principles:

- Pollution-causing activities—even those routine to our way of life and economy—should be made as safe and clean as possible, certainly to the extent that they do not cause illness or death.
- Optimism and confidence are necessary with respect to the technology and human ingenuity required to reduce risks to satisfactory levels, up to and including the belief that entirely new technologies can be developed to accomplish old functions at an affordable price.
- Government at the national, state, and local levels has a crucial role to play in preserving collective values and protecting the public interest via lawmaking and enforcement.

Progress since the 1970s has been halting, but public support for environmental concerns remains strong enough that politicians who visibly favor corporate interests over environmental concerns act at their peril. After taking control of the 104th Congress, the Republican leadership and its industry allies re-learned this lesson the hard way when they attempted the wholesale dismantling of the existing environmental, health, and safety regulatory structure. These efforts were met with public outrage at the prospect of weakening or rolling back valued protective measures, forcing their sponsors into a hasty retreat.

Despite the repudiation of such highly visible efforts, powerful special interests opposed to vigorous environmental protection have made important gains in the past 30 years. In fact, they increasingly dominate the public policy debate, continually putting regulatory programs on the defensive, starving government regulators of essential resources, blocking legislation needed to address emerging problems, and selectively rolling back crucial protections. They insist on framing the policy debate in terms of deep skepticism about regulation, arguing that public health and environmental risks are not proven or do not exist, that the costs of reducing such risks are too high, or that corporations should be allowed to police themselves, without pressure from the government.

In the 1960s and '70s, the nation's debate was framed very differently, and government at all levels was assigned the important job of mitigating hazards to ourselves and the environment. By focusing on the need to avoid supposedly excessive costs, waiting for scientific certainty, and reducing the role of the federal government, conservatives have obscured the true implications of their radical agenda. For example, when people are asked, "Do you want the federal government to impose more costs on you and the economy?" they tend to respond differently than when asked, "Do you want safer drinking water for you and your children?" To the extent that antigovernment, antiregulation interests continue to formulate the questions that are debated, it will be that much more difficult to move in a progressive direction.

Conservative think tanks, litigation centers, and opinion leaders have been sufficiently successful that sometimes it may seem that their questions are the only ones to be asked. For example, the language of cost-benefit analysis has become the *lingua franca* of elite public policy discourse. Emphasis on economic growth and competitiveness stimulates images of regulation as purely a cost that dampens the energies of private enterprise rather than as the expression in law of collective values that correct for the errors and omissions of private enterprise, ultimately producing a far better overall result. Prevailing cynicism toward government and the complementary allure of the free market create a structure that obscures the wisdom of collective action.

If the public remains fundamentally committed to the core ideals of national environmental laws—reducing risks, requiring industry to do the best it can to prevent pollution, and taking collective action to accomplish these goals—what explains the apparent success of regulated industries in reshaping the policy debate?

One significant reason for the disconnect is that the nature and complexity of the policy-making process permits two levels of activity, one of which the opposing special interests dominates. This split-level picture emerges from understanding that implementing public policy is more complex than simply enacting a piece of legislation, with a signing ceremony in the White House Rose Garden. Laws that protect health, safety, and the environment must be implemented by administrative agencies, and implementation requires the administering agency to make many more important decisions than even the most carefully crafted, detailed statutes can anticipate. For example, the Clean Air Act (CAA) mandates that the Environmental Protection Agency (EPA) establish ambient air-quality standards necessary to "protect public health." The CAA, however, does not precisely define the public health or what it means to protect it. Often the exposure to air pollution and its adverse effects are related, with the adverse effects becoming less severe and fewer in number as exposure decreases, but without any fixed level of pollution at which one can say that a certain exposure causes no harm. Instead, the choice of the appropriate level of protection essentially is left to the judgment of the EPA administrator, who must struggle with how much to demand from polluting industries that constantly threaten to challenge the Agency's decisions in court.

Regulatory policy is filled with examples of issues like these, many of them much more technical and with implications much more difficult to determine than setting an ambient air-quality standard. More often than not, the public is either completely unaware that these decisions are being made or unable to judge the justifications offered by those who oppose or support them. Yet each decision provides an opportunity for powerful interests to lobby for a favorable outcome.

Congress can play a substantial role in regulatory decisions, depending upon whether members of Congress are working in conjunction with powerful interests or fighting to protect the public's commitments. In recent years, the members who fight back have enjoyed some success largely because inertia favors existing programs. At the same time, important skirmishes are being lost to the powerful special interests capable of devoting huge sums of money to battles of attrition with under-funded government regulators.

Enforcement decisions are among the most important issues in translating public policy into actions that make a difference. No piece of legislation realizes its full potential without the credible threat of enforcement against those who break the law. Decisions not to enforce rarely attract much public attention, and even when they do, public concerns may be localized. Even when public concern prompts the relevant agency to provide a justification for its decision, it is difficult to probe that decision to determine its legitimacy. Enforcement decisions depend upon a host of relatively invisible and hard-to-challenge agency judgments, such as how to set priorities, how large a penalty to seek, and whether to pursue a cooperative or more adversarial enforcement strategy.

Congress also plays a crucial role in the enforcement process—one that can be constructive or destructive. Congress acts constructively when it conducts oversight to ensure vigorous enforcement and provides adequate funds for such efforts. It plays the opposite role when it reduces or eliminates funds for inspection and enforcement, which it has an opportunity to do annually in appropriations bills. Such decisions often are made out of public view and are prime candidates for being pushed in a direction that favors powerful interests.

When the public's commitment to public health and environmental quality encounters an obvious, transparent, and easy-to-understand government action that endangers the public and the environment, the public interest stands an excellent chance of prevailing, despite the powerful opposition of special interests. Even politicians who often may do the bidding of special interests are reluctant to face voters' wrath on Election Day. The Bush Administration's aborted effort to loosen restrictions on arsenic in drinking water is an example of what can happen when arcane regulatory procedural matters attract public attention. Unwilling to be seen as an enemy of clean drinking water, the Administration backed away from its efforts. But when media attention has been easier to avoid, or when the issues seem less tangible than a recognizable poison in drinking water, the current Administration has allowed industry to increase the levels of air and water pollution.

We know from the experience of the Republican-led 104th Congress, as well as from other evidence, that there are competitors to the dominant cost-benefit, scientific-certainty, antigovernment perspective on environmental, health, and safety issues. Most of us still respond to messages that point out the environmental degradation certain policy proposals will cause, and these pro-environment attitudes can be strong enough to block backsliding proposals. But resistance is only a small part of what is needed. Real progress requires that the entire progressive perspective be more accessible to more people. Today we too often engage in arguments with deregulatory forces that accept the way they frame issues.

To begin moving toward progress again, progressives face several different challenges. First, they should proudly champion policy changes that will make a difference rather than settle for half-a-loaf strategies or half-solutions that fit comfortably into the dominant antiregulatory framework. Second, progressives must promote their agenda in a cogent and compelling fashion—and in starkly different terms from the typical contemporary policy debate practiced in the states and Washington, D.C. Third, progressives need to understand how current government policy-making undermines initial advances and guard against it. Fourth, progressives have to insist on necessary institutional changes that will facilitate effective regulation and enforcement.

This book seeks to contribute to all four of these agenda items. It reflects the expertise of its authors, member scholars of the Center for Progressive Regulation, which supports protective regulations and rejects the dominant view in Washington that government's principal domestic function is to increase the efficiency of economic markets. The book largely focuses on environmental issues. However, it includes several references to other regulatory issues in order to demonstrate that the approaches proposed in these pages can be applied readily to other regulatory goals.

We begin with a brief discussion of the history of environmental protection efforts, and then proceed to an enumeration of the principles underlying our progressive agenda for the environment, contrasting those principles with the efforts of those who would halt and roll back environmental progress. From there we turn to a more detailed discussion of progressive approaches for guiding public policy, recommending specific policy measures and methods along the way. We consider how the United States should apply progressive principles to international environmental matters and highlight important elements of the political, social, and institutional structures crucial to bringing the progressive principles to fruition.

Among the specific recommendations offered in these pages:

- Climate change is the most serious, long-term environmental threat facing future generations. The United States must stop behaving like a rogue nation and join with the international community to take effective action to slow, and eventually halt, global warming.
- Cost-benefit analysis, which is intrinsically and fatally flawed, should not be used as a definitive approach to policy-making designed to protect human health and the environment.
- Whenever possible, polluters must install state-of-the-art controls to prevent harming the public. Current standards are too lax, and regulations often effectively encourage industry to pollute up to the legal limit.
- Congress should repeal laws that allow companies to hide evidence of their illegal acts, such as the Critical Infrastructure Information Act, and that give corporations the tools to harass and discredit valuable science, such as the Information Quality Act.
- Budgets for agencies that protect public health and natural resources must be increased dramatically. Spending for standard-setting, enforcement, and the preservation of public lands should double in the next

decade. These increases should be funded by new taxes on corporate polluters and by the dedication of fees collected from those who use public resources like the national parks to rigorous conservation programs.

- Provisions enabling citizens to bring lawsuits that force factories to abide by laws should be strengthened by eliminating restrictions on standing and by allowing penalties for past violations.
- We must end unwarranted government subsidies of activities that destroy natural resources.
- Emissions trading schemes can be cost-effective means of controlling pollution where overall quantities of less hazardous pollutants are subject to steeply declining caps. But such market-based remedies must never be used to control toxic hazards, such as mercury, that pool into "hot spots" and poison those unfortunate enough to live nearby.
- The dirtiest manufacturing facilities are often located in low-income and minority communities. This type of discrimination is compounded by a lack of affordable health care and adequate nutrition. Civil rights laws must be strengthened to outlaw discrimination, eliminating any requirement that intent be proved and instead concentrating on the disparate effects of such practices and activities.
- The current Administration has contradicted principles of federalism in an effort to prevent states from imposing stricter standards. Washington, D.C. should continue to be the epicenter of environmental regulation, but the states must have authority to implement more-stringent regulations.
- Current information gaps regarding toxic chemicals are appalling. We lack sufficient information about 80 percent of the high-production volume toxic chemicals sold each year. To close this gap, government must increase public funding for research and require new toxic chemicals to be screened before they enter the marketplace. The government should compel producers of such substances to complete toxicity testing or require products that contain such substances to be labeled as untested. Untested chemicals should be presumed harmful for legal purposes until comprehensive testing exonerates them.
- More public resources must be devoted to monitoring environmental conditions and trends in a consistent and comprehensive manner. In particular, we recommend that Congress establish an independent and truly impartial Bureau of Environmental Statistics, analogous to the federal Bureau of Labor Statistics, and that it provide this new agency with ample authority and resources to work effectively. This new bureau should be charged with assessing environmental data needs, creating

guidelines for collecting environmental data, collecting and analyzing comprehensive statistics on environmental quality, and disseminating the data it gathers to the public.

- EPA should shine a spotlight on state environmental agency performance by means of regular and public evaluations of how well state agencies are meeting their obligations, based on a uniform set of criteria.
- The National Environmental Policy Act (NEPA), which requires environmental impact assessments each time the federal government takes an action that could produce a major effect on the environment, must be extended to cover private corporations.
- To strengthen corporate accountability for harmful activities, Congress should enact a law requiring business to disclose promptly, accurately, and fully the nature, extent, and impact of any corporate activity or practice that poses a significant threat to public health and the environment, whether or not the activity is regulated, with appropriately circumscribed protection for confidential business information.
- Similarly, companies listed on national securities exchanges must disclose the adverse effects their practices have on human health and the environment so that investors are informed enough to decide whether the company is a sound and ethical investment.
- California's Proposition 65 has proven to be an effective tool for triggering needed product reformulations, as well as reductions in unnecessary toxic exposures. It also provides the public with the necessary information to make informed choices and avoid unnecessary risks. A similar requirement should be applied on a broader, national scale, requiring companies to provide clear and reasonable warnings prior to exposing people to toxic chemicals, with exposures below a certain level of risk exempted.
- In the context of so-called "advertorials" or "corporate image ads," companies under fire for poor environmental or labor practices have invoked their ostensible First Amendment rights to evade prohibitions on deceptive and unfair advertising. Those prohibitions are a cornerstone of the free market, protecting consumers and ethical competitors. The courts must reject claims that the First Amendment shields anyone from compliance with these provisions.

Chapter 2

The Unfinished Agenda

Success Stories

The social and political changes spawned by the reform movements of the 1960s and '70s were as ambitious in the environmental, health, and safety arena as they were with respect to civil rights. Regulated industries and their conservative political allies in Washington love to hate these programs, claiming they are economically inefficient and built on false assumptions. Progressives believe that laws protecting the environment, health, and safety have brought dramatic progress toward a safer, fairer world, but they also criticize the regulatory system's shortcomings, with the goal of expanding and improving regulatory effectiveness. While we have fallen short of the highest ambitions of such laws, we have made great progress. In short, there is far more in the existing system to preserve and extend than to jettison.

The laws passed in this period protect the air and water from pollution and mandate government screening of pesticides to ensure that their application does not threaten public health or sensitive ecosystems. They create programs to rid workplaces of occupational illnesses and accidents. They dictate the use of strict hazardous waste management practices and give government the authority to prevent the marketing of dangerous toxic chemicals. The laws say government should prohibit the use of environmentally destructive surface-mining practices and establish liability as an incentive for responsible parties to clean up abandoned waste dumps. The laws mandate that government act to reduce injuries and fatalities from automobile accidents and dangerous products. And considerable progress has been made in each of these areas.

Under Clean Air Act (CAA) regulations, known as National Ambient Air Quality Standards (NAAQS), we have achieved a 48 percent aggregate reduction in the emissions of six major air pollutants.[1] Between 1970 and 2002,

---

1. EPA, *Latest Findings on National Air Quality: 2002 Status & Trends*, August, 2003, 1, http://www.epa.gov/airtrends/2002_airtrends_final.pdf.

particulate matter emissions fell 34 percent; carbon monoxide decreased 48 percent; volatile organic compounds, which contribute to ozone pollution, dropped 51 percent; sulfur dioxide declined 52 percent; and nitrogen oxide emissions fell 17 percent.[2] In turn, these reductions decreased the incidence of adverse health effects attributable to air pollution, including lung damage, asthma, bronchitis, reduced oxygen flow in blood, eye irritation, and reduced resistance to infection.

The greatest CAA success story, however, is lead. The presence of lead in the air has proven to be extremely harmful to human health, especially to exposed children, who can experience brain damage and retardation. One major source was lead additives in gasoline. After scientists documented the harmful health effects of lead pollution in the air, EPA began to phase out its use in gasoline in the 1970s. In 1990, Congress banned the marketing of gasoline containing lead additives. As a result, lead emissions fell 98 percent between 1970 and 2002.[3]

In addition to lead, Congress has banned other pollutants that are potentially harmful to humans. In 1990, after scientists discovered a significant decline in the concentration of stratospheric ozone over the southern hemisphere, especially over Antarctica, Congress amended the CAA to phase out the production and use of chlorofluorocarbons (CFCs) and other ozone-depleting chemicals. The United States also led international efforts to negotiate the Montreal Protocol, an international accord to reduce drastically the global release of ozone-depleting chemicals. These restrictions already have begun to work. By 1998, CFC production had decreased 95 percent in industrialized countries, with a sharp decline beginning in the late 1980s and early 1990s.[4] Scientific evidence indicates that the rate of ozone depletion in the upper atmosphere also is slowing.[5] Trends such as these will help protect humans, animals, and plant life from harmful radiation.

Another notable success story in U.S. environmental regulation is the national effluent limitations program under the Clean Water Act (CWA). While the details of this program are complex, the basic idea is simple. In the 1972 CWA amendments, Congress directed EPA to adopt controls for certain types of industrial plants, such as paper mills or oil refineries, that reflect the best pollution-control technology considering cost and other factors, regardless of location. Congress required similarly uniform controls on the nation's mu-

2. Ibid., 2.

3. Ibid.

4. Ozone Secretariat, United Nations Environment Programme, *Action on Ozone, 2000 Edition*, 16, http://www.unep.org/ozone/pdf/ozone-action-en.pdf.

5. EPA website, Air Trends, Stratospheric Ozone, Trends in Stratospheric Ozone Depletion, http://www.epa.gov/airtrends/strat.html.

nicipal sewage treatment plants. EPA has issued enforceable guidelines for more than 50 major industries, covering as many as 45,000 facilities that discharge directly into the nation's waters, and another 12,000 that discharge into public sewage treatment plants.[6] According to EPA, these rules prevent the release of almost 700 billion pounds of pollutants every year,[7] including more than a billion pounds of toxic pollutants known to contribute to or cause cancer and other serious health problems, such as diminished mental and motor development in children as well as liver and kidney damage. The rules, which apply nationally, reduce water pollution in every river, lake, and coastal waterway that receives municipal or industrial effluents.

We have also seen notable victories involving regulations that protect public safety. In 1972, Congress established the Consumer Product Safety Commission (CPSC) "to protect the public against unreasonable risks of injury associated with consumer products." Among the CPSC's successes is child-resistant packaging for aspirin and oral prescriptions, which has saved the lives of about 700 children since the early 1970s.[8] In 1966, Congress passed the National Traffic and Motor Vehicle Safety Act, which directed the Department of Transportation to "reduce traffic accidents and deaths and injuries to persons resulting from traffic accidents." In 2001, 1.52 persons were killed per 100 million vehicle miles traveled— the lowest fatality rate in history.[9] In 1970, Congress created the Occupational Safety and Health Administration (OSHA) and directed it to "assure as far as possible every working man and woman in the Nation safe and healthful working conditions." Between 1974 and 2001, the average number of cases of workplace injuries and illness fell from 10.4 to 5.7 per 100 full-time workers.[10] In 2002, the fatality rate from workplace injuries dipped to 4 fatal work injuries per 100,000 workers—the lowest since 1992, the earliest date available for comparison.[11]

---

6. EPA, *A Strategy for National Clean Water Industrial Regulations, Effluent Guidelines, Pretreatment Standards, and New Source Performance Standards*, Draft, November 5, 2002, 4, http://www.epa.gov/guide/strategy/304mstrategy.pdf.

7. Ibid., 9.

8. Consumer Product Safety Commission, *Child Resistant Packaging Saves Lives* (CPSC Document #5019), http://www.cpsc.gov/cpscpub/pubs/5019.html.

9. NHTSA, *Traffic Safety Facts 2001: Overview*, 2001, (DOT HS 809 476), 1, http://www-nrd.nhtsa.dot.gov/pdf/nrd-30/NCSA/TSF2001/2001overview.pdf.

10. U.S. Department of Labor, Bureau of Labor Statistics, *News Release: Workplace Injuries & Illnesses in 2001*, December 19, 2002, 1, 15 (Table 6), http://www.bls.gov/iif/oshwc/osh/os/osnr0016.pdf.

11. U.S. Department of Labor, Bureau of Labor Statistics, *News Release: National Census of Fatal Occupational Injuries in 2002*, December 17, 2003, 1, http://www.bls.gov/news.release/pdf/cfoi.pdf.

In the area of information disclosure, the Toxics Release Inventory (TRI) is an important achievement. Public demands for information about releases after the deadly gas leak in Bhopal, India, led to the passage of the Emergency Planning and Community Right to Know Act of 1986 (EPCRA). Under EPCRA and the Pollution Prevention Act of 1990, facilities must annually report to the EPA the industrial release of more than 650 toxic substances. Once reported, EPA makes this information available to the public through the TRI. Armed with such information, the public and the media have pressured companies to reduce and better manage their releases of toxic substances and the EPA to provide stronger protections against such releases. As a result, companies have reduced toxic chemical releases and changed how they manage such substances. According to EPA, total on- and off-site releases of approximately 332 chemicals reportable under TRI fell 48 percent between 1988 and 2000.[12] In addition to being a crucial source of information for the public and a vehicle for reductions in industry releases, Congress used the TRI to identify the 189 toxic chemicals to be regulated as hazardous air pollutants in the CAA Amendments of 1990.

Another important success was the creation and implementation of the Superfund program for cleaning up U.S. hazardous waste sites. Spurred by the need to clean up abandoned waste sites such as Love Canal, which posed serious threats to public health and the environment, Congress enacted the Comprehensive Environmental Response Compensation and Liability Act in 1980 and amended it in 1986. The law established a federal fund that would be replenished by a stringent liability regime for holding responsible parties liable for cleanup costs. Cleanup activities have been completed on 846 of the 1,498 most toxic waste sites in the nation, up from 149 site cleanups in 1992.[13] Even more important, the powerful incentives created by Superfund liability have spurred waste reduction, improved waste handling, and prevented much intractable pollution across the country.

The Unfinished Agenda

These successes are undeniable as an objective matter, no matter how fervently deregulators try to debunk them. But these successes must not mask the reality that much remains to be done. By the time laws and regulations began to

---

12. EPA, *Draft Report on the Environment 2003*, iv, http://www.epa.gov/indicators/roe/pdf/EPA_Draft_ROE.pdf.

13. Ibid., v.

modulate the damage caused by unbridled industrial activity, there were many locations in dire need of cleanup. In an era when chemical pollution in Ohio's Cuyahoga River caught fire, abandoned toxic waste dumps leached gallons of hazardous waste into groundwater, and the air in Los Angeles choked its citizens, it was relatively easy to identify what is sometimes characterized as "low-hanging fruit." Deregulators argue that solving such obvious problems should mark the end of the road for efforts to curb the adverse health, safety, and environmental consequences of many activities. They insist that while such efforts may have been appropriate for these pressing problems, it is no longer necessary to impose such stringent controls.

So, for example, regulated industries and their conservative political allies often invoke the "90/10" rule, claiming that it is not worth spending large sums of money to tackle the last 10 percent of pollution. Deregulators assert that we are at the 90 percent point with the existing pollution-control strategies. Further efforts to eliminate the remaining threats to people and the environment will produce only minimal benefits compared with the huge costs such endeavors require, they maintain. Deregulators say it is time to switch to strategies that provide business with incentives to improve more, that allow them to choose whether to reduce pollution, and that apply the tools of cost-benefit analysis to environmental, health, and safety problems to ensure further cleanup is worth the cost.

We part company with these critics in their assessment of where we stand and where we need to go. The steps taken in the past 30 years provide a strong foundation. We must learn from the past. Complacency, or the belief that we are working on the last 10 percent of our problems, can lead us in the wrong direction. Significant challenges remain, and they will not be adequately met so long as the dominant frameworks for thinking about these problems are "government = bad; marketplace = good" and "cost-benefit analysis should guide our steps."

In subsequent chapters, we will lay out some of the central principles for the progressive approach to these issues. To understand the urgency of these recommendations, we must first explain the agenda of unfinished business and recent backsliding we face.

Clean Air

Smog and Soot in the Air: Despite the progress made in the past 30 years, some of the problems that prompted Congress to pass the CAA continue to pose serious threats to the nation's health and the integrity of its natural resources. Although air pollution has decreased, about 146 million people are exposed to air-pollution levels that put their health at risk because they live in counties that violate EPA standards for healthy air.[14] For example, in New Jersey alone, vehicle air pollution is related to the premature deaths of 2,300 to 5,400 residents; 7,800 to 15,000 respiratory and heart-related hospital admissions; 170,000 childhood asthma attacks, including the hospitalization of 290 to 440 children; and 600,000 missed school days each year.[15] And these troubling statistics are repeated in other, densely populated, urban and industrialized areas. Deadlines for the states to comply with air-quality standards have been extended many times, and only a small number of the worst areas will meet the latest set of deadlines in 2005.

Trouble also is brewing in the arena of hazardous air pollutants. Congress told the federal government to establish more stringent "maximum achievable control technologies" for such pollution sources and to ensure the installation of such technologies. Rather than follow the letter of the law, the Bush Administration has cooperated with industry in miring these rules in endless debates over whether controls are too costly. At this rate, meaningful controls on hazardous air pollutants will take decades to accomplish.

Old, Dirty Power Plants: The CAA exempted many existing facilities from the pollution controls required at new facilities on the basis that retrofitting such plants would be very expensive—an approach known as "grandfathering." Congress adopted grandfathering on the assumption that such plants would reach the end of their useful lives within a decade or two, and would be replaced by new, clean facilities. More than 33 years later, many of these old, dirty plants continue to operate and emit high levels of sulfur dioxides, which can cause permanent damage to lung tissue and reduce lung capacity, as well as high levels of mercury, which can damage the brain and kidneys and cause birth defects. Until the Bush Administration took office, however, there was one vital safety net established to prevent the immortality of these "old dirties." The CAA mandates that grandfathered factories undergoing renovations must apply for permits that bring them up to the standards for new facilities. Without such requirements, these outmoded plants could live forever. The imposition of state-of-the-art controls on new sources and newly renovated sources is known as "new source review."

To the dismay of state officials, public health experts, and public interest groups, the Bush Administration has abandoned this vital program, leaving the owners and operators of all the old dirties free to renovate them indefi-

14. EPA website, Air Trends, Six Principal Pollutants, http://www.epa.gov/airtrends/sixpoll.html.

15. NJPIRG, *News Release: Clean Air Advocates Call for Urgent Action on Air Pollution: New NJPIRG Study Shows Too Many Lives At Risk,* December 8, 2003, http://www.njpirg.org/NJ.asp?id2=11512&id3=NJ&.

nitely without implementing controls to meet public health requirements. The failure to regulate these sources of pollution may cause as many as 20,000 premature deaths, 400,000 asthma attacks, and 12,000 cases of chronic bronchitis each year.[16]

Global Warming: Some pollution problems continue to exist not because they have been dealt with inadequately under existing laws, but because the law does not cover them at all. The most pressing example is global warming. The "greenhouse effect" is the set of conditions that arise when the Earth's atmosphere allows radiation from the sun to pass through, while at the same time absorbing much of the energy and infrared radiation reflected by the Earth's surface. This trapping of heat helps make life possible on this planet, but the atmosphere now traps too much heat. According to organizations such as the Intergovernmental Panel on Climate Change and the National Research Council, global warming and associated climate changes will continue throughout this century. Experts believe the increase in global temperatures in this century will likely surpass anything in the last 10,000 years. There is little doubt that global warming is in large part caused by human activity.

While some of the consequences of the climate changes anticipated to occur in the future will be beneficial, such as increases in crop and forest productivity in some areas, global climate changes will generate extraordinary negative effects for people and the natural environment. The frequency of heat waves that cause discomfort, illness, and death is likely to increase as temperatures rise. Higher temperatures could cause an increased demand in electricity for air conditioning, producing overloads that lead to brownouts or blackouts. They are also likely to trigger increases in rainfall rates and violent weather conditions and make semi-arid regions more susceptible to drought, outbreaks of pests, and the diseases that accompany them. Natural ecosystems are particularly vulnerable to the harmful effects of climate change.

In light of these potentially catastrophic problems, immediate action is imperative, even though we cannot predict the exact nature and scope of the consequences of global warming. Policy-makers across the globe have found this

---

16. Clear the Air, National Campaign Against Dirty Power, *News Release: Statement of Angela Ledford, Director, Clear the Air, On Today's Bush Administration Changes To New Source Review,* August 27, 2003, http://cta.policy.net/proactive/newsroom/release .vtml?id=24900&PROACTIVE_ID=cecfcfccc6cfc6c9c6c5cecfcfcfc5cececdcac8c8c6cecbcdc5cf.

argument to be compelling. When representatives of more than 150 nations gathered in June 1992 at the Earth Summit in Rio de Janeiro, Brazil, they endorsed this approach by signing the United Nations Framework Convention on Climate Change, which provides that parties to the agreement should take "precautionary measures to anticipate, prevent or minimize the causes of climate change and mitigate its adverse effects." In the wake of this agreement, the industrialized nations agreed in the 1997 Kyoto Protocol to take steps to reduce emissions of carbon dioxide and other gases that contribute to global warming by 2012.

The United States signed the protocol in 1998, agreeing to cut emissions by an average of 7 percent below 1990 levels between 2008 and 2012, but the U.S. Senate failed to ratify the agreement. Just a few months into his Administration, President Bush repudiated the protocol and withdrew the United States from further participation. The president appears to have responded to pressure from the energy industry, which continues to rely on fossil fuels that generate enormous quantities of greenhouse gases, and has yet to propose any plan for preventing the adverse consequences of global warming.

Mercury: Power plants and other industrial facilities regulated under the CAA continue to emit high levels of mercury, which converts into extraordinarily toxic methyl mercury and bioaccumulates in fish. Low levels of mercury exposure can cause irreversible neurological damage in developing fetuses, infants, and young children. Each year, according to EPA, 630,000 of the country's 4 million babies are born with significantly unsafe levels of mercury in their bloodstream.[17] The Centers for Disease Control and Prevention estimate that 8 percent of American women of childbearing age have blood mercury levels that could harm their future children.[18] In addition, the FDA has issued warnings to pregnant women and young children about the dangers of consuming large quantities of fish, including white tuna, that may contain mercury. Despite this overwhelming evidence, the Bush Administration has sidestepped the CAA's mandate that power plants, the second-largest source of domestic mercury emissions, install pollution-control equipment. Instead, it proposes to allow them to buy and sell the right to emit such pollutants. The

---

17. Guy Gugliotta, "Mercury Threat to Fetus Raised, EPA Revises Risk Estimates," *Washington Post,* Feb. 6, 2004, A3.

18. Centers for Disease Control, *First National Report on Human Exposure to Environmental Chemicals,* March 2001, 18.

Administration also refused to impose meaningful controls on nine outmoded mercury cell chlor-alkali plants, which are estimated to emit 50 percent more pollution than power plants.

Clean Water

Nonpoint Sources of Water Pollution: Despite dramatic gains in the control of industrial water pollution and municipal sewage, 40 percent of streams, 45 percent of lakes, and 50 percent of estuaries are not clean or healthy enough to support fishing, swimming, water supplies, and sustenance of fish and wildlife.[19] Although factory pipes and other "point sources" are partially responsible for this pollution, the main source of the problem is "nonpoint sources"—pollution runoff from land used for farming, logging, mining, grazing, and construction—which are not regulated under the CWA. To date, Congress has addressed pollution runoff through state-driven, largely voluntary programs that encourage landowners to implement "best management practices" designed to reduce runoff or the amount of pollution it carries. Water-quality trend data in the past three decades indicates this approach is not working.

Backsliding on Point Sources: Although we have made tremendous progress in controlling large point source dischargers, growing evidence indicates we are losing ground as a result of federal and state budget cuts and the lack of political will to enforce such requirements. The CWA allows facilities to operate indefinitely on expired permits, so long as they have filed a timely application for a new permit, and the states are fighting a losing battle to stay current with their permitting work. Many state agencies lack the will and the resources to punish systematic violations of such permits, and citizen lawsuits authorized to supplement those efforts have run into a gauntlet of procedural barriers erected by pro-industry judges. Even more serious, the states have systematically failed to develop Total Maximum Daily Load (TMDL) standards, which are the safety net established by Congress to compel the restoration of waters so contaminated that they cannot be used for their designated uses—drinking, swimming, fishing, boating, irrigation, etc.

---

19. EPA, *Water Quality Conditions in the United States: A Profile from the 2000 National Water Quality Inventory,* August 2002, (EPA-841-F-02-003), 1, http://www.epa.gov/305b/2000report/factsheet.pdf/.

Ocean Pollution: The CWA restricts pollution discharges into the nation's streams, rivers, lakes, and ocean coastlines. In addition, the Marine Protection, Research, and Sanctuaries Act prohibits the transportation from the United States of any material for the purpose of dumping it into the ocean, without an EPA permit. The Oil Pollution Act, adopted in 1990 after the Exxon Valdez disaster, imposes further restrictions on ocean pollution. Despite this impressive body of law, excessive nutrient loading from made-made sources threatens oceans around the world. Although most algae are beneficial, indeed essential, to life, and comprise the base of the ocean food chain, algae sometimes bloom into dense, visible patches near the surface of the water. Some of these patches contain neurotoxins that can be carried through the food chain, causing mass deaths in fish, shellfish, birds, and marine mammals, as well as illness and death in humans who consume the contaminated products. Coastal winds also are capable of transporting these biotoxins through the air, causing severe eye, nose, and throat irritation. Beaches and fisheries have closed due to the proliferation of harmful algal blooms, largely resulting from anthropogenic sources causing nutrient enrichment, climate shifts, or transport of algal species through ship ballast water. Until recently, only a few regions were affected, but, according to the National Oceanic and Atmospheric Administration, "now virtually every coastal state is threatened, in many cases over large geographic areas and by more than one harmful or toxic species."[20]

Product and Workplace Safety

The High Cost of Avoidable Accidents: Although the number of persons injured or killed by consumer products or in the workplace has fallen significantly, thousands of Americans continue to suffer injuries or die as a result of avoidable accidents. On average, 23,900 Americans die and 32.7 million are injured in events associated with consumer products under the jurisdiction of the CPSC.[21] OSHA is similarly ineffective. In 2001, 42,000 people died in traffic accidents, and another 3 million were injured.[22] In the same year, nearly

---

20. NOAA, *U.S. National Research Plan for the Study of Harmful Algal Blooms,* http://www.redtide.whoi.edu/hab/nationplan/nationplan.html.

21. Consumer Product Safety Commission, *2004 Budget & Performance Plan (Operating Plan): Saving Lives and Keeping Families Safe,* March 2004, 2, http://www.cpsc.gov/library/foia/foia04/brief/operate.pdf.

22. NHTSA, *Traffic Safety Facts 2001: Overview,* 2001, (DOT HS 809 476), 1, http://www-nrd.nhtsa.dot.gov/pdf/nrd-30/NCSA/TSF2001/2001overview.pdf.

6,000 workers lost their lives in workplace accidents,[23] and there were 5.2 million work-related injuries and illnesses.[24]

Asbestos: A prime example of OSHA's failure to protect workers is asbestos. Mechanics who install replacement brakes in vehicles are routinely exposed to deadly doses of asbestos because most such brakes are imported from overseas and contain asbestos. Yet OSHA has taken almost no action to protect these workers. Thirty-one countries have banned asbestos on the grounds that no level of exposure is safe, but the United States imports about 30 million pounds of asbestos each year.[25] In 1989, EPA attempted to adopt a ban under the Toxic Substances Control Act, but the 5th U.S. Circuit Court of Appeals ruled the agency did not have the legal authority to ban this dangerous substance.

Natural Resources

Overfishing: The Fishery Conservation and Management Act of 1976, also known as the Magnuson Act and as amended by the 1996 Sustainable Fisheries Act, was designed to conserve and manage the fishery resources located off the coasts of the United States. Despite these laws, about 45 percent of U.S. fish stocks are overfished, and the populations of some species have fallen below 10 percent of optimum levels.[26] Stocks of Atlantic salmon, for example, have declined precipitously as a result of a combination of overfishing, pollution, habitat destruction, and aquaculture. Crab fisheries in areas bordering the Bering Sea have collapsed from similar causes. The depletion of cod stocks in Canada and the northeastern United States has deprived many fishermen of making a living.

Contamination of Fisheries: The contamination of fish and shellfish from mercury, dioxins, polychlorinated biphenyls (PCBs), and other contaminants

23. U.S. Department of Labor, Bureau of Labor Statistics, *Census of Fatal Occupational Injuries (CFOI) Current and Revised Data,* 2001, http://www.bls.gov/iif/oshwc/cfoi/cftb0166.pdf.

24. U.S. Department of Labor, Bureau of Labor Statistics, *News Release: Workplace Injuries & Illnesses in 2001,* December 19, 2002, 1, 15 (Table 6), http://www.bls.gov/iif/oshwc/osh/os/osnr0016.pdf.

25. Andrew Schneider, "Panel Urges U.S. To Ban Asbestos Imports," *St. Louis Post Dispatch,* May 4, 2003, A1.

26. Daniel A. Farber, "Building Bridges Over Troubled Waters: Eco-Pragmatism and the Environmental Project," *Minnesota Law Review* 87 (2003): 851, 857.

continues to raise significant concerns for public health and the environment. Rivers and lakes throughout the United States remain under fish-consumption advisories, including 14 percent of river miles, 28 percent of lake acreage, and all of the Great Lakes and their connecting waters.[27]

Water Shortages: Throughout the world, communities are experiencing severe water shortages. Overpumping of aquifers has become routine and water tables have fallen across the globe in China, India, and the United States—countries that produce half the world's grain.[28] For example, in the Klamath Basin in Oregon, farmers, fishermen, Native Americans, and environmentalists remain embroiled in litigation over a limited supply of water. In the Aral Sea Basin and along the Nile River, competition for water has provoked international discord. Water shortages have sparked conflicts as a decreasing water supply is rationed to meet a diversity of needs, including those of urban populations, industry, agriculture, and ecosystems. It is estimated that as much as one-third of the world's population will not have sufficient water supplies by the year 2025.[29]

Egregious Resource Extraction Subsidies: Other valuable natural resources are overused because the federal government improperly subsidizes their extraction or use. The General Mining Law of 1872 is the most egregious example of such government giveaways. Under this law, anyone who discovers a valuable mineral deposit on federal lands may mine the deposit virtually for free and purchase the land at a cost of $2.50 to $5 per acre. For example, several years ago, a mining company called American Barrick Resources, without paying any royalty fees, received a patent to mine land in Arizona containing $7 billion worth of gold.[30] Although Congress has forbidden further such transactions by appropriations riders, the General Mining Law, which continues to be fiercely defended by corporate mining in-

---

27. EPA, *Draft Report on the Environment 2003,* iii, http://www.epa.gov/indicators/roe/pdf/EPA_Draft_ROE.pdf.

28. Lester R. Brown, *Plan B: Rescuing a Planet Under Stress and a Civilization in Trouble* (New York: W.W. Norton and Company, 2003), 9, http://www.earth-policy.org/Books/PlanB_contents.htm.

29. Grant Ferret, "Water shortages threaten Africa," *BBC News World Edition,* last updated November 2, 2003, http://news.bbc.co.uk/2/hi/science/nature/3235829.stm.

30. David Bollier, *Public Assets, Private Profits: Reclaiming the American Commons in an Age of Market Enclosure* (Washington, D.C.: New America Foundation, 2001), 42, http://www.bollier.org/pdf/PA_Report.pdf.

terests, has not been amended or repealed. If Congress ever permits its moratorium to expire, the federal government again will be obliged to transfer titles to hard-rock minerals and the lands that contain them into private hands for a pittance.

The General Mining Law is not the only example of subsidizing private access to public natural resources. The costs to the federal government of conducting timber sales routinely exceed the revenues received by the United States from those sales. In 1997, the Forest Service estimated that timber sales in the national forests lost $88.6 million.[31] Annual forestry losses earlier in the decade were about $300 million to $400 million a year.[32] Between 1982 and 1988, the government spent $389 million building roads and providing other benefits to logging companies in Alaska's Tongass National Forest but received only $32 million in revenues.[33] Similar subsidies flow from federal reclamation laws. Between 1902 and 1986, for example, the government lost between $47 billion and $99 billion on public irrigation projects.[34] Federal grazing permits issued by agencies such as the Bureau of Land Management historically have charged ranchers grazing fees for using federal lands; however, the prices are far below fair-market value for the use of comparable private lands. Federal grazing fees amounted to as little as 56 percent of federal costs per animal unit in 1990 and were as low as 18 percent of private market rates.[35] It is clear that the federal government is providing corporate welfare in a wide variety of contexts through the sale, rental, or giveaway of valuable public natural resources.

A Different Agenda

Much remains to be done, but the Bush Administration has shown no inclination to continue the progress we have made protecting human health and the environment. Instead, it has worked energetically to deregulate many of

---

31. George Cameron Coggins, Charles F. Wilkinson and John D. Leshy, *Federal Public Land and Resources Law* (Thomson-West Group, 5th ed. 2002), 725.

32. Ibid.

33. Douglas A. Kysar, "Law, Environment, and Vision," *Northwestern University Law Review* 97 (2003): 675, 706.

34. Ibid., 707.

35. Robert W. Hahn, Sheila M. Olmstead & Robert N. Stavins, "Environmental Regulation in the 1990s: A Retrospective Analysis," *Harvard Environmental Law Review* 27 (2003): 377, 386.

the industrial sectors that cause the greatest harm. Unless we reverse this backsliding and get back on track soon, we will lose the progress we have made and fall further behind in the struggle to solve the new challenges we confront.

It is long past time to regulate power plants and other large industrial sources originally exempted from the CAA, but the Administration instead has proposed to continue the exemptions indefinitely. President Bush has no plan for addressing global warming after repudiating the 1997 Kyoto Protocol. Nonpoint source runoff is the most pressing problem under the CWA, but EPA adopted a watered-down version of a regulation proposed during the Clinton Administration to reduce the extent to which streams and rivers are polluted by the 220 billion gallons of liquefied manure produced each year by large factory farms.

The Clinton Administration proposed requiring automobile manufacturers to install monitors that would notify drivers that their tires were dangerously low, but the Bush Administration replaced this requirement with one that, according to the government's own data, would prevent only about half as many injuries and deaths as the original rule. The Bush Administration also withdrew efficiency standards promulgated by the Clinton Administration for air conditioners and heat pumps in order to propose weaker regulations.

After Congress vetoed a regulation adopted in the Clinton Administration to regulate the exposure of millions of workers to ergonomic injuries, the Bush Administration decided to rely on voluntary employer compliance, despite evidence that each year such injuries result in 70 million physician office visits and cost between $45 million and $54 million in compensation costs, lost wages, and lost productivity.[36]

Most of such recent agency actions were taken at the request of the Office of Information and Regulatory Affairs (OIRA), which is part of the White House Office of Management and Budget (OMB), based on estimates of regulatory costs and benefits. OIRA also pressured EPA to exempt firms that emit the hazardous air pollutant formaldehyde from installing protective controls despite compelling new scientific data that exposures cause cancer. OIRA also has leaned on EPA to weaken regulations that would: control runoff from construction sites that contaminates water supplies, reduce the trillions of fish killed each year in the operation of power plants, and cut the amount of pollution caused by snowmobile emissions.

---

36. National Academy of Sciences, Institute of Medicine, *Musculoskeletal Disorders and the Workplace: Low Back and Upper Extremities*, 2001, 1.

When it has not rolled back regulations, the Bush Administration has let the laws on the books wither through lack of enforcement. EPA has caught and punished fewer polluters than in the two previous administrations, in part because the agency has the smallest inspection and enforcement staff it has ever had. Since January 2001, the average number of violation notices EPA issues each month has dropped 58 percent compared with the average number in the Clinton Administration.[37] Nevertheless, in 2003 the White House sought to eliminate the positions of more than 200 enforcement jobs.[38] Similarly, the Bush Administration conducted fewer OSHA inspections than the Clinton Administration and, in 2003, proposed cutting OSHA's budget by $9 million dollars, which would eliminate 64 full-time enforcement positions.[39]

The Bush Administration also has been slower than previous administrations in finishing regulations and proposing new ones. According to a study by OMB Watch,[40] a Washington, D.C.-based nonprofit research group, EPA finished only two significant regulations in President Bush's first two years, but it finalized 23 such rules during President Clinton's first two years. In the same period, EPA proposed nine significant new regulations, compared with 28 during the Clinton Administration. Other agencies have been doing even less. The Department of Health and Human Services did not finish a single significant regulation in the Bush Administration's first two years; the Department of the Interior produced only two significant regulations; and OSHA completed only one such regulation, which actually involved deregulation.

The failure to address the problems we confront is a political failure, not an institutional failure. The political forces that oppose regulation have the upper hand at the moment. Clearly, not all regulations have been successful and regulatory innovation is necessary. But such reforms will not be possible so long as the Administration and its allies belittle the job ahead and the government as a tool to implement change.

---

37. Seth Borenstein, "Fewer polluters punished under Bush administration, records show," *Philadelphia Enquirer*, Dec. 9, 2003, http://www.philly.com/mld/inquirer/news/front/7446525.htm.

38. Rena Steinzor, Testimony before the Subcommittee on Fisheries, Wildlife, and Water of the U.S. Senate regarding Implementation of the Clean Water Act, September 16, 2003, http://www.progressiveregulation.org/articles/EPA_Enforcement_Testimony_091603 .pdf.

39. OMB Watch, *Ignoring Enron's Lessons, Bush Rollbacks Continue,* Nov. 6, 2002, http://www.ombwatch.org/article/articleview/1174/#limiting.

40. OMB Watch, *Administration Advances Few Health and Safety Protections,* Dec. 15, 2003, http://www.ombwatch.org/article/articleview/1256/1/110/.

Conclusion

In the 1960s and '70s, Congress adopted a wide-ranging group of laws that aspired to protect individuals from air and water pollution, dangerous consumer products, and unsafe workplaces. Congress also sought to protect the environment from being damaged and destroyed by human actions. The experience since that time confirms the government's ability to accomplish these important tasks.

By employing a cost-benefit methodology and other easily manipulated analytical tools, regulated industries and their political allies claim that the economic benefits of addressing the remaining important problems do not justify strict regulation, if any at all. Progressives believe in principles that require government action on the significant problems we face. The next chapter describes the principles that underlie the progressive agenda. Subsequent chapters expand on how these principles support that agenda, and why these principles require rejection of cost-benefit analysis and other utilitarian approaches favored by regulated industries and their allies.

CHAPTER 3

PROGRESSIVE PRINCIPLES

Progressive History

The New Progressive Agenda extends and refines ideas that first had a significant influence on public policy during the Progressive Era's heyday in the 1920s and '30s. Both the original and today's progressives start with a commitment to humanity's well-being. The original Progressives witnessed the development of concentrations of wealth and power to such a degree that a handful of corporations and holding companies were capable of controlling major segments of the economy. Progressive economic programs were designed to prevent these corporate concentrations of wealth and power from exploiting working people. Progressives' concern for working people led to legislation improving safety conditions and working hours, especially for women and children. We owe the first Pure Food and Drug Act and the federal law requiring meat inspections to the original Progressive Era. Gifford Pinchot's development of the Forest Service and the principles of sustained maximum yield also resulted from Progressive concerns.

The destructive capacity of concentrated wealth and power increased dramatically in the second half of the 20th century. Misuse of wealth and power threatens not only the health and well-being of the environment and the existing population but also that of future generations. In the final analysis, we hold the earth and all of its ecosystems in trust for our children.

Progressives understand that achieving progressive goals requires collective action to address social problems and that government is most often the best vehicle for change. We look to government to regulate excessive or unfair economic activity because it is by far the most powerful and ubiquitous institution capable of legitimizing collective social values. Laws can and should affirm and define social values as well as create rights and obligations within society.

Progressives accept the U.S. free-market system, but we argue that the market must operate within a framework that respects collective values. In truth, this principle has always been an accepted norm. Some forms of government regulation of market behavior predate the American Revolution, so progressives rely upon well-established ideals.

Progressives recognize that government sometimes does a poor job of translating collective values into action. We have a dual agenda—advocating values to promote well-being while at the same time calling for government reform so that it can contribute more fully to the expression and implementation of such values.

While progressives believe in the capacity of government experts to take the laboring oar in designing effective programs to protect human health and the environment, we also know that bureaucracies have their limits in a healthy democracy. Many of the most difficult environmental, health, and safety issues involve important value choices that must be made democratically, as opposed to being determined by scientists or other professionals. Experience has taught us that hiding value choices behind a scientific or technical facade provides additional opportunities for powerful corporate forces to capture the government and frustrate progressive goals.

Progressives measure the success of their country in terms of the progress it makes in living up to the social values that determine the well-being of all of its people. We base our agenda on bedrock principles that define what is lacking in society and what is appropriate to ask of others through the collective power of democratic decision-making. The principles central to the protection of the environment and public health are explained below.

Address the Source, Not the Victim

In America's religious and ethical traditions, no one life is less valuable than any other. People are entitled to protection from actions that could subject them to the risk of injury or death. Such protection is a primary goal of health and safety regulation.

When people harm others, we expect them to take responsibility for the consequences of their actions. The idea of personal responsibility for one's actions is also a core concept in most religious and ethical beliefs. This concept extends to businesses and corporations, which are not permitted to avoid this obligation simply because they are associations of individuals.

Regulated industries and their political friends in government have attempted to shift the responsibility for their actions to the victims who suffer as a result of their actions. For example, air pollution exacerbates asthma, a disease that has risen to epidemic levels in America's inner cities, especially among the poor. Parents of millions of asthmatic children are told to keep their children indoors on "Code Red" air-quality days, when air pollution is dangerously high. They bear the burden of treating their asthmatic children with expensive medicines, which they often cannot afford. Shifting the blame to the victims of pollution, and expecting them to deal with problems that aren't of their own making has somehow become socially appropriate because it is less expensive than cleaning up the pollution.

Corporate forces and their political allies urge Americans to base regulatory policy on this type of utilitarian calculation. They prefer that we use a cost-benefit analysis to decide the extent of regulation. This approach attaches no moral approbation to harming people. Instead, it attempts to justify a supposedly balanced approach, requiring the victims of pollution to do whatever they can to protect themselves in order to spare the corporations from "excessive" pollution-control costs. This formulation absolves corporations of responsibility for their actions, even when they kill people. In this scheme, people are not treated as people, but as economic inputs whose fates are determined by the goal of producing more goods and making more money.

Progressives passionately disagree with this approach. We believe government's most basic purpose is to protect people from being harmed by others. Our environmental, health, and safety laws are built on the premise that those who harm people are responsible for their actions and that they must act to reduce these harms. These goals have been subverted by deregulation, which allows corporations to avoid or deflect their responsibility for causing harm. In response, progressives believe that we must reorient regulatory policy to address the *source* of the harm rather than its *victims*. Such changes would reestablish the social principle that people who harm others are responsible for the consequences of their actions. Chapter 4 explains what we must do to shift the burden of protecting public health and the environment back onto the shoulders of those who cause such harm.

Do the Best We Can

While the basic role of government is to protect people from being harmed by others, public policy must take into account the cost of regulatory protection because economic growth and prosperity also are important public goals. No country, not even one as wealthy as the United States, can afford to protect everyone from all of the risks posed by modern technologies. Rather, progressives believe that we should try to "do the best we can" to protect individuals from injury and premature death by seeking the highest level of achievable protection using available technologies. In this manner, the country respects the sanctity of human life by doing all that is possible to protect people.

Existing laws adhere to this principle in a number of ways. The most common is to require any corporation creating a dangerous condition to provide protection using the best protective technology on the market. The availability of this technology usually indicates that some corporations already provide this level of protection and that most other firms can afford to adopt it without significant economic disruption. The existence of technology is also easy for regulators to verify.

Industries and their political allies oppose such technology-based approaches, saying they are too expensive. Rather, they argue, the government should be stuck with strict limits on how much it can ask corporations to spend to protect the public. Even when government has applied rigid cost-benefit analysis in making decisions, deregulators say that only those who can reduce pollution most cheaply should do so, and then only if they are financially subsidized by other corporations that do not clean up. These exchanges, commonly referred to as market-based solutions, leave communities located near polluting plants unprotected because the owners of those plants are allowed to pay a plant many miles away to assume its cleanup responsibilities.

Despite intense lobbying from corporations, Congress has not backed down from the nation's commitment to the principle that we must do the best we can when it comes to health and safety threats. In order to fulfill this commitment, however, additional progress is necessary, starting with an effort to reduce our ignorance about activities that cause harm. Chapter 5 explains how this principle can be used to address the unfinished agenda of urgent problems we described in Chapter 2.

Reduce Ignorance

One reason corporations escape responsibility for damage they cause is that as a nation we are disturbingly unaware of the full implications of their harmful activities. In the latter part of the past century, we experienced an unprecedented period of technological growth in terms of the rate of technological change and in technology's abilities to cause harm directly and indirectly. Although we have developed a good deal of knowledge about the effects of some of these activities, such as the use of lead, asbestos, pesticides, and mercury, there is an enormous amount we still do not know.

Quite often we acquire sufficient knowledge to activate norms of responsibility only after an activity has been going on long enough for there to be evidence of adverse environmental impacts, which often registers in the form of increased mortality or morbidity among significant portions of the population. Progressives want to establish practices and norms that give us this information in time to prevent these unacceptable consequences.

By comparison, regulated industries too often obstruct the development of scientific knowledge that would associate their activities with harm to individuals and the environment. When industries have information about the peril of their products and activities, they strongly resist disclosing it to regulators. They do so knowing that by avoiding disclosure they can avoid the potential for greater regulation. Corporations also try to prevent the generation of new scientific knowledge by university scientists and others and attempt to denigrate any information that goes against their self-interest.

Chapter 6 proposes a series of steps to preserve the integrity, objectivity, and independence of the scientific research we need to close this information gap. Chapter 7 proposes reforms that would create much stronger incentives to produce information about the implications of industrial activities. Chapter 11 explains what we can do to increase corporate accountability, produce more information about environmental, health, and safety risks, and enable regulators to act more expeditiously. Information disclosure also can empower citizens to engage in political and civic activities that could help reduce injuries, deaths, and environmental damage. Chapter 13 considers these possibilities and the types of information that people need in order to engage in them. It proposes steps to enable consumers to act on their social and environmental product preferences.

Better Safe than Sorry

A commitment to do the best we can to protect individual well-being requires us to act on the basis of reasonable evidence of anticipated harm, rather than waiting for more conclusive proof that some industrial activities injure and kill people. If we act on the basis of anticipated harm, then we prevent injuries and deaths, which is preferable to waiting for them to occur and then compensating the victims. No fair and moral society believes that compensating a family for the loss of a loved one is equivalent to preventing that person's death. This principle is also essential to preserving the environment for future generations. Not only is it impossible to anticipate all of the unfavorable consequences of technological change, some technologies change the world in ways that cannot be reversed. These ideas are often referred to as the application of the "precautionary principle," which is best understood as the application of the age-old injunctions, "look before you leap" and "it is better to be safe than sorry."

The better-safe-than-sorry principle requires the government to regulate when there is reasonable evidence of potential harm. Once we know an activity is likely to harm people or the environment, this principle requires regulators to assume there is no safe level of human or environmental exposure to a harmful activity in the absence of reasonable evidence that such a safe level exists. This approach places the burden on corporations to establish that their activities are safe below some level of harmful exposure. Where such evidence is not available, the government should reduce the harmful activity according to the first principle discussed: Do the best we can to protect people and the environment.

Corporations and their political allies oppose a precautionary approach to regulation because it requires them to take protective action on the basis of potential rather than actual harms. They would prefer to postpone regulation as long as possible in order to maximize short-term profits. While this stance serves corporations' economic self-interests, they try to avoid opprobrium by engaging in a disingenuous campaign to convince Americans that regulation is unnecessary. In lieu of a straightforward but wholly unsympathetic argument that we should wait until people have died or the environment has been destroyed before regulating, corporations attempt to convince the public that the government uses "poor science" when it bases regulations on incomplete information. But valid scientific studies often fail to establish conclusively the risk industrial activities pose to humans or the environment because it is difficult to prove such relationships. The question of whether to regulate based on incomplete knowledge is a policy issue, not a scientific one. Rather than attacking the policy preference, corporations and their political allies try to divert attention from their preference for profits over precaution.

Chapter 7 explains that existing statutes employ the precautionary principle, but that they also contain exemptions and loopholes that corporations have been able to exploit to prevent precautionary regulation. It proposes a number of steps the government can take to ensure that safety comes first.

Be Fair

The previous principles promote the well-being of individuals by reducing the health and safety risks they face. A commitment to improving the well-being of all Americans also requires that there be a fair distribution of environmental and other harms. Yet a large body of evidence indicates that low-income and minority communities are disproportionately subjected to hazardous waste facilities, air pollution, contaminated fish, pesticides, and hazardous work environments. A commitment to well-being also requires us to be concerned about access to parks, beaches, and other natural amenities that Americans use and enjoy. For many, these benefits are important to their quality of life, and a fair society attempts to give its citizens a chance to enjoy the things that make life special. Yet these opportunities are far less available to minorities and low-income populations.

Corporations and their political allies do not worry about the distribution of environmental harms or amenities because they consider distributional inequities as the inevitable outcomes of a free market system. This belief, however, ignores the fact that, due to economic and social handicaps not of their own making, not all Americans have an equal opportunity to prosper. By contrast, progressives believe that everyone should have the opportunity to be educated, enjoy their family, and contribute to society. Corporations defend outcomes, such as the location of hazardous waste dumps in poor neighborhoods, as appropriate because it is the cheapest solution for waste disposal. Today's progressives reject utilitarian approaches to public policy that treat people as economic inputs in order to make more money for corporations.

Chapter 8 proposes several steps to lead the country toward a fairer distribution of the burdens and benefits of living near industrial sources. It also proposes that environmental fairness offers an opportunity for the diverse groups that comprise the progressive movement, including civil rights advocates, Native American organizations, the labor movement, and environmental advocates, to come together to eliminate discrimination in employment, housing, and education.

Public Resources Belong to Everyone

The well-being of the American people depends on how well the risks of industrial pollution are regulated. Our well-being also depends on how well we manage our natural resources. For centuries, societies have recognized that our health, welfare, and survival are tied to our natural resources. Since this country's founding, the air, water, wetlands, and wildlife have had a public character under our laws, placing them under a public trust doctrine that regulates the conduct of private parties whose activities threaten these resources.

We also designate public resources that individuals cannot privately own or sell. National parks and forests are perhaps the best-known examples of such public ownership. In order to preserve these areas, we carefully regulate the uses of our public lands, including the exploitation of raw materials, such as wood and minerals.

Some of the original progressives were in the forefront of protecting public lands and public resources. As mentioned earlier, Gifford Pinchot was responsible for developing the Forest Service and limiting logging in the public forests according to their sustained maximum yield. Today's progressives continue to believe that public resources, which belong to everyone, should be used for the benefit of everyone. Government may permit corporations to undertake commercial activities that affect our natural resources and public lands. But government must ensure that such commercial activities reflect the public's interest in these resources.

Corporations want to minimize the regulatory burden that accompanies activities that adversely affect our natural resources. They also try to pay as little as possible for the right to exploit resources located on public lands. Both of these goals are motivated by their desire to reduce corporate costs and maximize profits. In light of the potential to save millions of dollars by reducing government regulations and fees, corporations are willing to donate large amounts of money to friendly politicians and spend equally large amounts of money on lawyers and others who can influence politically appointed regulators.

Corporations and their political allies realize the public may not agree that the country should degrade and despoil our natural resources and public lands just so U.S. industries can make more money. They therefore argue that it is in the public interest to allow such activities because it will spur economic development or lead to a more efficient exploitation of resources. Given their self-interest in the outcome, however, the government needs to review such claims with a great deal of care and skepticism. Unfortunately, corporations too often are able to put allies in key government positions— usually people who worked for the very corporations that they are to supervise and regulate.

Chapter 9 offers a series of steps the country should take to restore and improve protection of our natural resources and public lands. Our stewardship of these national treasures will not only determine our own well-being but that of future generations. Chapter 11 discusses the importance of government transparency. Decision-making behind closed doors facilitates corporate efforts to exploit America's natural resources.

Progressive Principles Do Not Have Borders

Progressives' concern for the fate of people and the environment does not stop at the U.S. border. Our religious and ethical traditions teach us that human life is sacrosanct no matter where an individual lives. The exploitation of the poor, for example, is no less objectionable when it occurs outside the United States. Moreover, our well-being is inextricably tied to what goes on in the rest of the world. Problems such as stratospheric ozone depletion and global warming will determine the fate of our children as well as the fate of the world's future generations.

Protecting ourselves from global risks and helping others abroad can be more difficult than achieving the same goals at home. Getting many nations to agree is a complex and daunting task, but progress cannot be made without such agreements. It is incumbent upon the United States to be a leader in the quest for progress, yet the business community and its political allies have vigorously opposed visionary U.S. leadership because they are more concerned with their short-term profits than with addressing pressing international problems. Indeed, the U.S. business community has been in the forefront of seeking international deregulatory agreements that make it more difficult for the United States and other countries to protect people and the environment.

Progressives believe the United States should reclaim the high ground as a leader in protecting people and the environment at home and abroad. Chapter 10 proposes a series of steps to replace the myopic policies of the business community and its political allies that currently dominate U.S. policy-making.

Democracy Demands Disclosure

The achievement of progressive goals requires an informed public. To make intelligent decisions about public policy, citizens must have adequate information about the risk to people and the environment, how private firms contribute to these problems, and what government is doing to address them. An effectively functioning democracy requires disclosure of government and corporate activities that affect individuals and the environment.

Corporations have a different objective. Government and corporate secrecy aids their goal of opposing new or increased regulation and exploiting natural resources with less government interference. Although corporations' wealth and power to influence the government give them a built-in advantage, they are less likely to be successful if the public is aware of their actions. Elected officials, for example, become more reluctant to do the bidding of corporations when their constituents could learn they are acting against their wishes. Recognizing this reality, corporations seek to capture key government institutions that are in a position to stop regulatory initiatives in ways that escape the public eye. Business groups, for example, have gotten their political allies to insert antiregulatory riders into large appropriations bills, where they are highly unlikely even to be noticed by other members of Congress, let alone the public. Corporations also have relied on conservative, business-friendly presidents to establish regulatory review programs in the White House that block regulations in ways that receive little public attention, and to appoint agency administrators who can operate behind the scenes to benefit their former corporate employers.

Progressives believe that we must develop strategies to make government and corporations more accountable to Americans. Chapter 13 details ways to ensure that government decision-making remains open and transparent. The chapter also includes proposals to make it easier for Americans to hold business accountable for the harms they cause and to develop effective regulatory programs to address those harms.

We Have a Right to Know

As previously mentioned, the religious and ethical beliefs of most Americans hold that no person's life is less valuable than another's. People are entitled to be protected from actions that subject them to the risk of injury or death unless they have knowingly accepted such risks with a full understanding of the dangers involved. Americans are therefore entitled to scientifically accurate information about health and safety risks.

Individuals are forced to make decisions every day about risks in market transactions. Purchasing products and services exposes consumers to health and safety risks; some people's jobs open them to such risks. People may have different preferences concerning the extent to which they are willing to accept risks. Individual circumstances often influence a person's decisions about risk. For example, safer products frequently cost more money, leaving many people unable to afford to reduce their risks. Similarly, workers may accept riskier jobs that pay more because a safer job may require education or training they do not have. But no matter a person's situation, the government should ensure each person has the proper information to make an informed decision.

More broadly, Americans need information about risks to participate in the political system. When corporations pollute the air or water, people are entitled to know the extent to which they and their environment are at risk.

Corporations have resisted government efforts requiring them to produce information about risks. They seek to avoid the expense of producing the information and the potential for being further regulated on the basis of new information. At the same time, the business community argues that the government should await more definitive information about risks before it regulates. Thus, corporations have resisted the very testing that would provide additional information about human and environmental risks while contending that regulation is not justified because of the lack of more definitive information.

Chapter 7 asserts that the burden of producing information about human and environmental risks should be shifted to the corporations responsible for creating dangers and proposes a number of steps to change law and policy in order to achieve this objective. Chapter 11 calls for governmental and corporate accountability and includes recommendations concerning how law and policy should be changed to ensure that both the government and corporations provide more information to Americans about human and environmental risks.

Make Government Work

The original Progressives sought to take control of government away from powerful corporations and trusts and reform it to better protect Americans. These early Progressives were behind the creation of the civil service system, which they intended would end political patronage and build a professional bureaucracy. Progressives continue to believe in the importance of designing and implementing policies that make government work better.

Businesses pursue their interests, not the public interest, when it comes to government reform. The business community, however, tells the American public a different story. It raises a barrage of policy arguments that contend their proposals will best serve the public interest. When Congress created the Occupational Safety and Health Administration in 1971, for example, employers convinced Congress that it should divide the regulatory responsibilities among three different agencies in order to establish a system of checks and balances in the implementation of worker safety. The business community knew that no other government agency had been structured this way because it could not work. True to form, this arrangement has frustrated OSHA's ability to promulgate and enforce regulations that protect American workers.

Making government work is not an easy task. Progressives must confront the sea of policy arguments put forward by corporations and their political allies. In some cases, the business community correctly identifies a program's failures, but proposes reforms that serve business interests rather than the public interest. In other cases, the business community claims a program is not working in order to weaken it through the adoption of a less effective approach.

To meet these challenges, progressives must identify innovations and changes that will make government more effective.

Chapter 12 proposes a series of programmatic and structural reforms to better protect humans and the environment. It distinguishes between approaches that have worked and those that require reform. The chapter then recommends the best way to bridge existing gaps between regulatory aspirations and actual outcomes.

Use Self-Help

Progressives look to government to achieve our collective values involving the welfare of all Americans. Many of the most profound risks to people and the environment stem from industrial activity that the public has no meaningful way to change through its purchasing power or other means. Nevertheless, there are significant self-help opportunities. For example, millions of individuals recycle, although it is more convenient and less costly for many of them simply to throw things in the garbage can. This type of self-help goes beyond consumers' decisions to take actions that personally benefit them, such as buying safer cars or reducing their exposure to potentially harmful foods. When consumers engage in self-help, they also are seeking to improve the well-being of others in this country and around the world.

The Progressive movement has a strong historical connection to political activism within private consumer markets. The sit-ins, boycotts, and purchasing campaigns that civil rights advocates used are perhaps the best-known examples of self-help. There are many modern-day equivalents, such as student campaigns to convince universities not to license their logos and insignias to clothing manufacturers that do not ensure fair pay and safe, healthy working conditions for their foreign workers. These activities indicate that consumption need not be viewed as an inherently private, self-interested, and nonpolitical activity. The progressive perspective is that self-help is an important outlet for Americans to express their social and political views, whether as individuals acting on their own or joining with others in organized campaigns to improve the welfare of others.

Corporations are threatened by the idea that consumers would regard corporate production and employee practices as relevant to purchasing decisions, and they have sought assistance from their political allies to stymie consumer self-help. Businesses have resisted providing information to consumers that puts their products and practices in a bad light, and they have sought to block governmental actions that would require them, or permit others, to publicize such information. Agricultural producers and food manufacturers, for example, have successfully prevented the Food and Drug Administration from requiring food labels to divulge whether a food or one of its components has been genetically modified, although this is a standard practice in Europe.

Chapter 13 identifies steps the government must take to effect progressive consumerism. It describes a number of market-enhancing programs aimed at improving the consumer's ability to function as an ethical and effective decision-maker within globally integrated marketplaces that too often cause undesirable social and environmental consequences.

CHAPTER 4

SHIFTING THE BLAME

The Blame Game

In recent years, industry and government political appointees have labored to shift responsibility for addressing the consequences of pollution from the polluters to their victims. A memorable scene from Jonathan Harr's book, *A Civil Action,* captured the approach: An industry lawyer asks victims of toxic pollution in Woburn, Massachusetts, whether they eat peanut butter and bacon, use Teflon pans, chew gum with artificial sweeteners, or use deodorant—all products that carry some risk. The lawyer's plain intent is to shift the responsibility—and the blame—for the victims' health problems from his corporate client to the victims.

Unfortunately, this doesn't just happen in books and movies. For example, some years ago the American Lung Association (ALA) asked the Environmental Protection Agency (EPA) to set a new standard for sulfur dioxide emissions based on scientific studies that concluded the existing standard would not protect asthmatics from recurring respiratory problems. Those problems were so serious that they prevented the afflicted person from doing strenuous outdoor work or necessitated a visit to the emergency room or even a hospital stay. In the first Bush Administration, the EPA's response was, in essence, to blame the victim. The EPA thought the sulfur dioxide-related problems the ALA cited were not serious enough to justify a new air-quality standard because the respiratory problems were caused by allowable sulfur dioxide emissions, they were within the range of problems asthmatics regularly faced, and the patients could improve their symptoms by taking medication. By this reasoning, people with asthma—not the polluters—are responsible for avoiding the health problems caused by pollution.

Similar examples of the same phenomenon abound. Childhood asthma rates are at an all-time high in the United States, and highest among the poor. Rather than acknowledge their complicity in the exacerbation, and perhaps even the initiation, of asthma, polluting firms have hypothesized that poor housekeeping habits, which can lead to household pests and their waste products, are behind the explosion in asthma cases. Likewise, lead-based paint poisoning, which is also prevalent among low-income families, often is blamed on parents allowing their children to eat paint chips when the real problem is the presence of microscopic lead dust in deteriorating, uninhabitable housing units—not to mention an industry that continued to add lead to paint for decades after learning that it posed a health hazard.

In many cases, the responsibility for avoiding the consequences of pollution can be shifted to the victims without most people noticing. Often, only a portion of society bears the greatest health risks from pollution—typically minority and low-income communities. It is relatively easy for industries or the government to insist that risk reduction is the job of a minority of citizens, since the majority of people either won't notice or won't understand why there is a problem. For example, some people might be satisfied when the government responds to water pollution by advising people not to eat certain kinds or amounts of fish, rather than by lowering pollutants to a level that makes the fish safe to eat. But fish occupies a central cultural and dietary role in the lives of many Native Americans that makes it difficult, if not impossible, to stop consuming fish. The same is true for subsistence fishermen and their families—a group of low-income Americans that relies on locally caught fish in order to eat. Shifting the responsibility for reducing the effects of pollution from polluters to such groups unfairly saddles them with a disproportionate share of the burdens of modern industrial society, particularly when these groups do not enjoy many of society's benefits.

Despite such imbalances, efforts to shift the responsibility for dealing with pollution from the polluters to their victims affect us all. Such efforts reduce the moral and political pressure for protective regulation, and long-standing theoretical foundations have put a respectable, intellectual face on this kind of shift.

The Ghost of Coase

British economist A.C. Pigou was the leading economic theorist on environmental matters in the first half of the 20th century. He observed that environmental harm resulted from the fact that polluting firms did not have to pay for their harm; they could "externalize" the cost onto pollution victims.[1] He thought the solution was for the government to make polluters pay for the environmental harm they produced, a concept referred to thereafter as a

---

1. A.C. Pigou, *The Economics of Welfare* (1960), 129–30.
2. Ibid.

"Pigouvian tax," known often today as a "green tax."[2] Thus polluting firms' externalities would become internalities, creating an incentive for firms to reduce pollution just as they have an incentive to cut any other business expense.

Pigou's solution to the pollution problem dominated economic discussions of environmental problems for decades. Then, in one of the most famous and influential law review articles of all time, Nobel Memorial Prize laureate Ronald H. Coase wrote that Pigou had gotten it wrong.[3] In "The Problem of Social Cost," Coase argued that Pigou was mistaken in assuming that it was the polluter who was doing the harm and the polluter who should be taxed. Rather, Coase wrote, it is equally true that pollution victims harm the polluter if they insist that the pollution be reduced or stopped. Thus, the appropriate response to pollution is not to tax the polluter, but to look at the social costs and benefits of the situation and select the alternative that creates the largest net social benefits. The most famous part of his article, published in the *Journal of Law and Economics,* outlined what has come to be known as the "Coase theorem"—the proposition that in the absence of obstacles to bargaining, or transaction costs, parties will reach the socially optimal solution to a problem, regardless of which party has the legal entitlement to pursue the desired outcome. Coase's essential point was that obstacles to bargaining often stand in the way of optimal social results and that, in these cases, the government might have to step in to accomplish the results that obstacles to bargaining have prevented. In any event, Coase maintained that the most important part of his argument was that there is no socially relevant difference between the polluter and the polluted; both, he asserted, can cause harm if they insist on having things their way without looking at the full social context.

Coase's article, written some 40 years ago, continues to influence how legal scholars, economists, and others think about pollution. Hailed as the most cited law review article in history by the *Journal of Law and Economics,* it is taught in law school courses ranging from property to torts to environmental law. If there is a canon in legal education, Coase's article is in it.

His theory makes an it's-all-relative attitude toward pollution acceptable: If we believe Coase, we can no longer say pollution is harmful or morally suspect without first looking at the polluter's reasons for polluting. With Coase, what had seemed like a straightforward idea—when pollution makes people sick or ruins their crops, the polluter is the one causing harm, not the victims who ask the polluter to stop—suddenly became suspect, even old-fashioned.

---

3. Ronald H. Coase, "The Problem of Social Cost," *Journal of Law & Economics* 3 (1960): 1.

This argument provided the theoretical underpinnings of, and impressive intellectual pedigree for, contemporary efforts to shift the responsibility for the harms of pollution to its victims.

Manufacturing Consent

If, as Coase argued, there is no socially relevant difference between being exposed to pollution and exposing someone else to it, then it must follow that there is no socially relevant difference between different kinds of events that cause or threaten people with the same kinds of objective harms. If people consent to one physical risk, for example, it must follow that they have implicitly consented to other physical risks that threaten harm of the same probability and magnitude. Once pollution and its harms have been stripped of their moral significance, it is possible to use all sorts of decisions people make to justify imposing pollution's burdens on them.

Most people are willing to take at least some risks for money. They might take riskier jobs for higher pay or buy a more dangerous product because it is cheaper than a safer one. In applying Pigou's theory, if a person accepts some risk by buying something other than the safest car on the road, that does not mean that the purchaser forfeits the right to be protected from health hazards from pollution, and that a firm whose pollution does the purchaser harm shouldn't pay for their damage. But according to Coase's theorem, there is no relevant difference between foregoing a safe car and having someone else's pollution harm you, so it is easy to say that the decision about a car implies something about one's attitude toward risk, and thus pollution. Today, we see the government taking a variety of market decisions—the choice of a riskier job, the decision to buy a cheaper car—and using them to estimate the value of protecting people from harms. When it turns out that this value is lower than the cost of protection, the government says that the people have spoken and they don't *want* more environmental protection. Look at the risky jobs they take and the shoddy cars they buy! This rationale is another way that responsibility for pollution control circles back to pollution's victims rather than its perpetrators.

The same strange logic surfaces when comparing the risks many people will take and the risks many would avoid. Economists, law professors, right-wing think tanks, and the media constantly remind us that the things that really scare us—shark attacks, snipers, toxic chemicals, and nuclear accidents—aren't nearly as dangerous as the ordinary things that don't—obesity, lack of exercise, and car travel. The implication is that our complicity in the creation of one risk is complicit in the creation of another. Pollution victims can be

Air Bags: A Case Study in Industry Intransigence

The story of how airbags came to be installed in American automobiles is an example of the disconnect between the interests of corporations and the public. Far too often, corporations strenuously oppose efforts to protect the health and safety of consumers, only to discover years later that an informed public demands those protections.

More than 40,000 Americans die each year in auto accidents. Another 5 million are injured, several hundred thousand severely. In all, 20 million automobiles are involved in accidents each year in the United States, a total monetary cost estimated between $60 billion and $100 billion, including the costs associated with property damage, bodily injury, and premature death.[4]

In 1966, Congress passed the National Traffic and Motor Vehicle Safety Act, directing the Department of Transportation (DOT) to "reduce traffic accidents and deaths and injuries to persons resulting from traffic accidents" by promulgating regulations that "shall be practical, shall meet the need for motor vehicle safety, and shall be stated in objective terms."

Efforts to reduce the number and severity of automobile accidents prior to the Act were confined to the tort system and to the auto industry's voluntary approach to auto safety. The staggering number of persons killed and injured each year was testimony to the failure of both approaches. Still, Congress did not act until the publication of Ralph Nader's book, *Unsafe at Any Speed*, exposed the design hazards of General Motors' Corvair automobile and highlighted the problems with a voluntary approach to auto safety. Indeed, for years, the auto industry had attributed auto accidents and the deaths and injuries that resulted to the "nut behind the wheel."[5]

For years, the auto industry insisted that safety does not sell, and so placed little emphasis on safety engineering.[6] Consumers were provided with little information about possible safety problems and solutions, and thus had limited ability to influence industry decision-making.

(Continued)

4. Thompson, "Regulating Motor Vehicle Safety Maintenance: Can We Make It Cost-Effective?," *Journal of Health Policy and Law* 9 (1995): 695.

5. Jon D. Hanson & Douglas A. Kysar, "Symposium: Rational Actors or Rational Fools? The Implications of Psychology for Products Liability, Taking Behaviorialism Seriously: A Response to Market Manipulation," *Roger Williams University Law Review* 6 (2000): 259, 347 (quoting Joan Claybrook & David Bollier, "The Hidden Benefits of Regulation: Disclosing the Auto Safety Payoff," *Yale Journal on Regulation* 3 (1995): 87, 91).

6. Ibid., 346.

Air Bags: *(Continued)*

While the Act's passage signaled a major step toward auto safety, a long road lay ahead. From the late 1960s to 1984, NHTSA promulgated numerous auto safety regulations, but each was either rescinded or postponed. For its part, the auto industry opposed safety regulations, including air bags, at every opportunity. In fact, General Motors opposed air bags even though three internal consumer polls showed that consumers wanted airbags, even at a high cost.[7]

In the 1970s, air bags became a political ping-pong ball after several failed efforts to require seat belts or airbags. William Coleman, President Ford's Secretary of Transportation, rescinded the existing regulations. In their place Coleman obtained the agreement of several manufacturers to supply at least 40,000 (and up to 400,000) air bag-equipped cars to demonstrate the feasibility of the technology. A few months later, after President Carter appointed Brock Adams as Secretary, DOT promulgated a revised standard. It required new automobiles to have passive restraints (either air bags or automatic seatbelts) by 1982. Congress did not veto the regulation, and it was upheld by the D.C. Circuit in 1979.[8] This regulation, however, did not survive even as long as the previous one.

The Reagan Administration took office with considerable deregulatory zeal. Vice President Bush was put in charge of a "Task Force on Regulatory Relief," which, after consultations with the auto industry, issued a report calling for a 34-point agenda of "Actions to Help the U.S. Auto Industry." Among the items listed was a proposal to delay the passive-restraints standard. Drew Lewis, President Reagan's Secretary of Transportation, told the National Automobile Dealers Association, "If I could do it, there would be a four-year moratorium [on new regulations]. I know four years is unrealistic, but my point is that this Administration opposes regulations."[9] In October 1981, Lewis took one action he could accomplish: he revoked the existing regulation. He explained that because manufacturers would likely choose to install detachable automatic seatbelts, rather than air bags, so many car occupants would detach the belts that DOT could not justify their cost. The Reagan Administration's opposition to auto safety regulation led General Motors to discontinue its airbag-develop

(Continued)

---

7. Gerald F. Tietz, "Strict Products Liability, Design Defects and Corporate Decision-Making: Greater Deterrence Through Stricter Process," *Villanova Law Review* 38 (1993): 1361, n. 213 (citing Ralph Nader & William Taylor, *The Big Boys: Power and Position in American Business* (1986), 136).

8. *Pacific Legal Found. v. Department of Transp.*, 593 F.2d 1338, 1349 (D.C. Cir.), *cert. denied*, 444 U.S. 830 (1979).

9. Joan Claybrook, *Retreat from Safety: Reagan's Attack on America's Health* (1984), 180.

Air Bags: *(Continued)*

ment project.[10] Rather than support safety regulations, NHTSA decided to promote a "National Safety Sabbath," a weekend during which all Americans would join in "a religious fellowship to rediscover the safety belt" by providing "National Safety Sabbath kits," replete with suggested prayers.[11]

In *Motor Vehicle Mfrs. Ass'n v. State Farm Ins. Co.*, 463 U.S. 29 (1983), the Supreme Court heard a challenge to the rescission brought by several insurance companies, which believed that passive restraints would lower insurance costs, and by several public interest groups. The suit was defended by DOT and the automobile manufacturers. When the dust of the legal battle cleared, the Court gave a clear victory to those who challenged the rescission. In noting that the auto industry's decision to use the passive belt over the air bag could not justify the rescission of the regulation, Justice White described the auto industry's strenuous opposition to airbags, stating that "surely it is not enough that the regulated industry has eschewed a given safety device. For nearly a decade, the automobile industry waged the regulatory equivalent of war against the airbag and lost—the inflatable restraint was proven sufficiently effective."[12]

In February 1983, four months before the *State Farm* decision, President Reagan appointed Elizabeth Dole to succeed Drew Lewis as Secretary of Transportation, and she found support for a new regulation in Congress.

Dole went on to devise an ingenious political compromise. In 1984, DOT promulgated a regulation that required automobile manufacturers to install either air bags or automatic seatbelts by 1989. The regulation provided, however, that it would not go into effect if two-thirds of the nation's population were covered by state laws requiring the use of manual seatbelts before April 1, 1989, and if those laws met the minimum criteria set out in the regulation.

After the regulation was promulgated, lobbyists from the automobile manufacturers swooped down on state legislatures in a $15 million campaign for the adoption of laws requiring the use of seatbelts.[13] The lobbying campaign

(Continued)

10. Gerald F. Tietz, "Strict Products Liability, Design Defects and Corporate Decision-Making: Greater Deterrence Through Stricter Process," *Villanova Law Review* 38 (1993): 1361, 1402 (citing Ralph Nader & William Taylor, *The Big Boys: Power and Position in American Business* (1986), 137–141).

11. Caroline E. Mayer, "You're in Really Good Hands with NHSTA," *Washington Post*, January 29, 1982, A19; "The Born-Again Seat-Belt Drive Loses Top Help," *Washington Post*, February 12, 1982, A21. The National Safety Council ultimately withdrew its support for the campaign after civil libertarians complained. Ibid.

12. *Motor Vehicle Mfrs. Ass'n v. State Farm Ins. Co.*, 463 U.S. 29, 49 (1983).

13. Pressley, "Public in Middle of U.S. Seat Belt Debate," *New York Times*, March 11, 1985, C1.

Air Bags: *(Continued)*

failed. Although most states did enact seatbelt laws, most of these did not meet the minimum criteria in the regulation. As a result, the regulation requiring passive restraints quietly went into effect on April 1, 1989, with little press coverage and no more outside interest than a handful of telephone calls to NHTSA from automobile manufacturers. The installation of air bags in automobiles in the United States has now become standard practice and what was once a target of industry opposition has become an integral part of the auto industry's campaign to market safety.

The end result of this lengthy regulatory battle was greater auto safety for consumers. But the decades-long delay in achieving these results could have been avoided had the auto industry channeled its vast resources away from blanket opposition to a regulatory approach and toward a better understanding of consumer preferences and demands for safety. After all, this latter approach is now serving the industry well, as it continues to market air bags as a selling point for its automobiles.

(Adapted from SIDNEY A. SHAPIRO & JOSEPH P. TOMAIN, REGULATORY LAW AND POLICY: CASES AND MATERIALS 29–33 (3rd ed. 2003).

blamed for their problems using this method, too. And they are not only blamed; they're criticized as irrational and maybe even a little crazy.

Ignoring Public Desires

The effort to manufacture consent to pollution by pointing to the risky decisions people make has run into a stumbling block: A large body of evidence from scholars who study people's risk perceptions and risk-related decisions shows that people do not take into account the numerical probability or magnitude of harm in shaping their attitudes toward risk. If someone drives a cheaper and less safe car, this doesn't mean the person will accept an environmental risk that has a lower probability of causing harm than the car does. People look at context in judging risk. If a hazard has certain qualitative features, such as being involuntary, uncontrollable, unfamiliar, and inequitably imposed, then ordinary people will likely find it scary even if the numerical probability of it occurring is rather low. In light of this evidence, it is not credible to say that people consent to one risk by accepting another kind of risk.

An additional argument, beyond consent, is necessary to justify shifting responsibility for pollution to its victims. If people judge risks according to factors other than the probability and magnitude of harm, they are being irrational and the government must step in to save them from themselves. In other words, it is better to ignore their wishes entirely.

Like Coase's ideas, this argument has an intellectual pedigree that prevents it from being dismissed outright. In a 1993 book, U.S. Supreme Court Justice Stephen Breyer, then chief judge of the 1st U.S. Circuit Court of Appeals, concluded that our approach to risk regulation was so misguided and ordinary people's demands for risk reduction were so wrongheaded that the best solution would be to turn over decisions about risk to an elite cadre of civil servants in the executive branch who were insulated from the pressures of politics—and from the crazy demands of ordinary citizens.[14]

Breyer's views, which were widely criticized as antidemocratic at the time he wrote them, have since taken on new life in the Bush Administration. John Graham, who heads the Office of Information and Regulatory Affairs at the White House Office of Management and Budget, has cited Breyer's proposal as his model in reshaping governmental responses to risk.[15] Not surprisingly, Graham has presided over what may be the swiftest shift in regulatory process and substance since the New Deal. He has centralized decision-making within the White House and frequently overruled the decisions of agencies specifically assigned certain tasks by Congress. In objecting to agency decisions, Graham has deployed a brand of economic analysis that shunts concerns about freedom, fairness, and other intangibles that permeate citizens' attitudes toward risk. This economic analysis also freely assumes that consenting to an exchange of money for risk in one context implies consent to risk in another context. According to this Administration, we have met the enemy, and it is us.

Making People Invisible

A related but distinct way of shifting blame for pollution is to make it seem as though no real person is hurt by pollution. Instead of avoiding pollution control by referring to victims' decisions and characteristics, here the strategy is to refer to their lack of identity. If no one sees or knows the victims of pollution, we can pretend they do not exist and no one has to be blamed for anything.

Pollution victims have been rendered invisible through the creation of the "statistical life," which is a collection of risks in a population. When these risks,

---

14. Stephen Breyer, *Breaking the Vicious Circle: Toward Effective Risk Regulation* (1993).

15. John D. Graham, Administrator OIRA, "Presidential Oversight of The Regulatory State: Can It Work?," Speech at Heinz School, Carnegie Mellon University, October 4, 2002, http://www.whitehouse.gov/omb/inforeg/graham_cmu_100402.html.

added together, will result in the loss of a life, this is a statistical life. The important feature of statistical life is that it doesn't belong to anyone in particular. Unlike the little girl trapped in a well or the soldier captured behind enemy lines, we can't attach a face or a name to it.

This lack of identity is partly due to the limits of science. Many of the harms caused by pollution, such as cancer and other illnesses, are also caused by other factors. It is often not possible to separate the harms caused by pollution from those caused by something else. It is only possible to say that, within a population, some people have gotten cancer as a result of pollution. Thus, some anonymity for pollution victims is an inevitable byproduct of the limits of our scientific knowledge.

But the statistical life has become much more than a tool of imperfect knowledge. It also has been used to justify placing a monetary value on risks to life and health; without this device, such an exercise would not be plausible.

Imagine trying to place a monetary value on the life of an identified person. An economist trying to value a person's life would have to try to figure out either how much the person would be willing to pay to go on living or how much money the person would be willing to accept in exchange for dying. Answers to the first question would be meaningless as a measure of willingness to pay because the answers would be dependent on capacity to pay. Bill Gates can pay a lot more money to go on living than could a poor person, but that doesn't mean the poor person wouldn't pay more if he could. Answers to the second question would be equally unhelpful. No sane person would accept a finite sum of money in exchange for certain death. It's not that people place an infinite value on their own lives; it's that they tend not to participate in markets for certain death.

Economic analysis of the benefits of life-saving programs goes nowhere if the benefit is defined as life itself. This is where the concept of statistical life starts to do some real work. Seeing the dilemma posed by valuing life itself, economists observed that there were no such dilemmas when the value of risk, not life, was at issue. Most people are willing to accept some risks in exchange for money. So rather than continue the futile quest for the value of life, economists began to talk about the value of statistical life. This maneuver saves the cost-benefit project by allowing a price to be placed on the benefits of life-saving programs. And, once again, the victims of pollution become responsible for the pollution levels allowed by the government and maintained by industry. If only people were willing to pay more, in wholly different contexts, to reduce their risk, the government would require industry to reduce pollution more.

The statistical life also obscures the invidious discrimination that underlies recent efforts to price lives differently depending on who owns them. When the EPA came under fire in spring 2003 for assuming lower monetary values for the elderly than for younger people, economists rushed to the EPA's defense to explain that these were statistical lives, not real lives. Apparently, the statistical nature of the relevant risk made discrimination acceptable.

This example also illustrates that the emphasis on statistical life has a final effect, which is to paper over the fact that even if we can't put a price tag on real people, they do fall ill and die as a result of pollution. In this way, the public can be lulled into believing that no moral dilemmas lie at the heart of pollution and its control. We can put a price on statistical lives, and even eliminate them if it's too expensive not to do so, without worrying about doing anything wrong. After all, they're just statistical lives, and who has ever met a statistical person? The normal human sympathy that accompanies suffering and loss shuts off when victims are portrayed as faceless, nameless statistics, which is very good news for the industries that kill thousands of people a year through preventable pollution. If their misdeeds were not so subtle, they might well be regarded as serial killers.

The Progressive Perspective

When people or companies cause harm, the relationship between them and their victims is not neutral. The people or companies that cause harm must be responsible for it. It is clear that the vast majority of Americans adhere to this view any time this subject is open for discussion. Consider the situation the EPA faced in the early 1980s in addressing the air pollution problems of a copper-smelting plant outside Tacoma, Wash. Risk assessments indicated that continued operation of the plant, even after installing what was then the best available pollution-control technology, would result in fatalities—the loss of statistical lives—due to the level of arsenic in the emissions. The plant owners said tougher pollution controls would force the plant to close, which would cost the community jobs. When residents of the affected communities had an opportunity to speak at the hearing, one person said the failure to insist on tougher controls was like "somebody standing on the other side of the city line with a thirty-ought-six and firing it into Tacoma."[16]

The idea that the polluter pays best expresses the non-neutral approach toward environmental hazards, but we should not ignore the real complications of implementing it. Job loss, for instance, causes serious hardship for fami-

---

16. Esther Scott, *The Risks of Asarco, in Ethics and Politics* (Amy Gutmann & Dennis Thompson eds., 2d ed., 1990), 163, 165.

lies who bear little responsibility for an employer's decisions. Adequate responses need to be worked out regarding such complications, but the bedrock idea is not to lose sight of the overriding responsibility, which is to avoid causing harm.

Those who cause harm through pollution or other effects on the environment continually try to shift the blame from themselves to the victims of pollution, with Coase's ideas about the moral equivalence of perpetrator and victim as their intellectual reference point. Fortunately, existing environmental laws generally have taken the opposite approach. Virtually all the major environmental statutes enacted in the 1970s were part of an era in which the U.S. legal system was fairly revolutionized by the simple insight that polluters should begin paying to prevent pollution and paying for the harms they could not prevent. Although these laws did not follow Pigou's advice insofar as they do not rely on pollution taxes to accomplish their work, their normative foundation was similar to his: The polluters are causing harm, and they ought to take this into account in going about their business. Coase's normative equalizing of the stature of both the polluter and the polluted was nowhere in the picture in those days. Countries outside the United States routinely impose green taxes as a means of controlling pollution.

When the modern Clean Air Act was passed in 1970, Congress made clear that it wanted the new statute to protect even the most vulnerable subpopulations—the elderly, the very young, people with respiratory diseases—from the harmful effects of air pollution. And when Congress in 1980 passed the Superfund law requiring cleanups of abandoned hazardous waste sites, it directed the EPA to choose permanent solutions to the problem of hazardous waste contamination rather than temporary ones. In practical terms, this meant the burden of avoiding the harms of contamination rested with the polluters responsible for it rather than with future landowners or land users. At core, the laws framed an important, critical, and straightforward question: "Why shouldn't the polluter pay?"

Federal law places the responsibility for avoiding pollution on polluters, not their victims, in many other ways. Nevertheless, the blame-the-victim mentality is an important development. It creates a public discourse that discredits new regulatory initiatives and threatens to roll back existing ones. It is time to lay this mentality to rest.

The Progressive Agenda

Change Attitudes

For many, a kind of resignation has developed around pollution harms. Environmental problems are framed as complicated and filled with trade-offs that require complex technical analysis to be resolved. We need to see these problems the way the Tacoma, Washington resident did. If viewed through that lens, attitudes toward problems and their solutions will begin to change. When we are told that our children should play inside because it is a Code Red air-quality day or that the fish in the river are filled with toxins so we shouldn't eat them, we should remember the alternative possibility: Perhaps those who pollute the air and water should have to change their behavior. This attitude shift will likely only come when we remember that the people who die from pollution are real, not statistical, people, and when we recognize that protecting individuals without blaming them for their personal traits or dismissing them as statistical ciphers protects and enriches our communities. Indeed, one of the surest ways to destroy a community is to contaminate it with toxic pollutants.

Let Children Play Outside

Turning from public attitudes to regulatory settings, the government should set standards to protect vulnerable subpopulations without requiring them to act in some way. For example, children should not be forced to stay inside in order to avoid becoming sick from air pollution. Asthmatics should not have to go to the doctor or emergency room because we haven't cleaned up the air. As we have seen, these are the kinds of results that existing law formally rejects. However, formal statutory commands from Congress can differ greatly from how an agency implements those commands.

Do Not Discriminate Against 'Statistical People'

If a fire station announced that it planned to stop sending fire trucks to nursing homes because the elderly weren't worth the trouble or if a hospital announced that it would start turning away people simply because they were very sick, public outcry undoubtedly would be fierce. In addition, the fire station and the hospital almost certainly would be found to be engaging in unlawful discrimination. Why should the public reaction and legal consequences be any different when the rescue squad is from the EPA? Using the tool of statistical life does not sanction discrimination against society's vulnerable groups.

Prefer Risk Reduction over Risk Avoidance

In the same vein, agencies should embrace risk reduction rather than risk avoidance. When a risk is reduced or eliminated, the entire system benefits. For instance, if you remove lead from a consumer product, you eliminate the consumer's exposure as well as lead-disposal problems, workers' exposure during the manufacturing process, environmental harms from mining, and so forth. Chapter 5 discusses this principle in greater detail.

Protect Workers

The blame-the-victim mindset has particularly affected workers. It is easy enough to assume, or at least hope, that people who work dangerous jobs have consented to the danger and either receive sufficient compensation for the risks they take on or that they like the danger. For example, we have a law that protects the public against the risks of pesticides far more than it protects farm workers, who have greater exposure to pesticides and are among the least powerful bargaining groups in this country. And we have an Occupational Safety and Health Administration that has been moribund for years, even as the EPA has made, however fitfully, significant strides in protecting the general public against pollution risks. We must eliminate the disparity between the protections afforded the general public and those afforded the workers who often are more exposed to hazards from which the public is protected.

Redress Harm

In recent years, courts have heard several cases in which plaintiffs allege that they were wrongfully exposed to harmful pollutants. In many instances, the plaintiffs are not yet sick, but they face an increased risk of illness and are afraid of what the future may hold. Courts have struggled with these cases, unsure about whether and how to compensate people who are not physically ill. Within these cases, one can discern a kind of hostility to pollution victims: Why are they complaining if they aren't sick? And why are they so afraid of something the judges think is benign? Many times, courts have simply thrown up their hands and denied relief. Even courts that have allowed these claims have worked hard to give them some predictable shape and scope and fit them within existing legal doctrine. They have done this work mainly by tying claims for risk and fear to claims for physical illness. In many cases, courts have required that compensation for risk and fear be related to the compensation that would occur in a case of physical illness. We believe that a more empathetic attitude to pollution victims would help courts see that they have been drawing the wrong legal analogies in these cases. When a person or, more commonly, a whole community is exposed to harmful pollution, the harm that occurs is to one's dignity—the kind people suffer when someone trespasses on their property. Thus, the legal analogy should be to assault and trespass, not to physical injury caused by negligence. Developing this theory of a toxic tort would steer attention away from a plaintiff's personal habits and traits, as illustrated by the excerpt from "A Civil Action" at the beginning of this chapter, and focus instead on the polluter's conduct. This new kind of tort, based on the harms that result from deliberately being exposed to a hazard, could help common law courts move away from the blame-the-victim mentality we have been criticizing.

Conclusion

Government's most basic purpose is to protect citizens from being harmed by others. Environmental protection has remained a bedrock value for most Americans, in part, because environmental problems are an example of citizens hurting other citizens. If the antiregulatory movement is to survive, it must take on the powerful image of what environmental problems do. Antiregulatory forces have tried to shift responsibility for pollution from the polluters to the victims of pollution by attempting to change how we think about harm. Our environmental laws, for the most part, do not sanction this shift. They are built on the premise that polluters should address the consequences of pollution. Nevertheless, influential forces are working to undermine this principle. We have offered several suggestions for reforms to environmental law that would strengthen and deepen the protection of pollution's victims. Above all, we hope we have exposed the tricks polluters use to make pollution's victims appear responsible for their predicaments.

CHAPTER 5

DO THE BEST WE CAN

Harnessing Technology

In the preceding chapter, we stressed the importance of reducing health or environmental risks, rather than blaming the victim. Progressives also have something to say about how the government should address risk-producing activities. In practice, the government uses two broad approaches. Some statutes require the government to determine an acceptable level of risk and then provide inducements or impose controls that reduce the risk to an acceptable level. Such "risk-based regulation" is an exceedingly complex and resource-intensive undertaking that typically results in little actual risk reduction because the burden is on the government to justify the acceptable level of risk and the method to reduce the risk. Chapter 7 addresses the progressive perspective on this approach and ways to improve it.

Other statutes use an easier and more effective approach, which insists that a source do its best to reduce risks. While the acceptable risk goal typically addresses the quality of the receiving medium (air, water, soil, etc.), the "best-efforts" approach focuses on the technologies that are capable of reducing pollution or other risk-producing activities. For that reason, it is sometimes referred to as a technology-based approach to regulation. Progressives generally prefer this approach to protecting health, safety, and the environment. This method is effective because it does not place huge informational and analytical burdens on the government. It also achieves risk reduction without significant economic disruption because the level of regulation is tied to existing or reasonably foreseeable technologies.

How the Best-Efforts Approach Works

Under a best-efforts approach, regulators begin by separating the sources of risk, dischargers of air or water pollutants for example, into categories and subcategories, attempting to include within each category a group of similar sources. Regulators then conduct a survey of a representative sample of sources and vendors of pollution-control technologies in each category with an eye toward identifying risk-reduction technologies that are currently available or capable of being developed in the near future. Statutes establish whether the regulator should select from currently available technologies or push technology development more aggressively by opting for one that will be available soon. After choosing a benchmark technology, the regulator determines the level of emissions reduction it can achieve and issues a standard set at that level. Sources can meet the standard by using the benchmark technology or any other method they choose.

Best Efforts in the Beginning

When the public interest movement emerged in the late 1960s, unions and public interest groups did not advocate intricate legislation under which the government would provide just the right amount of workplace safety or environmental protection. Rather than requiring the implementing agencies to gather and analyze data on the environmental, health, and safety effects of various pollutants and other risk-producing activities, advocates for change demanded that something be done to stop the carnage in the workplace, the eye-burning smog in the air, and the use of rivers and streams as industrial sewers. The advocates believed that corporations should do their best to reduce destructive behaviors. Efforts to calibrate the precise amount of necessary risk reduction inevitably result in the victims continuing to bear the burdens of exposure until time-consuming and controversial studies are completed and debated. Under the best-efforts approach, if exposures to pollutants, workplace chemicals, or other risks threaten to cause adverse effects, they should be minimized immediately and as much as possible. The goal is to ensure that all sources in the polluting industries make an adequate effort to reduce harm-producing activities.

The 1972 amendments to the Clean Water Act (CWA), for example, adopted a pollution-reduction goal for new and existing dischargers of water pollutants. The amendments required new sources to install the "best available demonstrated control technology" and called upon existing sources to install the "best practicable control technology currently available" by 1977 and the "best available technology economically achievable" by 1983.

In contrast, the primary goal of the 1970 Clean Air Act (CAA) was to meet the risk-based national ambient air-quality standards by 1977. As the deadline for reaching the standards passed with very little improvement in air quality, Congress shifted gears and launched several new technology-based regulatory programs aimed at achieving the highest level of pollution reduction possible. New major stationary sources in areas that did not meet the standards had to install technology capable of achieving the lowest achievable emissions rate. Existing stationary sources in such areas had to install less stringent "reasonably available control technology." Even in areas that met the ambient standards, major emitting facilities had to install the best-available control technology to prevent significant deterioration of air quality. Although Congress did not abandon the risk-based approach, it extended the deadline another 10 years. The best-efforts provisions it put into place, however, applied immediately to new facilities and began to have an effect on existing facilities within three years.

Best Efforts Expanded

When Congress overhauled the program for establishing national emissions standards for hazardous air pollutants (HAPs) in 1990, it embraced the best-efforts approach even more dramatically as a needed replacement for the risk-based approach. For nearly three decades, the EPA had struggled to promulgate standards for HAPs that would protect public health with an ample margin of safety. After more than 25 years, the agency had succeeded in promulgating HAP standards for only seven of the hundreds of well-known toxic chemicals emitted by U.S. plants.[1] The last straw was a decision written by a U.S. Court of Appeals for the District of Columbia Circuit judge, former Supreme Court nominee Robert Bork, that threw out the agency's decade-long effort to write a standard for vinyl chloride, a known human carcinogen.[2]

Pointedly abandoning the risk-based approach, Congress promulgated a list of HAPs and instructed the EPA to write best-efforts standards for all industries emitting them. The standards require new and existing sources of HAPs to install controls that reflect the maximum degree of reduction achievable, or "maximum achievable control technology" (MACT). In addition, Congress provided specific guidance for the best-efforts test. For existing sources, the requirement had to be at least as stringent as the "average emission limitation achieved by the best performing 12 percent of the existing

---

1. Office of Technology Assessment, U.S. Congress, *Identifying and Regulating Carcinogens: Background Paper*, 1987, 106.
2. *NRDC v. EPA*, 824 F.2d 1146 (1987).

sources" or, for categories containing fewer than 30 sources, as stringent as the "average emission limitation achieved by the best performing 5 sources."

While Congress' mandate was crystal clear, regulated industries still work to undermine MACT regulations. The most egregious example is the Bush Administration's decision to subvert these requirements with respect to mercury emissions from power plants and mercury-cell chlor-akali factories. These travesties of statutory misinterpretation will almost certainly be reversed by the courts.

Why Best Efforts Work Better

Congress' repeated return to the best-efforts approach reflects an understanding that it is generally easier to implement and, therefore, more likely to yield genuine improvement relatively quickly. Agencies can promulgate best-efforts requirements much quicker than risk-based standards. Indeed, agencies can write best-efforts regulations three to 10 times faster than risk-based regulations.[3] Moreover, the best-efforts approach is relatively easy to adapt any improvements in new risk-reduction technologies.

The primary reason best-efforts requirements are easier to promulgate is that they generally require much less information and analysis than risk-based standards. The agency needs information about the availability and cost of relevant technologies, but it does not need to engage in extensive hazard assessments, exposure analyses, modeling projections, or politically controversial allocations of responsibility for risk reduction. For the same reasons, the best-efforts approach is more accessible to ordinary citizens who lack expertise in toxicology risk assessment and exposure modeling.

Standards grounded in the best-efforts approach generally are more predictable and, therefore, more easily enforceable than most alternative approaches to pollution control. Although regulated firms may comply with such standards in many ways, they know that a technology capable of meeting the applicable standard will be available at a reasonable cost. Best-efforts standards are easier to enforce because the reference point is a definable technology with already developed numerical standards. Criminal sanctions also work effectively since it is hard for a source to argue that it was impossible to comply with a standard based upon the performance of one or more similar sources.

---

3. Wendy E. Wagner, "The Science Charade in Toxic Risk Regulation," *Columbia Law Review* 95 (1995): 1613, 1680 & n. 245.

Mercury: A Case Study on the Violation of Three Progressive Principles

Mercury is an extraordinarily toxic heavy metal that bioaccumulates in the environment. Approximately 60 percent of air deposition annually comes from human sources, particularly power plants and mercury-cell chlor-alkali facilities. Methyl mercury, the form of the metal most toxic to people, contaminates tuna, bass, swordfish, and other fish, providing the primary route of human exposure. The failure to control mercury emissions from major industrial sources violates three progressive principles: relying on clean science, doing the best we can, and avoiding disproportionate effects from environmental harms.

Exposure to high levels of mercury can cause mental retardation, cerebral palsy, deafness, and blindness. At significantly lower doses, children and fetuses can suffer more subtle neurotoxic effects, including poor performance on neurobehavioral tests that evaluate attention, fine-motor function, language, and verbal memory. EPA recently reported that 630,000 of the 4 million babies born each year have levels of mercury in their bloodstream significantly above safe levels. The Centers for Disease Control (CDC) estimates that eight percent of American women of child-bearing age have levels of mercury in their bloodstreams sufficient to harm a fetus.

The public health hazards posed by widespread methyl mercury contamination of the food chain have been recognized by every scientific body of experts to consider the question. After EPA and FDA established "reference doses" for levels of mercury intake that are considered "safe," the National Academy of Sciences (NAS) examined all available information and concluded that the weight of the evidence confirmed that the children of women who eat fish and shellfish regularly during pregnancy are at risk of permanent neurological damage, and also justified EPA's standard. The World Health Organization made a similiar decision in June 2003.

In light of the public health risks presented, the existing Clean Air Act dictates a "do the best we can" approach to methyl mercury air emissions. In particular, emissions from power plants should be reduced by installation of maximum achievable control technologies. Also, nine outmoded mercury-cell chlor-alkali plants cumulatively "lose" 65 tons a year in fugitive air emissions. They should be forced to shut down, leaving the 34 comparable facilities that use much cleaner technologies to pick up the slack in the market. Further justification for such actions, if any is needed, is that especially vulnerable groups of people—children, pregnant women, communities that rely on fish for subsistence—suffer the most harm. Tight controls are even justified by cost-benefit analyses that show the monetary values assigned to health benefits to be greatly in excess of the costs of controls.

Nonetheless, action on methyl mercury has so far been stalled by industry counterattacks and Administration reluctance to act. Deploying a familiar strategy, opponents of regulation fixate on a single epidemiological study on the

(Continued)

Mercury: *(Continued)*

Seychelles Islands that did not find a link between the consumption of contaminated fish and neurological damage in children. The author of the study failed to disclose that his study was funded in part by the Electric Power Research Institute, violating an important principle of clean science.

Rather than mandate controls as required by the Clean Air Act, the Bush Administration has instead proposed a "cap and trade" emissions trading system that would delay real reductions until as late as 2026. Such a system will almost certainly lead to concentrations of emissions—or "hot spots"—around major sources located in low income and minority communities. CDC statistics already reveal that white women have significantly lower levels of mercury in their blood than Mexican Americans or African Americans due to their proximity to major sources.

(Adapted from Lisa Heinzerling & Rena Steinzor, *A Perfect Storm: Mercury and the Bush Administration, Parts I and II,* 34 Envtl. L. Rep. 10297 (Part I) and 10495 (Part II) (2004)).

The Unfair 'Command-and-Control' Critique

Corporations try to denigrate the best-efforts approach because it can be implemented and enforced effectively—and it requires firms to change their behavior. Inaccurately labeling it command-and-control regulation, conservative think tanks aligned with industry argue that the best-efforts approach presupposes that a Washington, D.C. bureaucrat can know what technologies are more effective in reducing risk than the engineers who work for the regulated companies.[4] This criticism is misplaced, however, because the best-efforts approach does not require a firm to install any particular technology. Firms typically are free to implement any technology they choose as long as the technology performs at least as well as the model technology upon which the agency based the standard.

Other critics argue that the best-efforts approach is "wildly inefficient" because it requires regulated entities to expend limited resources to reduce risk even when the existing level of risk may be acceptable.[5] Why, they ask, should a company be forced to spend money on risk-reducing technology when it is not demonstrably needed to prevent greater harm? This criticism, however, erroneously presumes that a company should have a right to subject people and the environment to preventable risks so long as the profits derived from

---

4. Allen V. Kneese and Charles L. Shultze, *Pollution, Prices, and Public Policy* (1975), 58–63, 72–73, 82–83; Bruce A. Ackerman & Richard B. Stewart, "Reforming Environmental Law," *Stanford Law Review* 37 (1985): 1333, 1335–40.

5. Cass Sunstein, "Administrative Substance," *Duke Law Journal* 1991 (1991): 607, 628.

The Clean Water Act: Technology-Based Standards Achieve Substantial Improvements to Water Quality

One of the best documented examples of the successful application of the technology-based approach is the reduction in industrial discharges resulting from implementation of the Clean Water Act. Before 1972, efforts to improve the near-crisis state of the nation's waters focused primarily on providing federal funds to state water-control programs. Those federal dollars helped fund an initial set of upgrades to the nation's sewage treatment plants, but lax enforcement and an absence of federal controls hindered progress toward cleaner water. Water pollution, described by Senator Edmund Muskie as "'a cancer which threatens our very existence and which will not respond to the kind of treatment that has been prescribed in the past,'"[6] demanded "stronger medicine."[7]

Originally enacted in 1965, the Clean Water Act was significantly amended in 1972 and 1977 to require industrial dischargers to meet minimum control levels set by EPA based on the "best practicable technology" for conventional pollutants and "best available technology," for toxic pollutants. The implementation of these technology-based standards has been a remarkable success. As a direct result of this approach, industrial discharges of toxic and conventional pollutants have been substantially reduced. In 1998, EPA estimated the setting of these technology-based standards reduced pollutant discharges of conventional pollutants by 108 million pounds annually, and toxic pollutants by almost 24 million pounds annually.[8] Between 1987 and 1990, after these technology-based standards were first implemented, data from the Toxic Release Inventory showed that releases of toxic chemicals to surface waters declined from 412 to 197 million pounds per year.[9] Individual industrial sectors also achieved significant reductions that can be directly attributed to the implementation of technology-based standards. For example, in 1989, the EPA reported that toxic loads from the pulp and paper, aluminum, iron and steel, and leather industries were significantly reduced after implementation of best available technology.[10] Overall, between 1972 and 2000, the percentage of assessed waters

(Continued)

---

6. Robert W. Adler, et al., *The Clean Water Act: 20 Years Later* (1993), 7 (quoting Congressional Research Service (CRS), History of the Water Pollution Control Act Amendments of 1972, ser. 1, 93d Cong., 1st sess. (1972), 161–62).

7. Ibid., 7.

8. EPA and USDA, *Clean Water Action Plan: Restoring and Protecting America's Waters*, 1998, 3–4, http://www.cleanwater.gov/action/cwap.pdf.

9. Oliver A. Houck, *The Clean Water Act TMDL Program: Law, Policy, and Implementation,* (2002), Chap. 1, n. 6 (citing Robert W. Adler, et al., *The Clean Water Act: 20 Years Later* (1993), 17–18.

10. Ibid. (citing U.S. EPA, Water Improvement Study, tbl. 1-2 (1989)).

The Clean Water Act: *(Continued)*

that meet water quality goals has doubled.[11]

In addition to the substantial reduction in industrial discharges, the technology-based approach has also facilitated enforcement and public participation. The Clean Water Act is the federal environmental statute most often enforced by citizens groups, due in large part to the clear technology-based standards set forth in National Pollutant Discharge Elimination System permits.[12]

The success of the technology-based standards in the Clean Water Act led Congress to replicate the approach in the Clean Air Act, and other countries have followed suit.[13] While the work to be done to restore the nation's waters is far from over, particularly with respect to non-point sources of pollution, the use of technology-based standards has resulted in major improvements to water quality, particularly in waters subject to discharges from industrial sources.

---

the risk-producing activities exceed some calculation of the harm caused by those activities.

A related efficiency criticism is that it makes little sense for one industry to invest huge amounts of money in a technology, merely because it is available, when another industry that emits the same pollutant could achieve an even greater reduction in risk at lower cost. While there is some merit to this argument in theory, things do not work this way in the real world. Cost is always a consideration in establishing best-efforts standards, and agencies typically attempt to set standards for one industry that are not significantly more expensive than those that are applicable to industries posing equivalent risks.

Still other critics acknowledge the past successes of the best-efforts approach but claim that it is not capable of achieving similar progress in the future. In the 1970s, Congress could adopt relatively ambitious pollution-

---

11. EPA and USDA, *Clean Water Action Plan: Restoring and Protecting America's Waters,* 1998, 2, http://www.cleanwater.gov/action/cwap.pdf.

12. Wendy E. Wagner, "The Triumph of Technology-Based Standards," *University of Illinois Law Review* 2000 (2000): 83, 103.

13. Oliver A. Houck, "TMDLS IV: The Final Frontier," *Environmental Law Reporter* 29 (1999): 10,469, 10,479 & n. 223.

reduction goals on the assumption that pollution was so severe that the expense of installing the EPA-prescribed technology was nearly always justified by the resulting health and environmental gains. But, critics say, the low-hanging fruit has been picked, and society cannot afford the inefficiency of a best-efforts approach. As discussed below, this criticism is misplaced. There is much more low-hanging fruit to be picked, and its potential victims should expect sources of risk to do all they can to reduce these risks.

The Progressive Perspective

Progressives generally favor pragmatic solutions to social problems. New Progressivism is inclined to go with what works, and what clearly works in environmental, health, and safety regulation is a focus on technology. The movement away from the risk-based approach and toward technology-based standards reflected a congressional conclusion that agencies could not determine acceptable levels of risk and then ensure that the levels would not be exceeded. Until the information and analysis required by the risk-based approach can be collected and accomplished successfully, it just makes good sense to do the best we can to reduce or eliminate environmental, health, and safety risks.

Progressives prefer precautionary governmental approaches to environmental, health, and safety problems. The best-efforts approach is consistent with a precautionary method because it serves as a hedge against ignorance and uncertainty. Recognizing that data limitations and scientific uncertainties do not inspire confidence in the risk-based approach, progressives support the best-efforts approach as a stopgap measure that requires companies to do what they can to reduce the risk of unanticipated, but tragic, consequences until the threat is fully evaluated and comprehensively addressed.

The best-efforts approach has important moral dimensions that resonate with the progressive view of government's role in society. Even if the cost of achieving certain acceptable risk goals is too high, by some measures, for society to bear, such as the complete shutdown of an important industry or abandonment of the internal-combustion engine, we can at least be satisfied knowing that we are doing the best we can to protect those who are exposed to unacceptable risks. Doing all that is possible to protect people shows respect for human life. In the same manner, technology-based regulation en-

Regulation of Benzene in the Workplace: Judicial Intervention Delays Protections for Workers

Benzene is one of the top 20 chemicals produced in the United States, used in producing motor fuels, solvents, detergents, pesticides, and a host of other organic chemicals. It is also a human carcinogen known to cause leukemia, and it has non-cancer health effects as well, either from long-term exposure, or very high short-term exposure. Virtually the entire U.S. population is exposed to small amounts of benzene, and more than one million workers are exposed to larger amounts on a daily basis in service stations, petroleum refineries, coking operations at steel mills, chemical processing, benzene transportation, rubber manufacturing, and laboratory operations.

While scientists know benzene causes cancer, they have not yet identified exactly how exposure relates to the risk of cancer. Mindful of the risks, in 1977 the Occupational Safety and Health Administration, acting on a recommendation for a scientific advisory panel, promulgated a 1 part per million emergency temporary standard for benzene in the workplace, lowering its previous 10 parts per million standard.

Litigation ensued, and the matter eventually reached the U.S. Supreme Court. Writing for a plurality of only three judges, Justice Stevens wrote that the agency had acted improperly because it had failed to make an initial finding that the 10 parts per million exposure level was "safe," which Justice Stevens interpreted as requiring that there be a "significant risk" of harm. The burden of showing this fell on the agency, and because OSHA had not made such a finding for benzene, the court remanded to give OSHA a chance to do so.

The Court gave OSHA very little indication of how to meet this burden, but Justice Stevens did offer the following illustration of what the Court meant:

> Some risks are plainly acceptable and others are plainly unacceptable. If, for example, the odds are one in 1 billion that a person will die from cancer by taking a drink of chlorinated water, the risk clearly could not be considered significant. On the other hand, if the odds are one in a thousand that regular inhalation of gasoline vapors that are two percent benzene will be fatal, a reasonable person might well consider the risk significant and take appropriate steps to decrease or eliminate it.

The problem with this illustration is that it fails to take into account the number of people who are exposed to either risk. Nearly all of the 250 million Americans drink chlorinated water. If everyone drinks an average of four glasses of water per day, then a one in a billion risk per drink translates to an average of one case of cancer per day, or 365 cases per year. Many people might find this to be a "significant risk," particularly the unlucky 365. In fact, this risk is not meaningfully different from what might result from workers being exposed to a 1 in 1,000 risk from benzene. If we assume that this is the risk from an annual exposure (a necessary detail not specified by the Court), and that two workers in each of the country's approximately 200,000 service stations in

---

Regulation of Benzene in the Workplace: *(Continued)*

America are regularly exposed to benzene, then a 1 in 1,000 risk would yield 400 cancers per year.

Because the Court did not specify the frequency of exposure and the size of the population exposed in its ruling, it is difficult to know what to make of its examples. OSHA eventually interpreted the ruling to require it to employ quantitative risk assessment techniques in determining whether workplace carcinogens posed a "significant risk," even if it was not clear what degree of risk the Court intended to be considered "significant."

OSHA therefore conducted assessments based on new data, along with new analyses of prior studies. That effort confirmed the serious risks associated with benzene exposure, and after much delay, and even litigation to compel OSHA to act, in 1987—fully a decade after it first promulgated the 1-part-per-million standard—the agency finally issued a permissible exposure limit...of 1 part per million.

The Supreme Court's Benzene decision has had far-reaching implications for the regulatory process. The decision placed the difficult burden of demonstrating "significant" risk of harm on OSHA and the workers it was created to protect, rather than requiring regulated industry to show that its workplaces are safe. Additionally, the decision has solidified the use of quantitative risk assessment in areas of scientific uncertainty, a practice that eschews a preventive approach to regulation. Justice Thurgood Marshall warned in dissent that such a move toward quantitative risk assessment "would either paralyze the Secretary into inaction or force him to deceive the public by acting on the basis of assumptions that must be considered too speculative to support any realistic assessment of the relevant risk." Unfortunately for the American worker, Justice Marshall was right.

---

sures that we do the most we can to preserve a common environmental heritage for current and future generations.

Progressives also believe that no company has a right to pollute pristine areas merely because they are capable of assimilating waste. The best-efforts approach supports the antidegradation policy that many environmental statutes articulate. The phrase, "dilution is not the solution to pollution," best captures the moral imperative of protecting the integrity of existing environmental resources.

The best-efforts approach also is compatible with progressive concerns for fairness and equity. Unless a company can justify varying from a best-efforts standard, it applies equally to all similar companies. The laggards must get up to speed, and a company that has invested in risk-reduction technologies is not put at a competitive disadvantage. Best-efforts standards also protect all people equally by requiring the sources of risk to do the best they can regardless of their location.

The Progressive Agenda

Pick the Remaining Low-Hanging Fruit

Technology-based regulation should be the first tool considered in designing any program to protect health, safety, and the environment. The superiority of this approach over risk-based regulation has been demonstrated time and again. In deciding how to regulate new products and technologies, regulatory decision-makers should begin with a best-efforts goal and build on it to the extent necessary. For example, in deciding how to react to the discovery of the first case of Creutzfelt-Jacob (or Mad Cow) disease in the United States, the Department of Agriculture should have promulgated standards requiring that cattle be tested for the disease prior to slaughter and that slaughterhouses use the best-available technologies for separating risky materials, such as the brain, spinal cord, eyes, and upper intestines, from meat products. Technologies are readily available for both tasks, but it seems clear that the meat-production industry has not used its best efforts to reduce the risks of human exposures. Even though these technologies may cost more than the apparently inadequate status quo protections, USDA's failure to require the industry to take readily available steps to protect the food supply subjects U.S. consumers to unnecessary risk.

In addition to newly discovered hazards, plenty of low-hanging fruit remains to be picked by regulators adopting the best-efforts approach. Hundreds of major sources of air pollution are spewing uncontrolled emissions into the air because they have obtained grandfather status. Requiring them to install controls equivalent to what new plants installed 20 years ago would result in huge emission reductions. Large, concentrated animal-feeding operations have avoided controls under the CWA, despite the threats they pose to rivers, bays, and estuaries. If they were required to take modest steps to ensure that their waste does not flow untreated into rivers and streams, the risks they pose would be greatly reduced. Although the best-efforts approach has accomplished a great deal in the past 30 years, it can accomplish a great deal more at a reasonable cost.

Reach Higher

Beyond picking the remaining low-hanging fruit, progressives want to build upon the past successes of the best-efforts approach by forcing those who would impose unnecessary risks upon people and the environment to reach even higher. The nation's productivity continues to increase yearly, due primarily to innovations in production technologies that allow companies to do more with fewer resources. The primary obstacle to similar advances in risk-reduction technologies is industry reluctance to invest in research and development that is not directly tied to future profits even though such improvements would lower health care costs and help people have better lives. Despite initial grumbling, the auto industry has repeatedly achieved extraordinary advances in safety and pollution-reduction technologies when pressed by legal requirements to do so. There is no reason the auto industry's successes cannot be repeated in other industries and repeated again within the auto industry.

Force Technology

Some of the most successful government interventions have consisted of ambitious technology forcing—the phasing out and banning of especially risky activities. The EPA's effort to phase out tetraethyl lead used in gasoline was much criticized by the petroleum industry at the time, but that action is now cited as an environmental success story by observers at both ends of the political spectrum, despite the fact that it caused great industry disruption and put many small companies out of business.[14]

Radical technology forcing goes beyond the best-efforts approach to empower regulators to take a leap of faith in cases where source-oriented risk-reduction technologies are not clearly identifiable. An industry is told to cease a particular activity, such as selling a dangerous product, or achieve a particular level of control over its activity by a certain date. If it misses the deadline, it is subject to penalties. The agency is encouraged to trust the ingenuity of U.S. industry to develop effective control technologies or substitutes for risk-producing activities by the specified deadlines.

In addition to ease of implementation, radical technology forcing has the potential to induce genuine technological innovation. The best-efforts approach can bring the laggards up to speed, but it rarely brings about significant technological change.

---

14. George M. Gray, Laury Saligman and John D. Graham, *The Demise of Lead in Gasoline*, in *The Greening of Industry: A Risk Management Approach* (J.D. Graham & J.K. Hartwell, eds., 1997).

Although ambitious technology forcing is not a universal solution to the problem of regulating risk-producing activities, it is an important arrow in the regulatory quiver. The agency that adopts a technology-forcing approach must have courage and imagination. It must also have the flexibility to extend the deadlines when the facts prove that they are overly optimistic; but it must sternly resist attempts by the regulated industry to avoid change through artful brinkmanship. The approach works best in situations in which a major disruption of an unacceptable status quo will lead to a better future.

Conclusion

When coaches deliver impassioned pregame speeches to inspire their teams to victory, they do not exhort their players to "go out there and do your optimal" or to "find an acceptable level of exertion and sustain it throughout the game." Coaches urge their athletes to "do your very best and, if you do, I will be proud of you."

Regulatory agencies are not coaches, and regulated industries ordinarily are not enthusiastic protectors of worker safety and the environment. In fact, it is not always clear that they understand they are on the same team. Nevertheless, if we are to build on the progress already achieved in protecting public health and the environment, companies that engage in risky activities will have to do a better job. They may not be able to perfectly balance protection and economic development, but they should, at least, do the best they can.

CHAPTER 6

RESCUING SCIENCE FROM POLITICS

The Role of Science

Science has always played a key role in progressive environmental, health, and safety regulation. Indeed, scientists' warnings have been the motivation for the enactment of landmark regulatory programs. In 1960, biologist Rachel Carson's *Silent Spring* alerted the public to the unregulated pesticide use that was poisoning the nation's food supply and countryside.[1] In the 1970s, the Environmental Protection Agency (EPA) proposed airborne-lead regulations after scientists at the Centers for Disease Control and Prevention and the American Academy of Pediatrics found evidence that the substance caused neurological damage in fetuses, infants, and young children. In the 1980s, satellite data confirmed scientists' predictions of upper-atmospheric ozone depletion, which led to adoption of a worldwide treaty in 1987 that successfully reduced ozone-depleting substances.[2] In the 1990s, epidemiologists documented the tens of thousands of Americans whose premature deaths were caused by airborne particulates;[3] biologists recorded the worldwide crisis of species extinction; and more than 1,500 atmospheric scientists joined in proving global warming exists. All are part of the scientific case for enlightened public policies that could help us live in the kind of world we want.

Science is indispensable to advancing the progressive agenda, but science alone cannot determine its direction. Even when scientists agree that a serious problem exists, uncertainty always remains as to how serious a problem it is—both in terms of identifying the problem's magnitude (whether it is

---

1. Rachel Carson, *Silent Spring* (1962).
2. David L. Chandler, "MIT Scientist Shares Nobel for Identifying Ozone Damage," *Boston Globe,* October 12, 1995, 1, http://www.boston.com/globe/search/stories/nobel/1995/1995g.html.
3. Donald T. Hornstein, "Accounting for Science: The Independence of Public Research in the New, Subterranean Administrative Law," *Law & Contemporary Problems* 66 (2003): 227, 236–37.

measured in early mortalities, asthma attacks, or acres of lost coastland), and in terms of proving the problem's specific cause. Deciding how to respond to problems that inevitably involve some uncertainties is a political question, not a scientific one.

Drawing all the knowledge from science that it can provide at any point in time should be an ingredient in public policy-making. Progressives applaud when the application of science-based policy has that meaning. Increasingly, however, advocates of so-called "sound science" say that we should not take action to avoid potential problems until science has demonstrated that a potential harm has actually occurred and until science has pinpointed the exact cause of that harm. This approach does not base public policy on science but rather uses the absence of scientific certainty as an excuse to avoid taking precautions that reduce risk. It also assails democratic values, using a backdoor approach to undo statutes that command widespread popular support. The demand for sound science is no more—and no less—than a demand that we abandon the approach of preventing harm in favor of an approach that requires proof that harm not only has occurred, but is definitely caused by a specific type of industrial activity. That approach directly conflicts with the crucial threshold decision Congress made three decades ago to embrace the goal of preventing harm, as opposed to compensating victims after harm has already occurred.

In the next chapter, we discuss the positive role of science in the progressive agenda and how science can be an essential component of public policy. This chapter explains what we must do to rescue science from politics.

Suppression of Science

Ironically, the supporters of efforts to discredit precautionary policies as insufficiently science-based often deceive us about the conclusions science has actually reached. With almost-Orwellian language, they assert that policy should be based on sound science, but selectively ignore what sound science actually is. Even more perniciously, they resort to changing science itself when scientific conclusions they oppose can be suppressed no longer.

Consider the case of global warming. In 2001 and 2002, evidence of global warming mounted in reports from the National Academy of Science's National Research Council, the Intergovernmental Panel on Climate Change (IPCC), and the U.S. Global Change Research Program (USGCRP). As the scientific evidence unfolded, Republican strategist Frank Luntz conceded in a memo that "the scientific debate is closing [against us]" and "[s]hould the public come to believe that the scientific issues are settled, their views... will change accordingly."[4] Rather than let the public know about the scientific evidence, including data that questioned and highlighted the dangers of global warming, Luntz emphasized the "need to continue to make the lack of scientific certainty a primary issue."[5]

In July 2001, President Bush publicly promised that "my Administration's climate change policy will be science-based"[6] and announced expenditures for more research. At the time, President Bush had already commissioned the National Academy of Sciences (NAS) to investigate the issue. But when the NAS reported that global warming was all too real, a finding that was incorporated into a draft EPA report in 2003, White House officials demanded that the EPA delete any reference to NAS findings and to any other research corroborating the global-warming problem.[7] In its place, the White House instructed the EPA to cite an oil industry-funded study that questioned global-warming research. Again, opponents were hiding the science politicians didn't want us to hear and skewing the scientific record to exaggerate the uncertainties.

Another approach used by regulated industries and their political allies is aggressive interference with the process of scientific inquiry itself, harassing scientists who produce research that could lead to more stringent controls on pollution. For example, once publicly supported research has reached the point of publication, it becomes subject to the Shelby Amendment, a one-sentence rider added by Republican Sen. Richard Shelby of Alabama in 1998 to a massive appropriations bill, without the benefit of congressional hearings or committee investigation. The Shelby Amendment allows opponents of federally financed research to demand that they be given the data underlying any study with which they disagree—including scientists' laboratory notebooks. Although its political supporters defend the law as an effort to enhance transparency in scientific research, the NAS and

---

4. Frank Luntz, "The Environment: A Cleaner, Safer, Healthier America", excerpt from "Straight Talk," 137–138, http://www.luntzspeak.com/graphics/LuntzResearch.Memo.pdf; *see also* Jennifer 8. Lee, "A Call for Softer, Greener Language," *The New York Times*, March 2, 2003; "Environmental Word Games," *New York Times*, March 15, 2003 (referring to the memo as a "recipe for cynicism and political manipulation.").

5. Luntz, ibid., 137.

6. White House, *President's Statement on Climate Change*, July 13, 2001, http://www.whitehouse.gov/news/releases/2001/07/20010713-2.html.

7. Andrew C. Revkin and Katharine Q. Seelye, "Report by E.P.A. Leaves Out Data on Climate Change," *New York Times*, June 19, 2003.

the National Institutes of Health (NIH) warned that it "could invite[e] special interest groups to harass investigators engaged in controversial or competing work."[8]

A third legal tool used to interfere with scientific inquiry is the Data Quality Act, since renamed the Information Quality Act (IQA), which was also added to an omnibus spending bill, again without any congressional hearings, committee investigation, or floor debate. This fragment of a statute authorizes the White House to issue guidance on federal agencies' use or dissemination of quality information, including so-called sound science, requires all federal agencies to adopt conforming data-quality guidelines, and allows any "affected person" to "seek and obtain correction of information... that does not comply with the guidelines." In the eyes of its most ardent corporate supporters, the IQA allows them to threaten a lawsuit against any federal agency that has the temerity to reference a scientific study that, in their view, may violate these so-called sound science guidelines.

The White House Office of Management and Budget (OMB) has also invoked the IQA to establish new guidelines requiring peer review for scientific research deemed new or controversial.[9] The potential sweep of this new program is troubling because it could prevent the government from using science that had not run through this additional gauntlet.

The White House guidelines misperceive the appropriate role of peer review, which is not designed to certify *the* scientific truth. Rather, real peer review is a decentralized process by which groups of scientists not involved in conducting the original research work with the researchers to develop scientific theories and hypotheses. This pure peer review, run by scientists interested in pursuing discoveries to the full extent of current knowledge, follows a rigorous internal methodology that results in the dissemination of new science into the broader community for further inquiry, replication, criticism, and testing. Science is not dogma; it is freedom from dogma.

OMB's proposal will be superimposed on a system that already provides ample opportunity for peer review in a regulatory context. EPA has established

---

8. Joint Steering Committee for Public Policy, Website, A-110/FOIA Issue (March 23, 2000), http://www.jscpp.org/A-110.htm, citing testimony by Bruce Alberts, President of the National Academy of Sciences and Harold Varmus, Director of the National Institutes of Health at Hearings before the House Government Management, Information and Technology Subcommittee.

9. OMB, *Bulletin on Peer Review and Information Quality*, 68 Fed. Reg. 54023, 54024 (Sept. 15, 2003). The bulletin was later revised and was published in the Federal Register on April 28, 2004, OMB, *Revised Information Quality Bulletin on Peer Review*, 69 Fed. Reg. 23230 (April 28, 2004).

a Scientific Advisory Panel to review the scientific basis of pesticide risks, a Clean Air Scientific Advisory Committee to review the risk assessments underlying air quality standards, and a Science Advisory Board to review EPA's research initiatives and science-based policy determinations. Agencies also have the option of referring questions of regulatory science to the NAS or other specially constituted science advisory boards. The problem with existing regulatory peer review is not its scarcity but rather its extraordinary vulnerability to manipulation by regulated industries and their conservative political allies.

For example, the Bush Administration excluded three national experts on lead poisoning from the Department of Health and Human Services' Advisory Committee on Childhood Lead Poisoning Prevention and replaced them with individuals who had ties to the lead industry. The Bush Administration did not reappoint Dr. Robert Watson, former chief scientist at the World Bank and former director of the Science Division at NASA, to a key panel on global warming after he was attacked by the oil industry, prompting Princeton University scientist Robert Oppenheimer to say, "It is scandalous… This is an invasion of narrow political considerations into a scientific process."[10] And the Bush Administration appointed 15 members to an advisory committee of the National Center for Environmental Health (NCEH), many with ties to the very industries that potentially would be subject to regulations based on NCEH-reviewed science. This development led several scientists to write in *Science* that "stacking these public committees out of fear that they may offer advice that conflicts with administration policies devalues the entire federal advisory committee structure and the work of dedicated scientists who are willing to participate in these efforts."[11]

Capturing the Research Agenda

Efforts to suppress science that supports more stringent regulation are especially troubling because industry, in addition to controlling its own research, increasingly is able to influence public research, including publicly sponsored research on university campuses. Direct public support for higher education has dropped over the past 30 years, and universities have had to look elsewhere

---

10. Andrew Lawler, "Battle Over IPCC Chair Renews Debate on U.S. Climate Policy," *Science* (April 12, 2002): 232–233.

11. David Michaels, et al., "Advice Without Dissent," *Science* (October 25, 2002): 703.

for support. As a result, the number and extent of research relationships between private corporations and university-based researchers have unmistakably increased. By 1996, corporate funding comprised approximately 7 percent of overall university research budgets,[12] although on certain campuses and in certain areas of research the level of support is even greater. At Massachusetts Institute of Technology, for example, corporate funding constituted 15 percent of the campus research budget; at Carnegie Mellon University, the figure was 23 percent.[13] In the field of biomedical research, corporate funding is responsible for 62 percent of research spending nationally.[14] Before leaving his post as President of Harvard University in 1991, Derek Bok observed that universities were beginning to "appear less and less as charitable institutions seeking the truth and serving students and more and more as huge commercial operations that differ from corporations only because there are no shareholders and no dividends."[15]

The danger here is that corporations have opportunities to influence more directly the university-based research they finance. The problem of corporate influence over university-based research has been demonstrated statistically. A study of more than 1,000 peer-reviewed scientific papers found that, "[i]ndustry-sponsored research is 3.6 times more likely to produce results favorable to the company that helped pay for it."[16] Another study found that "96 percent of the researchers who wrote favorable articles about a controversial class of drugs for treating hypertension and angina also had financial ties to the makers of these drugs... [whereas among] those who published articles critical of the drugs, only 37 percent had financial ties."[17]

---

12. Donald T. Hornstein, "Accounting for Science: The Independence of Public Research in the New, Subterranean Administrative Law," *Law and Contemporary Problems* 66 (2003): 227, 234 (citing Dorothy S. Zinberg, "Editorial, A Cautionary Tale," *Science* 273 (1996): 411).

13. Ibid. (citing Wayne Biddle, "Corporations on Campus," *Science* 237 (1987): 353).

14. Ibid., 241 (citing Robert Lee Hotz, "Medical Tests Skewed, Study Finds," *L.A. Times,* Jan. 22, 2003, A14 (reporting on a study by Yale University researchers published in the Journal of the American Medical Association)).

15. Ibid. (citing Norman E. Bowie, *University-Business Partnerships: An Assessment* 57 (1994)(quoting Derek Bok)).

16. Ibid., 243 (quoting Robert Lee Hotz, "Medical Tests Skewed, Study Finds," *L.A. Times,* Jan 22, 2003, A14).

17. Ibid. (quoting Goldie Blumenstyk, "Conflict-of-Interest Fears Rise as Universities Chase Industry Support," *Chronicle of Higher Education,* May 22, 1998, A41, A42).

These problems are exacerbated exponentially by cuts in government-funded research. For example, no attempt was made to disguise the anti-science motivations of the 104th Congress, which slashed funding for the National Biological Survey because it feared scientists would discover threats to biodiversity that, in turn, might lay the scientific foundation for recovery efforts under the Endangered Species Act (ESA).[18]

The Progressive Perspective

Congress has incorporated expressions of our collective values into most environmental and public health statutes. These laws say that public health and natural resources should be protected when administrative decision-makers conclude, based on the best available scientific information, that the public may face environmental or public health problems. Courts long have interpreted existing statutes as authorizing, if not requiring, implementing agencies to act when scientific evidence is uncertain and to use the full arsenal of scientific information in making policy determinations. In the end, the sound science campaign is not about science. It is about undoing progressive regulations that serve the public interest because they are perceived as a burden to special interests.

Although progressive environmental and public health policy does not need endless science, it always needs clean science—information produced by experts whose inquiries are untainted by the need for preconceived results. Whenever possible, such research should be undertaken by neutral, government-sponsored research programs, run in a manner that preserves the freedom of scientific inquiry.

The basic economics of information tell us why clean science cannot be taken for granted and government sponsorship of research is so important. Much scientific information can be characterized as for the public good; whoever pays to produce it often cannot expect to enjoy exclusive rights to its economic use. No obvious or immediately available market exists for some types of science. Information about global warming or species extinction, for example, will not necessarily command any price in private markets, in contrast to marketing research about consumer preferences for breakfast cereals. There will be free-market incentives for information on

---

18. Jeffrey Brainard, "NSF Director Requests Big Increase for Research into Biocomplexity," *The Chronicle of Higher Education*, Feb. 26, 1999, A30.

breakfast cereals but not for scientific research on many environmental issues; therefore, market forces acting alone will under-produce such information. Other times, the free market creates perverse incentives not to study the environmental and public health consequences of human activities. In the absence of regulation, chemical producers, for example, have economic incentives not to produce information that reveals the adverse health or environmental effects of their products to avoid legal liability.

Much of progressive public law is designed to create corrective incentives leading to the development of the type of public health and environmental information free-market forces under-produce. For example, the federal pesticide statute empowers the EPA to order "data call-ins," by which the agency can require the registrants of already-marketed pesticides to provide public health and environmental information on their products' safety in order to justify continued registration. And the National Environmental Policy Act requires the federal government to prepare environmental impact statements for major federal projects that can significantly affect the environment. But even these ambitious measures are not enough to produce consistent, high quality research examining the implications of industrial activities for environmental quality.

In addition to filling data gaps through open scientific inquiry shielded from distortion by special interests, progressives believe that we must make far more concerted efforts to draw distinctions between the evaluation of existing science and the formulation of policies that protect the public from emerging threats. Until and unless Congress is willing to repeal the major federal health and safety statutes, the rule of law demands that we adopt a precautionary approach, not only tolerating, but accepting scientific uncertainty as inevitable, without using it as an excuse for inaction.

Progressives strongly oppose all of the measures adopted to facilitate a stealth attack on regulation through such deceptive rubrics as information quality or the selective harassment of scientists who document the adverse effects of government activities. The development of regulatory science must be shielded from such influences.

The Progressive Agenda

In contrast to the cynical and misleading call for sound science, scientists and others interested in basing decisions on the best available science should embrace the following principles to ensure we enjoy the benefits of clean science.

Preserve Scientific Freedom

Scientists must be allowed to conduct their research free of undue influence by private sector sponsors. Sponsors must never place restrictions or otherwise influence the design or conduct of a study in an attempt to obtain results favorable to their interests. Research must never be suppressed because it produces results that are adverse to a sponsor or other interested party. And no publication or summary of research should ever be influenced—in tone or content—by the sponsoring entity.

If vested interests use the legal system to harass scientists whose research or expert testimony calls into question the safety of their practices or products, the harassers must be held accountable with sanctions and must compensate injured scientists for the resulting interference with their research and damage to their reputations.

The government should circulate scientific research that forms the basis for regulatory decisions as widely as possible, withdrawing it only where there are compelling national security risks or other, similarly urgent justifications. However, unless data could help address pressing public health problems, or is otherwise submitted to the government as a basis for regulatory decisions, scientists should remain free to time the disclosure of the results of ongoing research.

Ensure Scientific Transparency

The data and results of research must be communicated honestly to the research community and broader public. The data and biomaterials underlying a published study, as well as a comprehensive description of the methods, must be available to other scientists and the public upon publication of the study or submission of the results to a federal agency, in compliance with prevailing rules for preserving the privacy of human research subjects. Researchers may be compensated for the "fair use" of their data. Regulatory agencies should rigorously review and challenge exaggerated claims that underlying data must be kept confidential for business reasons.

Encourage Scientific Honesty

Researchers and those using their data must be honest about the limits of the research and remaining uncertainties. If research is misrepresented by others to suggest an outcome not supported by the study, researchers must correct these misstatements as soon as they become aware of them. Research must never be dismissed or excluded because it does not provide a complete answer to a larger policy or science question. Research, by its nature, is incomplete, and to dismiss research because it does not provide a definitive answer could result in the exclusion of valuable science from regulatory decision-making.

Expand Public Funding

Government support of research is essential to produce discoveries that benefit the public good. Much research that benefits the public good does not generate private compensation for its production. Generous public funding of research is essential for advancements in scientific knowledge, especially in areas where there are no private benefits to be gained from the discoveries. All research produced or used by the government should be subject to basic quality assurance/quality control checks, especially if that research is not published or disseminated widely within the scientific community.

Use Peer Review Appropriately

In appropriate circumstances, peer review is an important step in the process of scientific discovery. Peer review should never be used to censor scientific research, but rather should be used to advance science, either by providing scientists with beneficial comments from peers regarding their research or to help academic institutions, independent journals, and decision-makers evaluate the quality of research. Legitimate scientific peer review does not encompass processes that enable outside stakeholders to pressure scientists to change their views in light of an anticipated effect on proposed policy decisions.

Peer review should be done by peer reviewers who have no present or past conflicts of interest likely to affect their review and specialize in the area. Peer reviewers should disclose the limits of their expertise in assessing the research. Practical realities of peer review have often fallen short of these normative ideals, and scientific peer review has been criticized for lacking objectivity. When peer reviewers cannot be found who do not have a have a financial conflict of interest, the entity selecting peer reviewers should select peer reviewers without financial conflicts of interest from a broader area of research. Entities that select peer reviewers should disclose any financial conflicts of interest and affiliations or perspectives that may influence their choice of reviewers.

Chapter 7

Safety First

Providing a Safety Net

Chapter 4 argued against a perspective on environmental, health, and safety policy that adopts a neutral stance toward the creators and the victims of environmental risks. In contrast, the progressive perspective demands that the creators of such risks bear both a moral and a legal responsibility for the risks they create. Chapter 5 illustrated one response to the legitimate claims of citizens who are exposed to environmental, health, or safety risks: We should adopt policies that do the best we can to avoid those risks.

Environmental, health, and safety risks raise complex, multidimensional issues, and while the preceding two principles go a long way toward pointing public policies regarding such threats in the right direction, additional principles are necessary to complete a progressive agenda for reform. The first such principle is the idea that we must always err on the side of safety. This safety-first principle encourages and even requires risk creators to characterize—and, if they can, eliminate—the risks they impose on society. This threshold mandate is appropriate because creators of such risks know best how their products and activities will adversely affect public health and the environment. When combined with do-your-best (or best-efforts) approaches, safety-first requirements not only ensure better protection of the environment and public health, they provide risk creators with incentives to produce information on the risks they impose on others. This chapter goes beyond the principles developed in Chapters 4 and 5 to flesh out this additional component of effective health and environmental protection.

Most people do not spend much time thinking about the safety of the food they eat, the water they drink, or the air they breathe. They simply trust the government to protect them from irresponsible companies that market dangerous products and discharge disease-causing pollutants. Reasonably sophisticated consumers know that the government's job is not to provide absolute safety and a pristine environment. A completely risk-free society would cost too much—in terms of dollars and foregone opportunities. But most of us expect the government to put safety first in deciding whether and how stringently to protect health, safety, and the environment.

The environmental, worker safety, and consumer protection laws Congress enacted in the 1970s generally did just that. Congress understood that a strong economy and a healthy environment must co-exist and that unbridled industrial production was generating ominous environmental, health, and safety hazards, so lawmakers directed administrative agencies to make safety the most important consideration in deciding whether and how stringently to regulate risk-producing private activities.

Best-effort statutes provide a powerful way to limit pollutant loads without requiring information-intensive decisions about the precise nature of the risk. Yet they do not provide enough protection in some instances. Especially in cases where many sources of pollution are contributing to the overall load on the air, water, or land, the requirement that facilities limit pollutant loads based on technological capabilities can leave unacceptable, residual environmental harm. If the laws stop at a best-efforts approach, then "hot spots" and other harmful activities can continue unaddressed and often undiscovered.

To deal with such residual risk, Congress has included a number of "safety net" mechanisms in environmental statutes. These safety-first approaches, although highly variable, are found in virtually all health and environmental statutes. One way Congress puts safety first is by setting a "risk trigger" to regulate air and water pollution as well as food and workplace safety, so that we do not have to wait for conclusive proof that actual harm has been caused before taking precautionary action. Congress often sets the corresponding risk target at a very protective level. For example, Congress may instruct agencies to err on the side of safety and to take action when an activity may reasonably be anticipated to endanger human health or the environment.

All of these mechanisms essentially shift the burden of proof to risk creators to justify the safety of their activities. This shift is accomplished either by enabling the agency to require the polluter or manufacturer to produce safety information as a condition of operating or by authorizing the agency to take regulatory action based on limited evidence of harm. In some cases, for example, Congress says an agency is authorized to regulate once a substance, process, or activity appears to exceed a specified level of risk based on the available information. If a risk creator finds the regulations too onerous, it must shoulder the burden of proving that its activities are not as harmful as originally supposed. While instructing agencies to set standards that try to ensure a certain level of risk is not exceeded, statutes also can err on the side of safety by allowing agencies to employ conservative assumptions and margins of safety in determining the stringency of controls. In fact, when applying risk triggers and imposing risk-based requirements, agencies are usually told to resolve uncertainties in favor of protection. The reduction of ambient air pollutants to levels that provide an adequate margin of safety is an example of this approach.

Congress can also put safety first when it establishes programs to review new products before they go on the market or are put to new uses. Congress can require the applicant to produce information on the safety of its products or activities as a precondition of entering the marketplace. The company must demonstrate to the implementing agency's satisfaction that the risks to health and the environment will not be greater than the statute's risk trigger. For example, food-additive manufacturers must use adequate scientific information to demonstrate that their products will be safe, meaning there will be a "reasonable certainty of no harm." Such statutes put safety first by making a demonstration of safety a precondition to entering the marketplace.

In these gateway statutes, once a product is on the market or a polluting activity is underway, the agency typically assumes the burden of demonstrating that the product or activity exceeds some risk trigger before taking action to regulate or ban it. Again, however, the agency typically is not required to demonstrate with certainty that the activity is causing particular harm. Under the Federal Insecticide, Fungicide, and Rodenticide Act (FIFRA), for example, the EPA must show that existing pesticides used on food crops cause "unreasonable adverse effects" on humans or the environment before taking action to stop the use of such chemicals. In making this determination, the agency can put safety first by resolving uncertainties against the pesticide and taking action without definitive evidence of toxicity to humans; proof that the pesticide causes cancer in other mammals is sufficient.

Land-protection statutes also employ a safety-first precautionary approach to environmental protection. The most notable is the Endangered Species Act (ESA), which prohibits actions that might jeopardize endangered or threatened species. Such actions are permitted only if a "god squad" of appointed officials determines that the proposed action threatening the species' survival is of regional or national significance and the project's cumulative social benefits so clearly outweigh the cost of losing the species that the action is clearly in the public interest.

The National Environmental Policy Act (NEPA) also employs a look-before-you-leap approach by requiring the federal government to analyze potential environmental effects prior to any development. Although NEPA does not necessarily lead to protective results, it does require enhanced information regarding major federal activities as a precondition to moving forward.

It places a precautionary speed bump in front of many development activities. Under the ESA and NEPA, the government may not engage in activities that have irreversible impacts without first analyzing those effects in a publicly available assessment.

Gaps in Coverage

While Congress has enacted numerous statutes that incorporate elements of a safety-first approach, U.S. law has always had gaps in its coverage. One of the most significant concerns is toxic chemicals. While food and color additives and pesticides must undergo mandatory safety testing before they can be marketed, most other toxic substances escape regulation because a safety-first approach has not been used.

Under the Toxic Substances Control Act (TSCA), a manufacturer is not obligated to test potentially dangerous chemicals unless the EPA can point to substantial evidence that the risk posed by the chemical exceeds a statutory trigger. Specifically, the EPA must establish that there may be a "more-than-theoretical probability" of an unreasonable adverse effect in order to justify requiring manufacturers to conduct safety testing on a product, even when no adequate data exists to assess the products' safety.[1] This standard creates a catch-22 for the EPA, since manufactures can—and have—challenged the EPA's efforts to impose test requirements by arguing that the agency has insufficient evidence to justify testing to develop more evidence. This burden of proof helps explain the alarming dearth of chemical toxicity information.

The burden imposed by TSCA is higher still for the EPA to initiate an actual regulatory response to protect human beings and the environment from chemicals known to be toxic. First, the agency must come up with sufficient information on the chemical's risks and benefits to support a threshold finding that one or more of its current uses causes unreasonable adverse effects on the environment. Once that standard has been met, TSCA allows the EPA to impose one of seven listed requirements on a toxic chemical. But the courts have interpreted that to demand that the agency first analyze the costs and benefits of every alternative regulation. Based on that extensive assessment, the EPA then must demonstrate that it has selected a regulation in which the benefits outweigh the costs and the selected alternative is the least burdensome for the regulated industry. The EPA attempted to regulate asbestos under this

---

1. *Chemical Manufacturers Association v. EPA*, 859 F.2d 977, 984 (D.C. Cir. 1988).

provision but gave up after a court held that the agency had not provided enough substantial evidence to support its conclusions.[2]

The European Union has proposed a new chemicals policy called Registration, Evaluation, and Authorization of Chemicals, or REACH, to address the remarkable absence of safety data concerning chemicals. The policy would require chemicals to be registered, tested, and granted a permit before being sold in the EU. In the white paper that describes the policy behind the legislation, the European Commission laid out the defects of the current approach, which, in effect, describes U.S. chemicals policy.

In recent years, U.S. statutory gaps have widened. The dominant direction of policy and its implementation is to open opportunities for opponents of protective regulation to exploit existing gaps and create new ones. Conservatives argue that existing laws are in need of reform because it is presumed that they go too far or are too rigid and uncompromising. The following section documents and explains some of these developments.

Burdens of Proof

The Food and Drug Administration (FDA) implements the Food, Drug, and Cosmetic Act (FDCA), a precautionary statute that puts safety first by requiring relatively extensive testing of drugs as well as food and color additives. It also imposes a safety demonstration as a condition to marketing these products. Despite this protective mandate, the FDA has effectively flipped the burden of proof in its regulatory oversight of genetically modified foods onto itself. The FDA has concluded that the products of biotechnology are "substantially equivalent" to foods that are not genetically modified. Therefore, these products presumptively fall within the "generally recognized as safe" exception to testing and pre-market clearance requirements, despite the absence of rigorous evidence to support that conclusion. Does this mean that genetically modified foods are necessarily dangerous? No, it means we don't know if they are because they have never gone through the testing required of other new food additives. It also means genetically modified foods are presumptively unadulterated, and companies are free to market them without identifying them as genetically modified. Moreover, the burden is on the government to establish that a particular genetically modified food is adulterated and, therefore, unmarketable.

Consumers face another serious protection gap in the case of dietary supplements such as ephedra. Dietary-supplement manufacturers historically

---

2. *Corrosion Proof Fittings v. EPA*, 947 F.2d 1201 (5th Cir. 1991).

have made ambitious claims about their products' capacity to enhance health or appearance. When companies went further by claiming therapeutic benefits, they risked running afoul of the FDCA requirement that drug manufacturers demonstrate that their products are safe and effective prior to marketing them. So they lobbied Congress, which eventually passed the Dietary Supplement Health and Education Act of 1994. The Act allows dietary-supplement manufacturers to market their products without FDA approval as long as their therapeutic claims do not go to the "structure and function" of the human body, a showing the FDA has the burden of sustaining. The new law also exempts dietary supplements from the definition of food additive, so the FDA must also demonstrate in court that a dietary supplement is adulterated before it can remove it from the market.

Neither of these experiments in shifting the burden of justification from the sponsor of risk-producing activity to the government—and the public, who act as guinea pigs—put safety first; and both have failed. The country witnessed a catastrophe in the food industry when potentially allergenic, genetically modified StarLink™ corn found its way into taco shells, despite assurances that it would be used only for animal feed. The National Academy of Sciences (NAS) recently issued a report concluding that more sophisticated approaches to biocontainment of genetically modified animals and plants are not likely to be successful.[3], Reports of adverse health effects caused byephedra other dietary supplements continue to pour in to a government agency that lacks the authority and the capacity to take effective protective action. See Case Study, p. 89, The government cannot put safety first when it has the burden of justifying protective interventions to protect people and the environment from risk.

Enforcement Loopholes

Manufacturers are able to avoid many protective regulations simply by deciding that the requirements do not apply to their activities. For example, waste generators can avoid regulatory requirements governing the disposal of hazardous waste if they determine that the waste does not qualify, in toxicity and volume, as hazardous. The EPA permits regulated entities to use their knowledge of the substance as the sole basis for the estimation; meanwhile the agency has limited grounds for bringing enforcement actions against those

---

3. National Research Council, National Academy of Sciences, *Biological Containment of Genetically Engineered Organisms* (2003).

A Case Study on the Erosion of Precaution: FDA Regulation of Dietary Supplements Containing Ephedra

Consumers often assume that dietary supplements derived from natural sources are safe. Such supplements are widely used in the United States to combat problems ranging from obesity to depression. More than half of all Americans are estimated to take vitamins, minerals, herbs, or other supplements.

Dietary supplements containing ephedra are widely popular in the United States, where they are marketed to promote weight loss and improve energy levels and athletic performance. As many as 3 billion servings are consumed in the United States each year. But researchers have linked supplements with ephedra to serious health effects, including heart attacks, liver failure, strokes, and seizures. The FDA has received approximately 17,000 adverse health reports on consumers who have used dietary supplements containing ephedra, including 155 reported deaths. One such incident garnered national attention in 2003: the ephedra-related death of 23-year old Baltimore Orioles pitcher Steve Bechler, who collapsed during practice and died the next day.

The prevalence of ephedra related health risks can be traced directly to the absence of a precautionary regulatory approach to dietary supplements. In 1994, Congress enacted the Dietary Supplement Health and Education Act (DSHEA), which amended the Food, Drug, and Cosmetic Act (FDCA) to provide that dietary supplements containing the natural form of ephedra would not need FDA approval before going to market. By contrast to the precautionary approach employed with respect to drugs, dietary supplement manufacturers are not required to demonstrate to the FDA that their products are safe or effective, before putting them on the market. In fact, manufacturers of such supplements have no obligation to test their supplements before they begin selling their products, nor are they even required to register themselves or their products with the FDA.

Instead of requiring manufacturers to demonstrate product safety, the DSHEA puts the burden on the FDA to prove that a supplement is unsafe. Even worse, manufacturers of dietary supplements are not even required to record, investigate or forward to the FDA any reports they receive of illnesses that may relate to the use of their products, as are drug manufacturers. As a result, the FDA must rely on voluntary reports of adverse health effects from consumers, health care providers, and manufacturers in order to determine whether dietary supplements are safe.

In 1994, the FDA issued a Medical Bulletin noting that it was "concerned about the seriousness of these reported adverse events and their increasing number." Nonetheless, the FDA's efforts to regulate ephedra were hamstrung by questions about the strength of its evidence and by DSHEA's provisions putting the burden of proof on the agency, instead of on the supplement manufacturers.

(Continued)

A Case Study on the Erosion of Precaution: *(Continued)*

In February, 2003, after the public outcry over Bechler's death, the release of a National Institutes of Health study that concluded ephedra may be associated with important health risks and may have limited health benefits, as well as other studies, the FDA renewed its regulatory efforts. Finally, on December 30, 2003, the FDA announced plans to ban the sale of dietary supplements containing ephedra, but the heavy burden of proof the DSHEA places on the FDA to show that a dietary supplement is unsafe before it pulls it from the market means that manufacturers will likely challenge such action.

On April 12, 2004, the FDA's final rule prohibiting the sale of dietary supplements containing ephedra went into effect, and if its action is upheld, the ban on ephedra will undoubtedly prevent thousands of future illnesses and deaths. Nonetheless, action on ephedra or other dietary supplements posing significant health risks will come far too late for those already harmed.

---

who use this information to their advantage. Indeed, the EPA has proposed rules for identifying hazardous waste that would rely on industry's self-determination even more.

Exemptions

Manufacturers and other risk creators also have won exemptions from protective regulation, even when their actions pose a clear risk of significant harm to health and the environment. For example, farmers and others who use pesticides and fertilizers that wash into rivers and lakes as nonpoint source runoff are now responsible for more than half of the water pollution in the United States, but they do not have to assess and reduce the environmental risks their activities pose because the EPA and the states have effectively exempted nonpoint sources of water pollution from regulation. Large petrochemical facilities do not need to monitor ambient concentrations of so-called "fugitive" releases of toxic air pollutants from leaks and spills, even though such sources cumulatively account for significant amounts of toxic air pollution.[4] Industrial sources of toxic releases resulting from malfunctions, shutdowns, and other changes in operations generally are not required to prevent such releases.

---

4. "Fugitive" releases are emissions from an unidentified source, or those not captured by containment methods as a result of equipment leaks, evaporation, or other unknown causes.

In all of these cases, the government cannot put safety first because it bears the burden of collecting and analyzing information, assessing the risks posed by the discharges, supporting a threshold determination that regulation is necessary, and justifying any regulatory controls it proposes to implement.

'Sound' Science

The subtle erosion of the protective core of U.S. environmental laws has accelerated in the past 10 years through the adoption of excess analytical and information requirements that further raise the EPA's burden of proof and add roadblocks to the swift promulgation of protective regulations. Such burden-shifting is most evident in demands by regulated companies for information-intensive prerequisites for regulation, such as cost-benefit analysis and regulatory sound science reforms. Such additions to the regulatory process typically require the agency to accumulate a definitive body of hard evidence before implementing a proposed regulation. The actual effect of the informational and analytical requirements is to prevent agencies from putting safety first, since the required data frequently do not exist, the information that does exist rarely supports definitive scientific conclusions, and the risk creator is not required to generate any evidence.

As discussed in Chapter 6, so-called sound science legal reforms use the rhetoric of objectivity to pursue an agenda that permits industrial risks. During the 104th Congress, for example, the unsuccessful wholesale regulatory reform bills typically included provisions requiring agencies to establish procedures for obtaining peer review of scientific studies that support significant regulations. Unable to secure such changes by directly amending environmental, health, and safety statutes, the opponents of protective regulation have inserted them into riders to lengthy and essential appropriations bills. One such rider, the Information Quality Act (IQA), allows disgruntled regulated entities to file formal complaints challenging the quality of information agencies use or disseminate to carry out their responsibilities, even if they cannot successfully challenge the regulation itself. More recently, the White House Office of Management and Budget (OMB) has proposed guidelines requiring agencies to obtain peer review of significant studies, despite Congress' previous failure to enact similar requirements into law. Curiously, sound science advocates within industry seldom apply the same standards of quality and peer review to the data they produce to meet gateway statutes such as FIFRA.

The wholesale regulatory reform legislation of the 104th Congress also included requirements for agencies to calculate the costs and benefits of major federal regulations. A cost-benefit analysis requirement was enacted in the Unfunded Mandates Act of 1996, and a similar condition has been imposed by executive order since the Carter Administration. Such requirements, increase the evidentiary demands on regulators by requiring them to demonstrate quantitatively that a regulation's benefits exceed its costs. A typical analysis for a major rule can cost more than a million dollars and take years. More importantly, regulatory actions that rely upon cost-benefit analysis almost never put safety first because such analyses typically ignore poorly understood and unquantifiable health and environmental benefits and exaggerate the cost of regulation.

Judicial Overreaching

Numerous studies have demonstrated that environmental, health, and safety regulation is an area in which federal judges are ideologically divided, with conservative judges favoring industry outcomes more often than liberal judges do. Consequently, legal challenges to protective regulations brought before conservative judges have an increased likelihood of success. Ideology has had a profound effect on judicial selection in recent Republican administrations, so it is often possible for regulated industries to find a judge who is not sympathetic to the safety-first principle.

A number of judicial decisions in the past two decades have hindered agency attempts to put safety first in implementing health, safety, and environmental laws by raising the evidentiary burden required for agency action and rejecting the evidence and policy judgments the agencies supply. As explained in the case study on page 66, the Supreme Court opinion that has most hampered agency efforts to apply the safety-first principle involved the Occupational Safety and Health Administration's (OSHA) attempt to regulate the carcinogen benzene.[5] A plurality of the court held that OSHA was required to perform a risk assessment prior to mandating lower levels of worker exposure to toxic chemicals. Only after finding that benzene posed a significant risk to workers, based on substantial scientific evidence, at existing exposure levels could OSHA require employers to reduce the level of exposure. Despite the court's assurance that the ruling would not strap agencies with a mathematical straightjacket, several subsequent federal appeals court decisions have moved in precisely that direction by imposing rigorous requirements for the scientific evidence needed to justify a protective standard.

---

5. *Industrial Union Dept., AFL-CIO v. American Petroleum Institute,* 448 U.S. 607 (1980) (the Benzene decision).

These court-imposed requirements, which are not found in the text of the authorizing statutes, represent conservative judicial activism rather than a fair attempt to interpret Congress' intent. For example, not long after the benzene decision, the 5th U.S. Circuit Court of Appeals held that the Consumer Product Safety Commission (CPSC) could not assume that the carcinogenic risk urea-formaldehyde foam poses to humans could be assessed on the basis of a large study of laboratory rats in light of inconclusive human epidemiological studies.[6] The court's opinion, which flew in the face of many cases upholding the frequently encountered agency assumption that laboratory animal data is relevant in assessing human risks, did not point to any statutory language that was inconsistent with the agency's safety-first policy choice. The 5th Circuit, which encompasses the heart of the U.S. petrochemical industry, particularly Texas and Louisiana, is notorious for cases that second-guess agency attempts to regulate chemicals.

The Progressive Perspective

Progressives believe that we need to return to and improve upon the protective safety-first approach that characterizes the foundation of health, safety, and environmental laws. The failure to adopt this approach for pervasive and harmful agents, such as asbestos, radiation, benzene, lead, polychlorinated biphenyls (PCBs), chlorofluorocarbons (CFCs), and diethylstilbestrol (DES), embody this too little, too late theme. Indeed, the multibillion dollar Superfund program is a testament to the expense and inefficiencies of taking action after the harm is done, rather than establishing ways to anticipate and prevent it.

Like an individual who purchases insurance to protect against personal catastrophe, legislatures enact protective laws to screen risky activities and to avoid public health and environmental harms. The private entities that would subject their neighbors and the environment to these risks frequently argue that protective laws cost too much money or cut too deeply into profits. They maintain that people who are injured can always collect damages for any injuries suffered as a result of unreasonable conduct in subsequent tort actions. Progressives respond that the possibility of having to pay victims in subsequent tort actions does not provide an adequate incentive to reduce risks because of the difficulties that tort claimants encounter in proving that the conduct of a particular private entity caused a

---

6. *Gulf South Insulation v. U.S. Consumer Product Safety Comm'n,* 701 F.2d 1137 (5th Cir. 1983).

particular disease and nonhuman environmental entities generally are not allowed to sue for compensation. Even if the tort system worked better, progressives believe a monetary payment is not the same as preventing harm to people and the environment. Companies that subject people and the environment to risks should be required to take precautionary action to prevent harm.

Progressives believe that government should protect its citizens with precautionary laws that effectively shift the burden to the risk creators, who should have to justify their risky activities as a condition of going forward. Risk sources should have to demonstrate, based on solid scientific information, that the risks are socially acceptable before public health and the environment are threatened. Companies must produce information about potential risks prior to engaging in activities that create those risks. This requirement would ensure that the government and potentially affected individuals would be aware of the risks and could take action to reduce or otherwise avoid the risks before any harm was caused.

Once such information is available, progressives expect the government to take effective action to limit or otherwise control risk-producing conduct. When technology-based controls are not enough to reduce risks to acceptable levels, government should require risk producers to go even further, up to the point of completely stopping the risk-producing activity if necessary.

In addition to being appropriately precautionary and protective, the safety-first policy is equitable. It builds on the assumption that the health and safety of every individual—from the wealthiest to the poorest American—is more important than the profits of a company that would impose risks on its employees and neighbors. Protective regulation under the safety-first principle also shows proper respect for the welfare of future generations because it carefully focuses on protection against irreversible harm.

The safety-first approach to public health and environmental protection is a mainstay of modern European and international law. After debuting in a number of general guidance statements in the 1980s, the precautionary principle, which incorporates the safety-first approach, has been integrated into at least 14 multilateral agreements. The proposed new European chemicals policy, REACH, adopts a safety-first approach by requiring chemical manufacturers to conduct prescribed toxicity tests as a condition of marketing the chemicals. Despite the fervent opposition of the chemical industry on both sides of the Atlantic, the cost of implementing the testing, which must be

7. Commission of the European Communities, *Commission Staff Working Paper, Extended Impact Assessment*, Oct. 29, 2003, 20, http://europa.eu.int/comm/enterprise/chemicals/chempol/bia/eia.pdf.

completed by 2012, is estimated at roughly 3 percent of current research and development expenditures,[7] a small price to pay for greater safety.

The progressive approach to risk-based regulation also has a solid pedigree in the economic concept of credible worst-case analysis. Unlike cost-benefit analysis, which assumes that sufficient information is available to assign reasonably accurate probability distributions to the possible consequences of risk-producing activities and risk-reducing interventions, credible worst-case analysis begins with the understanding that decision-makers usually have very little information about these probability distributions. Nobel Memorial Prize-winning economist Kenneth Arrow has demonstrated that in contexts in which the decision-maker knows very little about the distribution of probabilities it is generally not appropriate to simply make a best-case estimate by averaging all available expert predictions, which is the technique most practitioners of cost-benefit analysis apply. Rather, any reasonable approach to decision-making depends only on the best and worst possible outcomes.[8] In the case of complete ignorance of the relevant probabilities, all useful information for decision-makers is contained in the extreme outer bounds of possible outcomes. Subsequently, other economists have demonstrated that if society is risk-averse or prefers to keep its options open in the face of uncertainty, then it is sensible to choose a regulatory option that leads to the least harmful worst-case outcome, sometimes called the "maximin approach," even when some information on the relevant probability distribution is available.[9]

The progressive approach to regulation accepts this wisdom and urges risk assessment to be based on an analysis of the worst-credible outcomes. This ensures that health, safety, and the environment receive at least some degree of protection, even if the worst-case scenario does play out in the real world. Using such credible worst-case and maximin approaches to risk-based decision-making may, of course, result in decisions that provide more protection than would be provided by decisions relying solely upon best estimates. Since the essence of the progressive approach to risk-based regulation is to err on the side of safety, however, this possibility is consistent with sound progressive decision-making.

---

8. Kenneth J. Arrow and Leonid Hurwicz, "An Optimality Criterion for Decision-Making under Ignorance," in C.F. Carter and J.L. Ford, editors, *Uncertainty and Expectations in Economics: Essays in Honour of G.L.S. Schackle* (Clifton, NJ: Augustus M. Kelley, 1972), 1–11.

9. Itzhak Gilboa and David Schmeidler, "Maximum Expected Utility with Non-Unique Prior," *Journal of Mathematical Economics* 18 (1989): 141–53; David Kelsey, "Choice under Partial Uncertainty," *International Economic Review* 34 (1993): 297–308.

In the progressive view, environmental, health, and safety statutes, and the agencies implementing them, should adopt a safety-first approach toward assessing and managing risks in situations in which the best-efforts approach has already been implemented or is unavailable. For those situations in which Congress has specified a risk-based approach to regulation, agencies should take regulatory action whenever a risk creator's activities present a credible worst-case risk of harm to health or the environment. The nature of this regulatory action will depend on the statute and the context, and it should be proportionate to the threat presented, but the agencies should employ credible worst-case analysis in both cases to determine the nature and extent of any risk-based response.

The Progressive Agenda

Although progressives generally support an overall requirement that those engaged in risk-producing activities use their best efforts to reduce those risks, progressives also have something to say about regulatory programs that require agencies to regulate based on an assessment of the risks posed by the regulated activities. Based on the safety-first principle, progressive prescriptions for risk-based regulation include the following suggestions.

Adopt a Credible Worst-Case Analysis for Risk-Based Regulation

When a regulatory agency's statute requires it to make a threshold finding of risk as a precondition to taking protective action, it should employ credible worst-case risk analysis based on available information and conservative assumptions in making that finding. This approach will ensure that the agency does not fail to protect against activities that pose uncertain risks with major or catastrophic consequences. When an agency's statute requires it to consider risk in determining the nature and extent of the regulatory response to risk-producing private activities, the agency should employ credible worst-case analysis in choosing among regulatory options. In either case, the regulated entity should have an opportunity to rebut worst-case assumptions with reliable information produced under generally accepted scientific standards. Absent a thorough and effective rebuttal, the risk-based decisions concerning whether and how stringently to regulate should adopt the credible worst-case risk scenario as the starting point for determining the appropriate regulatory response.

The worst-case approach outlined above puts safety first by placing the burden of justifying risk-producing activity on the source, rather than leaving it to the government. It has the added advantage of providing a strong incentive for risk-producing companies to conduct risk-related research in order to meet the burden of rebutting worst-case assumptions, rather than rewarding them for suppressing information and shirking responsibility for researching the effects of their activities on health and the environment. Regulation based on credible worst-case analysis encourages responsible innovation in which new goods and services are developed in conjunction with solid safety information.

Make the Polluter Justify the Pollution

Regulatory programs are doomed to failure if they require the government to demonstrate that restrictions on risk-producing activity will reduce risks from unacceptable to acceptable levels. In an administration that is not inclined to impose potentially burdensome regulations on its industrial friends, the need for additional study and analysis is always available to excuse the government's failure to take protective action. In administrations that are inclined to be more protective, targets for potential regulation will have an almost infinite variety of opportunities to challenge an agency's data and analysis. The number of risky products and activities can overwhelm even an administration that is friendly to workers, consumers, and the environment. Therefore, Congress should empower agencies to impose risk-reducing requirements on pollution sources, dangerous workplaces, and other risk-producing activities based upon reasonable worst-case assumptions. If flexibility is needed to avoid overly burdensome regulation, Congress should give regulated entities the opportunity to justify less-stringent controls by adequately demonstrating that such controls will sufficiently protect public health and the environment.

Fix the Broken Statutes

TSCA is not a gateway statute like the FDCA or FIFRA because its supporters were forced to compromise with the chemical industry at the time it was enacted. TSCA is better characterized as a selective interdiction statute, under which a company is free to introduce potentially toxic chemicals into workplaces and the environment merely by providing notice to the EPA that it intends to do so. As discussed, the burden of proof is on the EPA to justify testing and any regulatory requirements, so the statute has been a near-complete

failure. It has been successful only in areas in which the burden is on the manufacturer, such as the control of PCBs.

Congress should amend TSCA to give the EPA authority to require testing of any chemical substance or mixture of chemical substances when the
amount of that chemical or mixture crosses a threshold volume. The Euro-
peans' REACH proposal is a good working draft for these amendments.
High-volume production chemicals should be tested whether or not the EPA
can support the threshold determination that a risk trigger has been exceeded. In addition, Congress should allow the agency to regulate new and
existing chemicals without bearing the burden of demonstrating that the
benefits of the regulatory requirements exceed the costs. Instead, Congress
should allow the EPA to rely upon a reasonable worst-case analysis to place
the burden on the manufacturer of a chemical substance or mixture to
demonstrate that the substance does not pose an unreasonable risk to humans or the environment.

Put the Burden on Risk Creators

Congress should reverse the recent trend toward exempting risk-producing
activities from safety-first regulatory requirements. Those who profit from
such activities should justify the risks they impose on humans and the environment. After almost a decade of implementation, it is clear that the experiment embodied in the Dietary Supplement Health and Education Act of 1994
went too far. It is also clear that the FDA's excuse for not regulating genetically
modified foods is a wholesale violation of the safety-first principle. Congress
should replace these and other failed attempts at regulatory reform with laws
that place the burden of justifying risk-producing activities on the companies
that make such products before they claim more victims. When congressional
action is not required to accomplish these results, the agencies should move
as quickly as possible.

Eliminate Paralysis by Analysis

Opponents of the safety-first principle have been very successful in persuading Congress and the OMB to impose unnecessary information gathering,
data quality and cost-benefit analysis requirements on agencies that promulgate environmental, health, and safety regulations. Although these requirements appear to be reasonable, the effort to impose detailed analytical requirements on agencies amounts to little more than sophisticated sabotage of
safety-first legislation. The consequences of these efforts on agency attempts

to promulgate protective regulations are painfully obvious. The process of writing rules has become so cumbersome that agencies are reluctant to initiate the process at all and, when they do, it takes years of intense effort to complete it.

Congress should re-examine the regulatory analysis requirements it imposed in the Regulatory Flexibility Act and the Unfunded Mandates Act with an eye toward simplifying them and reducing the burden of needless analysis on agencies that must, in the absence of such requirements, still provide sufficient analytical support for rules to survive judicial review. Both Congress and the White House should conduct a similar review of the analytical requirements contained in what, over the years, has become a proliferation of analyses that agencies must undertake prior to promulgating regulations. In addition, as recommended in Chapter 6, Congress should repeal the IQA, which has the potential to cause enormous mischief if opponents of regulation persuade the courts that information-quality challenges to agencies are subject to judicial review. Finally, Congress and the president should strongly resist any attempts to impose additional analytical requirements on agencies trying to apply the safety-first principle to environmental, health, and safety regulations.

Judges Should Be Judicious

The general principle of judicial deference to legislative and administrative policy choices is well accepted. So long as Congress has not trespassed on the Constitution, the courts should defer to the policy choices embodied in statutes. Likewise, the courts should not lightly set aside agency policy choices based upon their interpretations of the statutes Congress has enacted. In other words, unelected judges should not substitute their views of appropriate regulatory policies for those of Congress. When Congress either explicitly or implicitly articulates a safety-first policy in a regulatory statute, courts should insist that the implementing agency adhere to that policy choice. Courts should not substitute a less precautionary policy merely because an individual judge strongly believes that a safety-first policy is not warranted in the context of a particular assertion of regulatory power.

Unfortunately, many members of the federal bench were selected largely for their views on the proper role of government in society, and those views frequently clash with the safety-first policies underlying many of the existing environmental, health, and safety statutes. Evidence is rapidly accumulating that the antiregulatory policy preferences of these judges unduly influence their decisions. The growing tendency of conservative judges to substitute their views of appropriate regulatory policy for those of Congress must stop. More importantly, future presidents must not select candidates for the bench based on their proclivity for putting the economic well-being of corporations ahead of the health and safety of individuals and the integrity of our shared environment.

Conclusion

Congress and regulatory agencies should continue to develop and adopt protective approaches to regulating risk-producing private activities. The European Union is developing successful models of regulatory programs that take a safety-first approach and should result in much more information from private entities about the nature and extent of the risks of their activities. When information about risky activities becomes available to regulators, they should use it to determine whether and how stringently to regulate. When adequate information is unavailable, the government should employ worst-case analysis in administering risk-based regulatory programs.

CHAPTER 8

FAIR DISTRIBUTION OF ENVIRONMENTAL HARMS AND BENEFITS

Environmental Fairness

Until relatively recently, many people did not know or care much about the distributional effects of environmental policy. Environmental protection was almost exclusively concerned with defining and controlling *total* pollution levels with little regard for distributional patterns.

Over the past decade and a half, we have realized that patterns of environmental insults are distributed quite unevenly. Smog is rare in rural areas and common in cities. Dump sites, often scarce in the suburbs, are abundant in poor communities. The dirty river that loops past your neighborhood produces contaminated fish for the subsistence fishermen just around the bend. The "good" parts of the environment—the parks, the ponds, the tree-lined drives—also are distributed unevenly.

The irregular distribution of environmental harms and benefits in the United States often means unequal environmental protection for people who happen to live on the wrong side of the ecological tracks. A large body of evidence accumulated since the 1980s shows, for instance, that low-income and minority communities are subjected disproportionately to hazardous waste facilities, air pollutants, contaminated fish, and pesticides. The concern for inequalities based on income, race, age, sex, or other personal traits is called environmental justice.

Spawned by grassroots activists in the 1980s, the environmental justice movement originally began as a protest against locating polluting industries and waste facilities in low-income and minority communities. The agenda quickly expanded to address inequalities in other areas, including environmental health standards, worker safety, and political decision making.

Environmental justice issues span a broad spectrum. While the diverse and overlapping nature of environmental inequalities makes categorizing them difficult, we might divide environmental justice problems into inequalities associated with geography, weak health standards, and legal and political processes.

Geographic Inequality

The most familiar form of environmental inequality involves location. Reports of polluted inner cities or contaminated Indian reservations regularly capture headlines now. However, in the early 1990s, it was Oprah Winfrey who introduced Americans to "Cancer Alley," a stretch of small and almost entirely black Louisiana communities between Baton Rouge and New Orleans that had been poisoned by hundreds of chemical plants.

In addition to the anecdotes, a substantial body of evidence now documents the alarming extent to which low-income and minority communities are home to polluting facilities. One particularly influential report, released in 1987 by the United Church of Christ's Commission for Racial Justice, found that communities with the most commercial hazardous waste facilities also had the highest concentration of racial and ethnic minorities. While residents' socioeconomic status was an indicator for the presence of hazardous waste sites, the report concluded that race was the most significant indicator.

A correlation between air pollution and race also exists, in part because minorities are more likely to live in urban areas. When the EPA boasts that U.S. air quality "is much cleaner today than it was 30 years ago," it is telling only half the story.[1] In many metropolitan areas, air quality has actually worsened in the past 10 years, which has contributed to asthma rates more than doubling in all children since 1983. Even this focus on metropolitan areas masks the true disproportionate impact of our nation's air quality: Asthma is almost twice as common among blacks as it is among whites, even when controlling for income levels.[2] Black children also are three times more likely than white

---

1. EPA, *Draft Report on the Environment 2003*, ii, http://www.epa.gov/indicators/roe/pdf/EPA_Draft_ROE.pdf.

2. Surface Transportation Policy Project, *Clearing the Air: Public Health Threats from Cars and Heavy Duty Vehicles—Why We Need to Protect Federal Clean Air Laws*, 2003, 22 (citing American Lung Association, Minority Lung Disease Data), http://www.transact.org/report.asp?id=227.

children to be hospitalized for asthma treatments.[3] As Daniel Swartz, executive director of the Children's Environmental Health Network, said, "When there are more kids carrying inhalers to school than lunchboxes, you know you have a problem."[4]

The cleanup of contaminated property raises other environmental justice issues. The divestment and blight that accompanies areas that have more than their share of contaminated sites leaves low-income and minority communities in a difficult situation. The first problem is that these areas have to compete with other contaminated sites for government cleanup resources. A 1992 *National Law Journal* report supports the claims that contaminated sites in minority communities often are neglected or are cleaned up less effectively than sites in wealthier predominantly white areas.

Following this report, EPA-sponsored "brownfield" initiatives—efforts to clean up land developed for industrial purposes, polluted, and then abandoned—have offered some improvement by promoting community involvement in cleanup decisions, but there are serious holes in the program. First, many contaminated sites, despite their danger, do not qualify for federally sponsored cleanup because the federal program attacks only the "worst of the worst." Sites that don't qualify for the federal program usually end up in state brownfield programs, which vary greatly in terms of the degree of community involvement and cleanup standards. Second, brownfield redevelopment programs have a built-in tension between encouraging cleanup and protecting residents' health.

For decades, contaminated sites lay abandoned in industrial areas because performing a top-notch cleanup was more expensive than letting the land go to waste. Brownfield initiatives try to change this pattern by lowering the standards for deciding how much to clean up, and thereby lowering the cost of an acceptable cleanup, in order to encourage developers to reclaim the land. In exchange, the developer places land-use restrictions in the property deed to ensure that it will only be used for industrial purposes in the future. The advantage is that the reclaimed land will no longer threaten residents with toxic leaks, and the increased development will create local jobs. But the disadvantage is that such industrial areas, which are home mainly to low-income and minority communities, now are legally prevented from changing the character of their neighborhoods. Residents could leave, but relocating people who

---

3. Ibid. (citing American Lung Association, Minority Lung Disease Data).

4. Environmental Media Services, *Press Release, New Report Ranks Top Metro Areas with Worst Air Pollution*, August 19, 2003, http://www.ems.org/transportation_bill/clearing_air_release.html.

live near contaminated sites fractures communities. In Cancer Alley, for instance, corporate buyouts of contaminated homes separated people from their extended families, divided churches, and interrupted lifelong friendships. In addition, the contaminated surroundings of residents' homes are taken into account so that the "fair-market value" prices residents are paid are sharply discounted.[5]

Just as environmental threats are distributed unevenly, certain neighborhoods and communities enjoy more environmental amenities than other areas—and a large share of these lucky communities are affluent and white. In Los Angeles, there are 1.7 acres of parkland per 1,000 residents in areas that are disproportionately white and relatively wealthy, compared with 0.3 acres of parkland per 1,000 residents in the more racially diverse inner city.[6] In New York City, greenways, marinas, and bodies of water safe for swimming are all more common in predominately white areas. In the city's five boroughs, not a single designated fish-and-wildlife habitat area exists outside of a white community.[7]

Environmentally regressive transportation policy also harms minority communities. In addition to polluting the air, the government's emphasis on highway systems over public transportation hurts residents of low-income and minority communities, who are more likely to rely on public transportation than own a car. According to a 2003 study cosponsored by Harvard's Civil Rights Project, only 7 percent of white households do not have a car. In contrast, 24 percent of black households, 17 percent of Hispanic households, and 13 percent of Asian households do not have a car.[8] In urban areas, blacks and Hispanics make up 54 percent of public transportation users.[9] To add insult to

---

5. Environmental Defense maintains a helpful Website that "maps" environmental justice inequalities county-by-county. *See* http://www.scorecard.org.

6. Robert Garcîa, Erica S. Flores, Sophia Mei-ling Chang, Elizabeth Pine, *Building Community and Diversifying Democracy from the Ground Up: Strategies from the Urban Park Movement*, unpublished manuscript.

7. Samara F. Swanston, "Environmental Justice and Environmental Quality Benefits: The Oldest, Most Pernicious Struggle and Hope for Burdened Communities," *Vermont Law Review* 23 (1999): 545, 557 (citing New York City Dep't of Planning, *New York City Comprehensive Waterfront Plan: Reclaiming the City's Edge*, 23 (1992)).

8. Thomas W. Sanchez, Rich Stolz, and Jacinita S. Ma, *Moving to Equity: Addressing Inequitable Effects of Transportation Policies on Minorities*, 2003, vii (sponsored by the Civil Rights Project at Harvard University, Cambridge, MA, and by the Center for Community Change, Washington, D.C.), http://www.civilrightsproject.harvard.edu/research/transportation/MovingtoEquity.pdf

9. Ibid.

injury, the main public transportation routes in some metropolitan areas do not adequately serve poorer areas.

One-Size-Fits-All Health Standards

Weak health standards often fail to protect vulnerable classes of people. As discussed above, the incidence of asthma cases illustrates the need for strong air standards to protect children and the elderly, who are particularly at risk for respiratory illness. Women are more susceptible to polychlorinated biphenyls (PCBs), dioxins, and other dangerous chemicals that accumulate in fatty tissue. Pollution also threatens women's capacity to bear and nurse healthy children. In some cases, pollution susceptibility physiologically varies by race. In addition, minority and low-income populations—who suffer disproportionately from anemia, heart disease, and low birth weights—are more vulnerable to the cumulative effects of toxic exposure. Despite these important differences, many environmental health standards continue to be based on healthy white males between the ages of 25 and 35. This model becomes the measure of health for us all.

Unfair health standards arise from inaccurate assumptions about who we are and how we live. Consider fishing. Federal water-quality standards aspire to keep most bodies of water safe for fishing and swimming. In setting acceptable levels for waterborne toxins, the EPA had assumed that the average person ate fish only once per week, but this average concealed dramatic variations. In the South, the rural poor rely heavily on subsistence fishing and so do Native Americans in the Northwest. Some tribal populations in the Puget Sound consume many times the EPA "average."[10] Today, thanks in part to the efforts of environmental justice advocates, the EPA now uses a separate consumption standard for subsistence fishermen. But more work remains. The newer standards can only take into account the consumption patterns of subgroups whose habits are known and documented; however, most subgroups, tribal or otherwise, have not been studied. Without more information about subsistence fishing habits throughout the country, environmental protection is incomplete for these groups.

In developing standards to protect farm workers from pesticides, agencies estimate exposure without recognizing that children, even infants, often accompany their parents in the fields. These young people are much more vulnerable to pesticide fallout. And since farm workers in the United States are

---

10. Catherine A. O'Neill, "Variable Justice: Environmental Standards, Contaminated Fish, and 'Acceptable' Risk to Native Peoples," *Stanford Environmental Law Journal* 19 (2000): 3, 51–52 (citing Kelly A. Toy, et al., *A Fish Consumption Survey of the Tulalip and Squaxin Island Tribes of the Puget Sound Region* (1996)).

mostly Hispanic and generally poor, such regulatory oversights result in additional race-based and class-based inequalities.

From a broader perspective, the current chemical-specific approach to assessing environmental health risks fails to account for the fact that low-income and minority communities often are simultaneously exposed to several different pollutants. The cumulative and synergistic effects of multiple exposures can be dramatic. Some combinations of two or three chemicals can be hundreds or thousands of times as powerful as any single chemical.[11] An effort to regulate toxic mixtures began in the Clinton Administration but has not moved forward under President Bush.

In addition to physical differences in risk, people's perceptions of risk vary according to race and sex, suggesting that political decisions about acceptable health risks should incorporate the views of a wider range of the population. A national survey conducted by researchers James Flynn, Paul Slovic, and C.K. Mertz found that, even when correcting for differences in education and income, "white males tended to differ from everyone else in their attitudes and perceptions—on average, they perceived [environmental and non-environmental] risks as much smaller and much more acceptable than did other people."[12]

Unfair Process

Environmental justice advocates consistently raise issues about environmental decision making and public participation. Environmental decision-makers traditionally have heard the views of industry giants, conventional environmental organizations, state and local governments, and federal land managers but not the people who actually live in the most-affected areas. Influence on environmental decision making is a main priority of environmental justice organizations. But as activist William Shutkin writes, "Participation entails more than simply showing up. It demands recognition, equitable treatment, and deliberative responsibility."[13] Gaining this type of access is difficult.

---

11. Robert W. Collin & Robin Morris Collin, "The Role of Communities in Environmental Decisions: Communities Speaking for Themselves," *Journal of Environmental Law & Litigation* 13 (1998): 37, 55; Steve F. Arnold et al., "Synergistic Activation of Estrogen Receptor with Combinations of Environmental Chemicals," *Science* 272 (1996): 1489.

12. James Flynn, et al., "Gender, Race, and Perception of Environmental Health Risks," *Risk Analysis* 14 (1994): 1101.

13. William A. Shutkin, *The Land that Could Be: Environmentalism and Democracy in the Twenty-First Century* (2000), 129.

Conventional stakeholders have significantly more time, money, and other resources to participate in these processes and influence agency policy and implementation. Environmental justice advocates often lack the resources to participate as effectively in such a highly technical arena, and this fundamentally lopsided playing field significantly compounds the previously discussed problems and produces bad decisions that harm public health.

Since local environmental justice organizations must rely heavily upon publicly available information because they operate on such slender budgets, they bear a greater burden when government restricts public information, as the Bush Administration did after the terrorist attacks on Sept. 11, 2001. Government claims for exemption under the Freedom of Information Act (FOIA) are almost routine in some agencies. The Homeland Security Act and the Information Quality Act (IQA) also significantly limit many types of formerly public information that is relevant to environmental protection. Together, these initiatives could allow firms to withhold information about hazardous emissions, accidents, and other risks posed by power plants, nuclear facilities, refineries, chemical plants, and other large facilities. In a democracy, information is power; but this move toward greater secrecy can only disempower our most environmentally vulnerable communities.

The Progressive Perspective

The distribution of environmental harms and benefits throughout society does not occur randomly. Race, sex, and other immutable characteristics affect one's likelihood of exposure and susceptibility to environmental threats. Some environmental justice advocates point to intentional bias among corporate or governmental decision-makers. Defenders of the existing system often respond that distributional patterns result from market forces and consumer choices. The landfill, the smelter, and the chemical plant do not move to low-income or minority communities in order to harm residents, the argument goes; they are built to take advantage of affordable land and friendly land-use regulations. In other instances, "market dynamics" cause low-income or minority populations to congregate around existing facilities.

But the debate between malice and market is largely a ruse. Like any human system, the free market reflects the biases and power imbalances of broader society. When told that dumps are attracted to low-income and minority neighborhoods because the land is cheap, one must ask why the land is so cheap. The answer will often involve social prejudices held by landowners, rental agents, lending institutions, and others. The truth is that many sectors

Applying 'Civil Rights' While Ignoring Distributional Harms

The EPA has provided communities of color with an administrative procedure under Title VI to challenge facilities whose emissions will cause disproportionate environmental harms to communities. But this civil-rights remedy has proven illusory because the EPA's "one size fits all" utilitarian approach to measuring health risks distills environmental effects to a common measure that ignores distributional effects on the most vulnerable communities.

As is now clear from the history of EPA's Title VI complaint procedure, this narrow approach has even forced the agency to ignore equity considerations in the enforcement of its civil rights obligations. The first adjudicated Title VI decision decided by the EPA cemented its approach to environmental justice permitting challenges. The *Select Steel* case involved a challenge to an air pollution permit granted by the Michigan Department of Environmental Quality to the Select Steel Corporation for the construction of a steel mill in a community of color. The proposed plant was to be located in the city of Flint, Michigan, whose residents are already exposed to various sources of outdoor pollution from hazardous and solid waste facilities, proximity to major highways, and truck traffic. The challengers in the case, a predominantly African-American community, raised specific concerns about the facility's potential to add to this exposure with its emissions of lead, air toxins, and dioxin.

The EPA dismissed the challenger's complaint within a few months of receiving it, without requiring any additional documentation from the permit applicant or the state. The EPA concluded that since emissions from the proposed facility would not lead to any violations of the national ambient air quality standards (NAAQS) for ozone-depleting substances and lead emissions, the environmental effects of the facility's emissions did not rise to the level of "adverse." Since no population would suffer an "adverse" effect, the EPA found it unnecessary to consider whether the facility would add to the "disparate" impact of pollution exposure on the African-American population. In other words, the EPA never considered the cumulative health impact of even technically "safe" (under the NAAQS) levels of emission from the facility, especially when combined with other pollutants or when combined with other polluting sources in the community. Instead, the EPA assumed that when health-based standards, which do not consider cumulative or synergistic impacts of multiple exposures to different pollutants, have been met, there is no impact to remedy.

The *Select Steel* principle has guided the EPA in its adjudication of Title VI complaints, leading it to dismiss 12 of its 20 adjudicated decisions under Title VI because of failure to show "adverse impact," without even bothering to determine whether the complaining communities were being disproportionately exposed to environmental pollutants. To date, none of the citizen complaints to the EPA under Title VI has been successful.

(Continued)

Applying 'Civil Rights' While Ignoring Distributional Harms *(Continued)*

For more information, see Michael Gerrard, EPA Dismissal of Civil Rights Complaints in New York Law Journal, November 28, 2003. As of late 2003, the EPA has received a total of 143 Title VI complaints since 1993. Of those 143, 114 are closed and 29 are still pending. Of the 114 closed complaints, the EPA rejected 82 outright without further investigation, usually for technical reasons, and of the 32 remaining complaints, the EPA issued 20 decisions.

---

of society bear responsibility for environmental unfairness, including consumers, industry, developers, government planners, health experts, and mainstream environmentalists. The issues have been ignored for too long.

Whatever the cause, it is hardly fair for low-income and minority communities to suffer environmental harm when so many others do not. The unfairness mounts when one considers that the middle- and upper-classes produce more of the country's extraordinary levels of pollution and waste because they are able to consume more. Aspiring to distributional equality would actually lead to better and more efficient environmentalism by internalizing consumption costs. If consumers of wasteful products shared more equally in bearing the environmental costs of production and disposal, the result might well be more eco-friendly products, more pollution prevention, and fewer and smaller landfills. Environmental justice activists, therefore, do not think of themselves as NIMBYs ("Not in My Backyard"), but as NOPEs ("Not on Planet Earth"). A greater emphasis on environmental costs would awaken privileged groups to the environmental vulnerabilities they share with the less privileged. In turn, such awareness can lead to more forceful and unified environmental protection campaigns.

The Progressive Agenda

Provide Fair Access to Decision Making

Struggles for environmental justice begin to gain traction when local groups and coalitions become politically active and begin to pry open the decision-making procedures that are ignoring their concerns. Some examples include: a group of organizations in Emelle, Alabama that fight for higher standards for the town's hazardous waste dump; the multiracial organization in Oakland, California that educates residents about lead poisoning; and Mothers of East Los

Angeles, a group that successfully protested a proposed incinerator in their already blighted community. Some parts of the country, particularly New York City and Los Angeles, are in the midst of an urban parks movement, in which a diverse coalition of city dwellers join together to encourage and protect parks and other environmental amenities.

But grassroots activism cannot succeed by itself. Government must play the leading role in both a practical and a moral sense because the mission of government is to protect the welfare of citizens, regardless of income, race, or other characteristics. The overlapping nature of environmental justice problems suggests the need for a broad array of strategies in many fields.

Incorporate Fair Distribution into All Government Decisions

Officials obviously should avoid the circumstances that allow the many previously described ills to take root. Local governments and the federal officials who sometimes oversee them should not permit polluting factories or waste dumps in areas already plagued by such facilities. State and federal enforcers should investigate violations in the inner city as aggressively as they do in the suburbs. Standards for toxic cleanup and brownfield development should remain consistent across race and class lines.

California provides one example of such efforts. Its new city-planning statute requires long-range development plans to equitably distribute public services and avoid over-concentrations of industrial facilities near schools and neighborhoods. According to the state's guidelines, "[o]ver-concentration occurs when two or more industrial facilities or uses, which do not individually exceed acceptable regulatory standards for public health and safety, pose a significant hazard to adjacent residential and school uses due to their cumulative effects."[14]

The federal government also has work to do. Concern for a decision's distributional effects would lead to a rethinking of many policies. For instance, the federal government should revise national transportation policy to champion cleaner vehicles, reduce air pollution, and emphasize public transportation in minority and low-income communities. In addition, agencies responsible for setting health and safety standards should revise their risk-assessment methods to take account of differences among various subgroups and adverse health effects caused by cumulative exposures and synergistic interactions between pollutants.

---

14. State of California, Governor's Office of Planning & Research, *General Plan Guidelines 2003*, October 2003, 26, http://www.opr.ca.gov/planning/PDFs/General_Plan_Guidelines_2003.pdf.

A Clinton-era executive order on environmental justice provides a vehicle to achieve all of these goals. The 1994 executive order, which remains in effect, requires all federal agencies to pursue environmental justice goals "to the greatest extent practicable."[15] Specifically, it directs agencies to do two things: identify and address disproportionately high and adverse health or environmental effects on minorities and low-income populations through their programs and activities; and ensure that future programs and activities that substantially affect the environment do not create unequal burdens on the basis of race, color, or national origin.

At the very least, this language requires that: (1) federal agencies carefully inventory the demographic effects their actions have had on the human environment and investigate ways to relieve the most dramatic imbalances; (2) federal agencies evaluate the demographic effects that future initiatives would have on the human environment, through environmental impact statements or other devices; (3) agencies issue guidance documents specifically outlining courses of action for divisions within their offices to address environmental justice concerns; and, perhaps most importantly; (4) all agencies undertake regular, comprehensive evaluations of their programs and activities under the executive order.

Unfortunately, President Clinton's executive order seems to have lost steam. In 2003, the U.S. Commission on Civil Rights found the order was floundering, at least as it had been implemented by four key agencies, the EPA, Department of Transportation, Department of the Interior, and Department of Housing and Urban Development. Specifically, the report found that no agency had reported any comprehensive assessments of their environmental justice efforts in nine years. The degree of success in this area is impossible to evaluate without such assessments. The EPA was the only agency that had shown any support for environmental justice objectives in its top leadership. Internal leadership is essential to the success of this executive order, especially since its requirements lack enforcement provisions.

---

15. Executive Order 12,898, *Federal Actions to Address Environmental Justice in Minority and Low-Income Populations*, 59 Fed. Reg. 7629 (1994) amended by EO 12,948, 60 Fed. Reg. 6381 (1995).

Apply the Letter—and the Spirit—of the Civil Rights Laws to Environmental, Health, and Safety Decisions

One might look to the constitutional guarantee of equal protection under the law or to federal civil rights laws for relief since environmental justice so directly involves racial discrimination. However, such laws have serious limitations, in part because they were written without environmental justice in mind and, in part, because the federal judiciary has narrowly interpreted the laws.

The Constitution's equal protection clause provides scant defense against the disparities in treatment under our environmental statutes because, as currently interpreted, it bars only government conduct that produces a discriminatory outcome and reflects a clear discriminatory intent. In practice, this dichotomy usually means that, to establish the intent requirement, a government's laws or conduct must explicitly mention race. But government conduct that abets environmental injustice, such as poor zoning or siting decisions and inadequate permit requirements, almost never meets this test. Consequently, it is possible for a county to locate most of its landfills in minority communities without failing the equal protection test.

While some civil rights statutes allow plaintiffs to prove discrimination based only on discriminatory outcome, most of the major statutes cover discrimination in education, housing, and employment. Environmental justice claims fit poorly within these categories. The one major statute that should apply to these claims is Title VI of the 1964 Civil Rights Act, which authorizes agencies to bar recipients of federal funds from engaging in conduct that produces disparities in results. So far, however, effective administrative enforcement of Title VI in the environmental area has been stalled in the EPA; and a recent Supreme Court decision held that the only part of Title VI that provides a right for private citizens to sue is the law's protection against actions that have both discriminatory effects and discriminatory intent. In other words, it offers the same protection the Constitution already provides.[16]

The progressive agenda includes effective administrative implementation of Title VI as it applies to all federal environmental, health, and safety programs that generate the types of disparities the environmental justice movement has brought to our attention. It also continues to advocate changes in Title VI that will provide an effective legal remedy for citizens denied equal treatment under environmental, health, and safety programs.

---

16. *Alexander v. Sandoval,* 532 U.S. 275, 293 (2001).

17. Barry Commoner, *The Closing Circle: Nature, Man and Technology* (1971), 39.

Conclusion

If the belief that in nature "everything is connected to everything else"[17] has nurtured American environmentalism, the environmental justice movement now affirms that everyone is connected to everyone else. But until we address the role of fair distribution in regulatory policy, true environmental protection will elude us.

CHAPTER 9

PUBLIC RESOURCES
FOR PUBLIC USES

Sound Stewardship

Up to this point, we have focused on those aspects of the progressive agenda that affect the regulation of private sector activities undertaken largely through private decisions using privately owned resources, or public sector activities that have similar results (e.g., military pollution). In a society and an economy that relies heavily upon private initiative and private ownership, this focus reflects the reality that many of our most serious environmental hazards result from private sector activities, especially manufacturing.

This chapter extends that focus to two other important classes of resources. First, some of our most important lands and the natural resources found on them are publicly owned, including our national parks, national forests, wilderness areas, public rangelands, and wildlife refuges. As a society, we have identified these lands and their ecosystems as being of particular public value by not allowing them to be privately held. We have given the government control over these lands and resources, or otherwise given them special status, in order to protect a wide array of public values.

Second, some resources are not publicly owned or located on public land, but we still mandate their protection because the public has a collective interest in the fate of these interdependent elements of our environment. Accordingly, the U.S. legal system has a long-standing tradition of recognizing the public trust in coastal areas, wetlands, wildlife, endangered species, fisheries, and other important aspects of our environment.

This chapter will collectively refer to public lands, including the resources they contain, and protected public trust resources as "public resources." Private consumption of these public resources raises special concerns because they are finite and overexploitation can permanently exhaust them. The progressive agenda aspires to revitalize the guiding principle that public resources should be preserved for public uses, meaning that decisions to allow private consumption or degradation of public resources are proper only where private usage serves public goals.

Polls consistently show that the American public's concern for public resources extends to protecting them for future generations. Just as we depend on the store of natural environmental wealth that our parents and grandparents left us, our children and grandchildren will depend on the resources we leave them. Our stewardship of these treasures will define our legacy as a society and affect the well-being, even the survival, of future generations.

Society's interest in public resources encompasses the nonmarket value it places on human health and well-being, including recreational, ecological, symbolic, aesthetic, economic, spiritual, strategic, and inspirational values. Because there is a limited stock of natural capital that can be exhausted or impaired by private or inappropriate public uses, society has a great interest in the sound stewardship of these resources. Decision making about whether to allow the consumption or exploitation of public resources must consider the effects of such activities on all relevant values. If such uses are allowed, they must be subject to terms and conditions that minimize adverse effects and determine adequate financial compensation for the public through payments to the government.

Historically, the United States has been a world leader in maintaining a vibrant public sphere of natural resources. The country showed vision and leadership with the establishment of the National Park System in 1916. The adoption of the landmark Endangered Species Act (ESA) in 1973 inspired much of the world and has been copied widely.

In recent years, this tradition has been placed in jeopardy, as the pressure to open previously protected public resources to private exploitation has mounted. Public resources have been managed to benefit short-term economic interests without adequate consideration of the long-term effects on other public values. The balance we have historically maintained between public and private interests in the protection of public resources has shifted. As technology has advanced in the past 50 years, patterns of public resource exploitation and use have grown more intense. Some new technologies have minimized the attendant effects of exploitation, but many others have enabled depletion of resources faster and over larger areas. And government agencies and departments too often lack the resources to enforce the laws that were enacted to meet the challenge of protecting public resources over the long term. Restoring and maintaining the proper relationship between private and public interests is an integral part of the progressive agenda.

The Public Interest at Risk

While the Endangered Species Act (ESA) and other laws enacted since the late 1960s represent important steps toward preserving critical resources, they have not succeeded in halting the ongoing degradation and unsustainable use of public resources. Half of the wetlands in the contiguous United States have disappeared.[1] California has lost more than 90 percent of its wetlands, nine other states have lost 70 percent or more of their historic wetlands, and another dozen states have lost more than 50 percent.[2] While the pace of destruction has slowed, we continue to lose ground. Louisiana loses 25,000 acres of coastal wetlands each year.[3] Despite the protections of the ESA, many species become extinct each year as their habitats are destroyed.

Sustainability is the guiding principle of our fisheries laws, yet more than a third of the nation's coastal fishing stocks are considered overfished; and in most cases the overfishing continues.[4] The fate of the North American cod fishery, which many believed to be endless, illustrates the devastating effects of overfishing. After intense fishing tripled the total catch in the 1960s, the stock declined dramatically. The Canadian cod fishery, which was estimated to have produced more than 200,000 tons of fish per year for many years, was decimated by 1992, prompting the Canadian government to impose a two-year moratorium.[5] Two years later, the moratorium was extended indefinitely, and it remains unclear if the fishery will ever recover.[6]

Resources on our public lands also are being overexploited. Despite legislative constraints, damaging forestry practices have decimated areas of our national forests, destroying habitat and watersheds. Unsustainable grazing

---

1. U.S. Department of the Interior, *Wetlands Losses in the United States, 1780's to 1980's,* 1991, 1.

2. Ibid., 5 and Table 1.

3. U.S. Department of the Interior, Fish and Wildlife Service, *Wetlands of the United States: Current Status and Recent Trends,* March 1984, 38.

4. U.S. Department of Commerce, National Oceanic and Atmospheric Administration, National Marine Fisheries Service, *Sustaining and Rebuilding, NOAA Fisheries 2002 Report to Congress, The Status of US Fisheries,* April 2003, 8, Figure 3, http://www.nmfs.noaa.gov/sfa/statusoffisheries/cover_sos.pdf.

5. Canada Department of Fisheries and Oceans, *Backgrounder, The Fisheries Crisis in the Northwest Atlantic* (B-HQ-95-16E), July 1995, updated June 6, 2003, http://www.dfo-mpo.gc.ca/media/backgrou/1995/hq-ac16_e.htm.

6. Ibid.; National Academy of Sciences, Commission on Geosciences Environment and Resources, Ocean Studies Board, *Sustaining Marine Fisheries,* 1999, 33–34, http://books.nap.edu/books/0309055261/html/33.html#pagetop.

on public lands is widespread. Irreplaceable groundwater and scarce surface water are disappearing rapidly in the arid West, permanently altering fragile ecosystems.

We have also made terrible decisions about the financial terms that govern private consumption of public resources, creating what amounts to a welfare program for logging, mining, and ranching interests. Rather than sell public resources for economic uses at market prices, we give them away or sell them at a fraction of their market values. We subsidize forestry and grazing. These misguided policies encourage wasteful and unsustainable uses of our surface and groundwater, the biodiversity on public rangelands, the trees in our national forests, and the minerals contained in our public lands. While limited extraction of public resources can serve the public good, Bush Administration policies assume that it *always* does. Noneconomic values are systematically ignored, with predictably adverse results.

Our energy-related public resource policies are a case in point. At the urging of the oil and gas industries, Congress repeatedly entertains proposals to open highly valued wild areas such as the Arctic National Wildlife Refuge and the Florida coast to energy development and pipelines, despite the limited role this kind of development would play in securing energy for the nation. (See Case Study, "The Arctic National Wildlife Refuge and the Maintenance of the Public Trust," p. 122). When these controversial proposals fail, other less visible wild areas are sacrificed in their place. Environmentalists narrowly managed to defeat proposals to authorize drilling in the Arctic Refuge. Soon after, the Bush Administration announced plans to open large portions of the Rocky Mountain West to mineral and energy exploration and development. It has also approved plans to install more than 50,000 methane wells in Wyoming's Powder River Basin, which will pump vast quantities of groundwater and generate trillions of gallons of high-sodium wastewater.[7] These and other shortsighted energy and conservation policies make us the largest energy consumers in the world; Americans use four times the global per capita consumption.

---

7. U.S. Bureau of Land Management, Miles City Field Office and Billings Field Office, *Final Statewide Oil and Gas Environmental Impact Statement and Proposed Amendment of the Powder River and Billings Resource Management Plans,* January 2003, http://www.mt.blm.gov/mcfo/cbm/eis/; U.S. Bureau of Land Management, Buffalo Field Office, *Final Environmental Impact Statement and Proposed Plan Amendment for the Powder River Basin Oil and Gas Project,* January 2003, http://www.wy.blm.gov/nepa/prb-feis/; *see also* Powder River Basin Resource Council, *Press Release, Ranchers and Environmentalists File Suit on Largest Oil and Gas Project Ever Approved by Agency,* May 1, 2003, http://www.powderriverbasin.org/press_releases/5_03_worc_%20may.htm.

New initiatives that weaken biodiversity protection reflect the same fundamental flaws. The Bush Administration recently announced a policy that will strip protection from some of the most sensitive and ecologically valuable areas of Alaska's Tongass National Forest, and it has issued a plan to allow commercial logging in California's Giant Sequoia National Monument, home to trees that have lived more than 3,000 years and grown more than 300 feet tall. The Administration has eliminated protection for more than 2 million acres of Utah wilderness, opening it to commercial exploitation.

The Bush Administration's so-called Healthy Forests Initiative blocks the U.S. Fish and Wildlife Service from participating in decisions about endangered species, ensuring that the nation's experts on biodiversity do not have a seat at the table when activities that threaten such species with extinction are considered. Initiatives to provide broad exemptions from environmental laws for all military operations will leave the public lands the military controls with less protection than many private lands. Meanwhile, the Administration's failure to seek adequate funding for the implementation of the ESA has virtually halted the listing of species and blocked enforcement. Steady pressure to narrow the class of protected wetlands threatens to increase the pace of destruction. All of these policies advance short-term private economic interests at the expense of the broader public interest.

Privatization and Expanded Private Control

Supporters of these new initiatives argue that the government is inept and that expanded private control over land and public resources would prompt better decisions. The most extreme advocates of privatization propose that all public resources should be owned or managed privately. More moderate proposals would expand the ability of private interests to extract and degrade resources with fewer restrictions and less government oversight. While different in degree, both approaches overlook the effects of exploitation on biodiversity, clean air and water, wilderness, scientific knowledge, and aesthetic and spiritual values.

Depending on private landowners to undertake the stewardship of public resources can only result in the accelerated elevation of private profit over noneconomic values. For example, some claim that a private landowner would take better care of rangeland than a public manager. The argument is based on the assumption that a private landowner has an economic stake in the land, including its future value, and, therefore, will be a sound steward. This reasoning overlooks the likelihood that many landowners' sense of what the land is worth is based only on its market value, such as for grazing. Landowners may ignore all of the land's nonmarket values in using and managing the land. Instead of protecting the biological integrity, aesthetics, water quality, or wildlife values, such landowners may alter the land to promote only grasses that livestock will eat. When we privatize public resources or allow private interests to dictate their fate, nonmarket values often get left out of the picture. These nonmarket values are more important over the long term than the short-term interests of private landowners.

A similar dynamic is at stake in efforts that give commercial fishing interests quotas in an attempt to protect collapsing fisheries. In theory, target fish quotas will make those harvesting the fish good stewards: their ownership of these rights will give them an incentive to prevent decline in the target fish species. And by creating these private rights in the target fish, regulators hope to harness the economic self-interest of the fishing interests. However, if the targeted fish population is the only value in which there is an interest, then only that interest will be protected. There is no incentive to protect other species that may be caught incidentally. The target fish population may be protected, but the many other species that commercial fishermen catch will continue to be caught and discarded without constraint, continuing the spiral of marine decline. The incentives created by private rights to a particular resource do not replace a broad consideration of the public interest.

The move toward greater private control over our public resources is a dangerous distraction from the central focus of our natural resources policies: to ensure protection of the public's interest in these resources. If only the market values of these resources mattered, there would be no need to maintain them as public resources. Statutes that protect our public lands and resources reflect a desire to protect their nonmarket values. The goal of such statutes is to ensure that these values are considered in decisions that affect these resources. But experience shows that even with statutes that mandate the consideration of intangible values, we often fail to protect them in the face of the special interests that want to exploit our resources for conflicting economic purposes.

Understanding the Pressure to Expand Private Control over Public Resources

The pressure to consume public resources should not surprise us. Three related forces are at work. First, public resources represent an enormous stock of wealth that can be used to generate private profits. Second, individuals and for-profit entities acting in markets as landowners, shareholders, or business owners often do so with a narrow view toward increasing their wealth. Third, the profit motive, on which our system of private enterprise depends, is magnified by the legal structures through which most business is conducted. Corporations and the many variants of the corporate form were created to protect investors from liability and help them acquire wealth. At its core, the for-profit corporation is an engine for creating shareholder wealth.

It is tempting to think that the people who represent and run corporations will act to ensure the public good when they make corporate decisions because they are part of the public, breathing the same air, drinking the same water, enjoying the same natural wonders, and so on. But, by law, these individuals are bound to serve their investors or shareholders; they don't have the option of making decisions that are contrary to these interests. It sometimes may be in a corporation's financial interests—for public relations purposes or otherwise—to engage in civic-minded activity, but the core mission of private firms is not to preserve the public interest. Clarity about the effects of these intersecting forces is essential if we are to protect the public interest in public resources.

Moreover, although well-meaning individuals may run many companies, the revelations regarding Enron, WorldCom, and a host of other large corporate entities show that corporations, just like individuals, are vulnerable to corruption. One of government's most important roles is to guard against such abuses in order to protect the public interest. It is the government's job to ask the tough questions, obtain information that may not be in the corporation's interest to disclose, and determine the public interest. We should not expect companies interested in short-term profits to make decisions that will protect our interests or those of future generations.

In some cases, the resulting policies are obviously bad deals for the public, even if we think purely in terms of easily quantified values, such as the publicly owned minerals, trees, or grazing lands that we grant to private entities for a fraction of their market value. In other cases, the bad deals may not be so obvious if we apply an exclusively economic test because not all of the costs the public bears can be expressed monetarily. There may be unquantifiable losses of the sort of intangibles that led to the resources being held for the public good in the first place. In addition to the non-market values we lose during private exploitation of public resources, the public may lose the opportunity to pass resources on to future generations—something the American people consistently say is of great value to them.

The Arctic National Wildlife Refuge and the Maintenance of Public Trust

In 1960, the Arctic National Wildlife Refuge was designated a federal wilderness area by President Eisenhower. Today, with 19 million acres, the Refuge is the size of South Carolina and sits hundreds of miles north of the Arctic Circle next to Prudhoe Bay, hugging the Arctic Ocean. The Alaska Conservation Foundation describes the Refuge as one of the only places on Earth that protects the complete spectrum of subarctic and arctic habitats for abundant populations of migratory birds, polar bears, porcupine caribou, snow geese, and other wildlife.[8]

The Refuge's uses can only be changed by an act of Congress—and advocates of oil exploration have been urging just that for decades. President Bush's National Energy Plan supports opening the Refuge to oil exploration, estimating that between 5.7 billion and 16 billion recoverable barrels of oil lie beneath its fragile tundra. Even the optimistic upper estimate would only be equivalent to 800 days of domestic oil consumption; and the Refuge could never produce enough to be the exclusive source of domestic oil. Instead, the Energy Information Agency estimates that, at its peak-production levels, the Refuge would produce 800,000 barrels daily, reducing foreign oil imports from 62 percent of current U.S. demand to 60 percent.[9]

Securing the Refuge's oil could require 2,000 acres of oil pipelines and facilities. While a 2,000-acre "footprint" for oil production does not sound like much out of 1.5 million acres, production would require 20 different sites to exploit 30 or more oil fields, with roads and oil transportation networks connecting those areas. In its environmental impact statement, the Department of the Interior concluded that oil development would have serious impacts on the wildlife and the ecosystem.

According to New York Times columnist Nicholas Kristof, the choice may have been best summarized by an oil industry geologist who said: "We can build cleanly, we can drill without hurting the caribou. But we can't drill and keep this a wilderness."[10] To drill or not is the question. The accepted way of deciding to drill or preserve is to balance extra energy against environmental damage, balance contributions to the local economy against degradation of the wilderness, or balance the preservation of a land few will ever see against limited exploration by those willing to pay.

Such balancing proves both too much and too little. It proves too much because it hides two deep assumptions—that current costs and benefits are what matter, and that willingness to pay should determine the outcome. But it also proves too little because it concentrates on today's needs and neglects the future.

(Continued)

8. "Monumental Choice for the Arctic National Wildlife Refuge," *Alaska Conservation Foundation's Dispatch*, Fall 2000, http://www.akcf.org/pdf/acf_dispatch_fall00.pdf.

9. "ANWR oil could cut U.S. Need Slightly," *Juneau Empire*, March 14, 2002.

10. Nicholas D. Kristof, "What Price Drilling," *The New York Times*, Sept. 5, 2003.

The Arctic National Wildlife Refuge and the Maintenance of Public Trust *(Continued)*

The New Progressive agenda insists that we meet the needs of the present without compromising the ability of future generations to meet their needs. Alternatives to the marginal benefits of oil from the Refuge are feasible. The public interest in this case tips decisively in favor of maintaining the Refuge's wilderness status.

The Progressive Perspective

We should not be surprised when private interests lobby, negotiate, and use publicity to secure an arrangement in which the public bears the lion's share of the costs while private interests keep the lion's share of the profits. They are fulfilling their role as generators of private wealth, which leads to undesirable consequences and inequitable results that shortchange the public. These are the forces that produce below-cost timber sales, subsidies for logging interests to build roads in national forests, repeated proposals to drill in treasured wild areas such as the Arctic Refuge, and policies that are draining aquifers throughout the country.

The body of law that protects our parks, endangered species, forests, and rangelands has done much to slow the degradation of these priceless resources. If we are to ensure their future protection, these policies must be strengthened. The recent trend toward expanding private interests in these resources at the expense of the public interest is leading us in the wrong direction. If we are to protect our resources and our legacy, we must decisively and deliberately re-examine our values. Abdicating public control of public resources does not serve the public interest. Private control of public resources makes sense only when it is compatible with the public interest. In all other cases, the full range of public interests in natural resources can be protected only through public ownership and close government supervision of resource use. Long-term protection depends on long-range vision and commitment. We must develop funding and regulatory strategies that demonstrate our commitment.

The Progressive Agenda

There are many ways to improve our policies to better protect the public interest in public resources. First, we need to maintain and strengthen substantive controls on government decisions to promote sustainable use of our public resources. Second, we should demonstrate our long-term commitment through long-term funding strategies. Third, we need measures to promote greater government accountability.

Better Assessments Mean Better Decision Making

Some statutes, such as the Federal Land Policy and Management Act, National Forest Management Act, and National Environmental Policy Act, already purport to require an assessment of the environmental effects of public resource use prior to their extraction. However, as implemented, these programs set the threshold for permission to extract public resources too low. The results of weak enforcement are severely degraded public rangelands, harmful logging practices, toxic pollution, and biodiversity loss caused by mining and drilling operations. Too often, we discover the unacceptable levels of degradation after it's too late. To address these problems, we need to design better regulatory standards that require comprehensive assessments of the environmental effects of a proposed activity *before* it is authorized. Although some statutes claim to require cumulative assessments of impacts on public resources, these are ineffective in practice.

Another important problem is our attitude towards uncertainty: when information about impacts is lacking, the presumption is that there is no harm and the activity is generally approved. To help ensure sustainability of any permitted activities, we need standards that reverse this burden of proof. Where uncertainty exists, the proponent of the potentially degrading activity should bear the burden of proving that the activity will not cause unacceptable adverse impacts. In light of the time it may take for impacts to develop, we need standards that demand longer-term impact assessments. Standards requiring that sustainable alternatives be among those considered and analyzed would help to ensure that resource extraction is conducted in ways that will not preclude future alternative uses.

Beyond requiring more comprehensive disclosure of the anticipated effects of public resource use and its alternatives, a fair accounting of the anticipated benefits to the private interest would provide useful information and enable agencies to accurately assess the value of the resources. The dollar amount of anticipated private benefits would help the public assess whether the terms under which private interests are being granted access to resources are in the public interest.

Is it an added expense for businesses to collect and disseminate the necessary information to make these decisions? Yes, it can be. But that is a cost of private profit-making activities affecting public resources, and one that we have allowed companies to avoid to the public's detriment. There is no excuse for giving away public resources without carefully assembling and considering the facts. No corporation would do that with its resources, and no government that cares about its citizens' interests should either.

Harmful Exploitation Must Not Be Exempt

Recent legislative and executive measures that loosen standards for energy exploitation and logging on public lands and create exclusions from and limitations to the scope of NEPA are steps in the wrong direction that must be reversed. Similarly, measures to exclude public land used for military purposes from environmental standards would cause irreversible damage that will be very difficult to repair.

Fund Long-Term Protection for Public Resources

Inadequate funding has stymied agencies charged with the stewardship of our public resources. Lack of funds has prevented the U.S. Fish and Wildlife Service from listing species known to be endangered. Chronic understaffing coupled with the volume of applications to fill wetlands has placed undue pressure on Army Corps of Engineers staff to grant permits without adequate review. Even funds earmarked for conservation, such as the Land and Water Conservation Fund, are held in reserve and never spent, as a way to offset large budget deficits. A comparison of funding levels currently committed to conservation with those committed to agricultural subsidies reflects a lack of commitment to public resources.

This ambivalent and ineffectual approach to funding is at odds with the well-documented, consistent public commitment to protecting public resources. Poll after poll shows public support for higher levels of funding, even at the expense of other important programs. Moreover, efforts to weaken the protection of these resources have consistently met with tremendous public outcry. Indeed, since the uproar against Congress' efforts in 1995 and 1996 to weaken protections for our natural resources, groups attempting to undermine conservation programs have resorted to less visible budget cuts as a more effective way to accomplish their goals without the public's knowledge.

To protect public resources as a legacy for future generations will require funding that matches our goal. Recent initiatives such as the National Park Service's Fee Demonstration Program suggest one solution. By statute, Congress can bypass the annual appropriations process and direct that funds from designated sources, such as park entrance fees, permit fees, or taxes, be automatically applied to conservation programs. If our goal truly is to sustain our parks, forests, wildlife refuges, and the biodiversity they contain for the long term, then funding a broader-scale approach built on this model could help achieve that goal. Otherwise, we may claim to be committed to preserving these resources, but each appropriations bill merely postpones for another year the decision on whether to protect these legacies or sacrifice them. An automatic appropriation that funds its intended purpose gives credence to the American public's long-standing, undisputed commitment to these resources, rather than making it the subject of an annual money struggle. It's time for our leaders to take seriously the public's commitment to conservation and design a funding mechanism that matches the public's strongly held values.

Ensure Government and Corporate Accountability

As we recommit to government's responsibility to protect the public interest, it is appropriate for the government agencies that manage public resources to enhance their accountability. At the most basic level, existing rules governing ethics, conflicts of interest, and government's revolving door should be monitored and enforced. The many recent revelations regarding open-door access for advocates of public resource extraction suggest that protecting the public interest may also demand reforms in current standards. The Bush Administration's refusal to disclose the identities of the participants in its National Energy Policy Development Group demonstrates a disregard for the public's interest and a policy to prevent accountability that undermines the public interest. Although the president has a need for confidentiality in order to ensure a candid exchange of views, a president also has a responsibility to assure citizens that decisions are being made with the public interest in mind. Groups such as one established by the EPA to advise the agency on appropriate pesticide-control levels, which was comprised entirely of agricultural and chemical industry interests, raise similar concerns when they meet in closed sessions that thwart public scrutiny.

We need government decision-makers to consider carefully issues that affect the public interest in public resources following full disclosure of the relevant facts and without the pressures that financial conflicts of interest create. Only then can we count on sound decisions and adequate stewardship for our shared natural legacy. Strong conflict-of-interest rules and vigorous enforcement are minimum requirements.

In addition to preventing inappropriate influence by those who deplete public resources for private profit, we need to ensure that intangible non-market values are being considered in order to level the playing field. Expanded opportunities for public participation in decisions affecting public resources, including judicial review, can help achieve this. Funding for technical-assistance grants is essential if the process is to allow effective consideration of the public interest in public resources. Given that protected public resources have often been set apart because of the noneconomic values they represent, it is essential that these values, and not just the values associated with commercial exploitation, be considered fully.

Conclusion

The government makes an essential contribution to our health and well-being and to that of future generations by protecting public lands, water, and biodiversity. Preserving public resources is a core aspect of U.S. law and policy. We can and must improve our efforts to protect the diminishing stock of public resources. The incalculable aesthetic, spiritual, wilderness, inspirational, and other intangible values of our cherished public lands as well as the practical value of wetlands, biodiversity, and our stock of other natural capital demand greater energy. Renewed efforts will benefit our physical well-being and ensure we leave a worthy legacy for future generations.

CHAPTER 10

THINK GLOBALLY

The Imperative of Multilateralism

Many environmental problems spill over the borders of one country, even one as vast as the United States. Bilateral or regional agreements among nations address some problems, such as pollution that crosses national boundaries between Canada and the United States. Other issues, such as stratospheric ozone depletion or global warming, are universal in scope and require multilateral action. Achieving agreement among many nations is a complex and demanding undertaking. Unless nations consent to international agreements they are not bound by them, so approaches to global problems must be formulated in ways that circumvent or accommodate objections raised by individual states that see their participation as potentially harmful. Global problems present enormous challenges requiring the cooperation of many nations and the leadership of others, particularly the United States.

The Montreal Protocol, which restricts the manufacture and use of ozone-depleting gases, and the Kyoto Protocol, which attempts to reduce the emissions of greenhouse gases, are two of the best-known examples of multilateral agreements addressing environmental, health, and safety issues. The Montreal Protocol has been largely successful, while the Kyoto Protocol has encountered numerous difficulties in implementation. A critical distinction between them was the strong leadership the United States showed in promoting the Montreal agreement compared with U.S. failure to lead—and our government's eventual repudiation of—the Kyoto effort.

As the Montreal Protocol illustrates, the United States can mobilize the political will to effectively exercise international leadership in response to foreign policy challenges that are similar to current global environmental threats. The Reagan Administration was the principal architect of the Montreal Protocol, a precautionary solution to a problem then characterized by considerable scientific uncertainty. The preferred domestic and international policy adopted in this forward-looking agreement was aggressive technology forcing catalyzed by the total elimination of a class of chemicals that had been regarded as essential a few years earlier, well before alternatives had been clearly identified.

Other examples of the United States exercising critical leadership in addressing global issues include the successful efforts of the Reagan and first Bush Administrations in calling for environmental reform of the World Bank during the mid-1980s and early 1990s. The United States was also one of the major proponents of the Convention on International Trade in Endangered Species, the principal international mechanism for protecting the black rhinoceros, large cats, the great apes, and other endangered and threatened species. Perhaps the most significant example of U.S. leadership to date is the Marshall Plan, a comprehensive, massive intervention based on a farsighted, precautionary approach to a problem—the spread of communism—that was poorly characterized and cumulative in nature. More recently, prior to the 1991 Persian Gulf War, the U.S. government worked with its allies to secure the approval of the U.N. Security Council, a watershed moment in post-Cold War international cooperation.

Today's international system is a far more sophisticated machine than at any other time in history. In the early 21st century, numerous opportunities, in the form of international organizations and multilateral cooperation, are available to the United States as vehicles for cooperation with other countries to craft meaningful solutions to international environmental threats while simultaneously protecting our national interests.

The United States' rejection of the Kyoto Protocol is only one of a growing list of examples that demonstrate the government's current disdain for multilateralism and its pursuit of unilateral, go-it-alone policies that disregard the interests of other nations and the global environment. Other instances of recent U.S. hostility to multilateral cooperation include the U.N. Convention on the Law of the Sea, the Comprehensive Nuclear Test Ban Treaty, the Convention on the Rights of the Child, the Rome Statute of the International Criminal Court, and conventions adopted by the International Labor Organization. Our approach has been similar at other important international environmental gatherings, such as the World Summit on Sustainable Development in Johannesburg, South Africa in 2002.

As we discussed earlier, the United States often disguises unilateralism as a disagreement over scientific certainty. When the Bush Administration announced in 2001 that the United States was pulling out of the Kyoto Protocol, it acted in a fashion contrary to the virtually unanimous view of every independent, reputable atmospheric scientist on the planet. To cover its tracks, the Bush Administration then requested that the National Academy of Sciences (NAS) review an international consensus document agreed upon by a group of more than 1,000 scientists. To the embarrassment of the Administration, the NAS endorsed these international conclusions. Nevertheless, presidential advisers continue to urge the disingenuous misuse of nonexistent scientific uncertainty as a rational for opposing U.S. policy action on global warming. Administration policy proposals rely on the misleading gauge of carbon intensity per unit of economic output as a policy indicator on global warming—a formula that could lead to increases in greenhouse gas emissions as economic activity intensifies.

The Consequences of Unilateralism

Many of the recent deficiencies in U.S. foreign policy on environmental, health, and safety issues can be traced to a mode of thinking that places short-term national interests above the benefits of international cooperation. Foreign policies formulated from such an outmoded approach inevitably give short shrift to threats that are:

- long-term rather than immediate, shifting the burden of short-sighted policies onto future generations that had no say in shaping them;
- cumulative rather than immediate in their effects, resulting from the gradual buildup of environmental insults and toxins rather than catastrophic events;
- uncertain in nature or poorly characterized scientifically, giving reluctant government officials a convenient excuse for costly delay; and
- multilateral or global rather than domestic or bilateral, requiring additional leadership to convince other countries to voluntarily accept proactive solutions.

In a world in which serious threats to the global environment increasingly exhibit one or more of these characteristics, a refusal to participate in multilateral agreements:

- risks irreversible harm from unforeseen catastrophes such as the Antarctic ozone hole, a result of failing to act early and sufficiently;
- shifts environmental burdens onto regions of the world that have fewer economic resources to respond;

- squanders the immediate benefits that could come from wider and deeper international cooperation on environmental challenges that cannot be addressed otherwise; and
- saddles future generations and the world with a legacy of environmental devastation.

The Progressive Perspective

Both Republican and Democratic administrations generally have found it useful to articulate a high standard of international environmental performance for others to emulate. Serving as an environmental model makes good business sense for a country that already has high environmental standards in place and whose industries face competitive pressures and incentives to move overseas, where regulatory controls are more lax. Leading the international pack on environmental issues also generates significant foreign policy benefits, creates goodwill among our allies, and enhances a sense of U.S. strategic vision as an element of geopolitical leadership. And, of course, creative and assertive international diplomacy on the environment is essential to ensuring the integrity of the planet for present and future generations.

The U.S. government can and should again take a visionary leadership role on international environmental issues. The obvious starting place would be to assess all aspects of foreign policy to ensure that they are responsive to environmental imperatives. Then the nation will be well-positioned to advocate an integrated approach to the environment internationally and to implement the results domestically. The National Environmental Policy Act (NEPA) provides a domestic vehicle for accomplishing this goal, but there is no analogous comprehensive planning mechanism for international environmental issues.

As the pressures of globalization intensify, it is readily apparent that we need to do a forward-looking, critical evaluation of foreign policy areas previously thought to have little effect on the environment. For example, the rules formulated by the World Trade Organization (WTO) to govern international trade require an in-depth examination to determine whether they are encouraging or undermining sustainable patterns of consumption. Current trade policy is fixated on cracking open foreign markets to improve U.S. business' access to lucrative overseas trade and investment, often at the instigation of domestic industry. While it is legitimate to take this goal into account when formulating U.S. foreign policy, other social welfare considerations also should be considered in deciding, for instance, whether to dispute the food-safety regulations of other countries. The Bush Administration's challenge to the European Union's reluctance to import genetically engineered food, which is currently pending in the WTO, seems to have been undertaken primarily to promote domestic business interests, such as those of Monsanto Co., with little or no regard for its potential to create an unfortunate precedent that could constrain our domestic ability to regulate this emerging, unproven technology.

We must also renew public commitment to good-faith participation in multilateral processes. This commitment includes assurances that the United States is prepared to accept compromises that involve trade-offs between short-term national interests and long-term global benefits. When the United States turns its back on the rest of the world, it pays a high price in the loss of goodwill abroad. Opposition to multilateralism is not in the interest of the United States or the global environment.

The Progressive Agenda

Provide for Transparent and Participatory Engagement

To improve the effectiveness of multilateral efforts, the executive branch should adopt more accountable and more participatory processes at the domestic level and advocate for similar change internationally. Instead, much of recent foreign policy has been conducted in a close-to-the-vest mode that is more appropriate to a poker game than to facilitating informed public debate on international issues that affect Americans' basic quality of life and the integrity of the global ecosystem. Free-trade agreements, with their compressed "fast-track" processes for domestic implementation—now innocuously known as "trade promotion authority"— are a prime example of the need for reform.

There should be genuine, open debate in Congress on all aspects of pending and completed trade agreements and an opportunity for public comment on negotiating drafts. Congress also should adopt statutory guarantees for public participation in foreign policy-related activities, such as international treaty negotiations, through an international version of the Administrative Procedure Act—a set of basic legal guarantees that has facilitated much of the substantive environmental law and progress to date.

Multilateral processes are subject to multiple obstacles that discourage speed and efficacy. Requirements for consensus in the adoption of treaties; multiple subsequent decision points in the form of signature, ratification, and entry into force; and the perceived need for unanimity in decisions taken by international organizations tend to delay critically needed coordinated action and dilute the efficacy of international agreements. Nonconsensus decision-making processes, such as majority voting, should be considered as methods for dealing with holdouts, scofflaws, free riders, and laggards. While governments are understandably reluctant to relinquish absolute control over the nature of the international obligations they assume, various forms of nonconsensus procedures have been successful in diverse arenas, such as the Montreal Protocol, the International Maritime Organization, and the World Bank.

Apply NEPA to Actions with Global Effects

At a minimum, NEPA should apply to U.S. government activities that affect overseas environments. Wholly apart from recent fighting in Afghanistan and Iraq, the United States takes many day-to-day actions that have environmental consequences on our numerous overseas military bases. Examining the effects, many of them adverse, of the many government-sponsored activities overseas is essential to ensuring that, at the very least, the United States is a good environmental neighbor while pursuing its legitimate foreign policy interests.

Ensure the Use of Science in Global Affairs

Science is a widely accepted touchstone worldwide for establishing the need for interventions to protect public health and the environment. Early insights into the potential for refrigerants and propellants in the form of chlorofluorocarbons (CFCs) to harm the ozone layer earned a visionary group of scientists the Nobel Prize in chemistry. Mounting scientific evidence about the harm lead exposure causes children retrospectively demonstrated the wisdom of aggressive early action to eliminate this toxin from gasoline and paint. Conversely, demands for excessive scientific proof under the slogan of "sound science" can stall needed action and cause paralysis by analysis.

Fortunately for the ordinary person on the street, not to mention diplomatic negotiators and other nonexpert decision-makers, there are useful models to ensure science is used wisely in international decision-making. Multilateral panels of scientists consisting of governmental experts, academicians, and independent researchers from many countries have been assembled to advise the world community on such critical global threats as stratospheric ozone depletion and the greenhouse effect. While occasionally susceptible to political manipulation from governments, these international scientific fora generally have been independent and effective in clearly articulating for the public the state of key international environmental threats.

The potential for environmental hazards, particularly those of a global scale, to outstrip scientific understanding has led to calls for precaution as a fundamental principle of international environmental policy. Variously dubbed a "precautionary approach" or "the precautionary principle," there is widespread recognition of the need for early, effective policy action on threats that may be poorly characterized from a scientific point of view. Stratospheric ozone depletion and lead are historical examples of the need for cautious decision-making in the face of scientific uncertainty. As we learn from sometimes painful and costly inaction, it is worth noting that, without exception, the scope and magnitude of emerging environmental threats that seemed uncertain at first have turned out to be more severe than originally perceived.

Bridge the North–South Gap

To bend conservationist and Sierra Club founder John Muir's words only slightly, like it or not everyone is connected to everyone else. In our rapidly globalizing world, the fate of others increasingly is our destiny as well. For example, while the bulk of greenhouse gas emissions have been and are currently being produced by industrialized countries—the United States chief among them—emissions from developing countries will predominate sometime during this century as their economic development progresses. This situation calls for a global accord that preserves the integrity of the Earth's climate for the benefit of all, coupled with the responsibility to make meaningful emissions reductions worldwide and equitably distribute them among countries in light of past contributions and present needs.

On a different level, it is in the interest of the United States and other northern industrialized countries to bridge the gap with developing southern countries. While foreign aid will always be modest by comparison to the economic needs of the developing world, development assistance can stimulate important structural change in needy countries and demonstrate the good will of more fortunate countries. Consequently, maintaining and enhancing levels of development assistance should be a priority. The United Nations has established an international standard of 0.7 percent of GDP,[1] and some nations, such as Ireland, have made good-faith efforts to reach this target. The United States, the wealthiest and most energetic economy on the planet, is clearly in

---

1. European Parliament, *European Parliament's Resolution on Financing of Development Aid, Summary,* April 18, 2002, http://europa-eu-un.org/article.asp?id=1327.

a position to do so as well. Instead, Republican presidents and Congresses have dramatically reduced foreign aid over the past decade.

Recognizing the reality that foreign aid will always be limited, even under the most favorable of circumstances, external financing must be strategically targeted for maximum multiplier effects—environmental and otherwise. At the same time, there have been genuine environmental concerns about the quality of bilateral aid and multilateral financing from international institutions such as the World Bank. Development assistance from all donors, including the United States, should meet strict tests of sustainability. We can and should relieve the developing world of the necessity to repeat the mistakes that already-industrialized countries made on the path to economic development.

Promote Corporate Responsibility and Trade

Nation-states, as represented by their governments, are but one category of actors on the international stage. While intergovernmental agreements in the form of treaties and conventions are important, and in some cases necessary, private corporations play a crucial role in shaping the global environment. It is critical to create incentives that encourage private businesses to make choices that move the planet toward sustainability and away from unhealthy environmental policies and shortsighted patterns of resource exploitation.

Unfortunately, the fragmentation and decentralization of legal and political authority into more than 185 nation-states creates gaps in international governance that can be exploited by multinational corporations to the detriment of consumers and the environment. As globalization accelerates and business pressures intensify to move finished goods as well as parts and components across national borders, the inadequacy of the current legal and political system for regulating corporations—particularly multinationals—becomes ever more apparent.

A multilateral regulatory framework, such as a global convention, is required to meet this pressing need. Such an agreement might, for example, establish minimum environmental performance standards in order to remove competitive distortions from varying environmental policies and reduce the incentive for an international race-to-the-bottom, or regulatory competition, during which different countries are tempted to compete for global business by lowering their environmental standards. At present, no such international framework exists. The closest models are the WTO and the Multilateral Agreement on Investment (MAI). Those negotiations were conducted under the auspices of the Organization for Economic Cooperation and Development (OECD). They were derailed, in part, because of concerns for environmental quality.

While these settings are venues for multilateral cooperation on establishing rule-based systems of potentially global reach, to date they have focused exclusively on a deregulatory agenda with the premise that governmental action is always suspect as a potential impediment to trade or investment. Instead, these vehicles should be redirected to identify sustainability as the key goal—sustainable trade, sustainable foreign investment, and, more generally, sustainable business practices.

One area in which trade and the environment can reinforce each other is in encouraging the dissemination and transfer of environmentally beneficial goods and technologies. As a component of sustainable trade, manufacturing goods in ways that preserve rather than plunder the environment, finding alternatives to toxic chemicals, and creating the expertise for energy-efficient production processes should receive preferential treatment. Unfortunately, existing international rules governing trade and protection of intellectual property make no such accommodations and may in fact impede environmental progress.

More generally, the public should be much more involved in shaping, channeling, and focusing the current and future direction of globalization and consumerism to guarantee sustainability. The task is large but not insurmountable. For example, the international community should re-examine rules governing trade, foreign investment, and bilateral and multilateral aid to ensure that intellectual property rules encourage rather than undermine the preservation of indigenous cultural knowledge that may be of tremendous use in protecting biological diversity as the "raw material" of the recent boom in genetic engineering.

The current approach to realizing the benefits from trade and foreign investment, which both Democratic and Republican administrations and Congresses have advocated, has been massive deregulation of a kind that the public would not tolerate domestically. Through the WTO, the North American Free Trade Agreement (NAFTA), and ongoing negotiations of new trade and investment agreements, support for international trade has been interpreted myopically as disempowering and disabling governments from structuring trading relationships.

When a deregulatory approach is applied to governmental actions designed to promote environmental integrity or public health, however, it has severe and obvious limitations. In contrast to liberalized trade, in which the ideal endpoint is an unregulated market, environmental, health, and safety goals require affirmative and sometimes aggressive limitations on private actions, which are usually put in place by and enforced through the coercive power of governments. Unfortunately, environmental, health, and safety regulations have come under increasing scrutiny as potential impediments to trade. For example, the European Union's approval requirements for genetically modified food, its ban on hormone-treated beef, and U.S. restrictions on the importation of shrimp caught in ways that harm endangered sea turtles have all been challenged in the WTO. Public policies designed to encourage sustainability, such as labeling environmentally preferable products, have also been thwarted as potential violations of WTO rules.

While advocating changes that encourage sustainability in the United States and abroad, we should lead by example. Developing countries routinely have stated that they expect industrialized countries to reduce consumption before the Third World can be expected to take on meaningful obligations on issues such as global warming. The United States can deliver on at least a part of this expectation with few or no negative implications—and many positive ones—on the American way of life. Low-hanging fruit in the form of policies that are easy and cheap to implement include energy efficiency standards for appliances and automobiles, both of which would reduce or at least improve greenhouse gas emissions.

We live in a consumer-oriented capitalist society, meaning that each of us has the freedom—indeed, the responsibility—to consume wisely, which is another goal that can be realized without sacrificing our standard of living. However, the U.S. government is promoting many policies internationally that are pushing us in the exact opposite direction. The Bush Administration, like the Clinton Administration before it, opposes environmental conditions in trade agreements, which will virtually assure the encouragement of overconsumption with little or no regard for the environmental consequences.

Conclusion

The government, private sector, and citizens of the United States can and should overcome the current malaise in Washington and reclaim the high ground as a leader in protecting the international environment at home and abroad. Myopic policies that fail to consider the long-term consequences of today's actions are incompatible with our national interest and the health of the planet. The U.S. government should subject all its policies to critical scrutiny to ensure sustainability with a focus on economic strategies to promote trade and investment, which can have a profound effect on the flow of material and capital worldwide. As a good international citizen, environmental leader, and promoter of the national interest, the United States should restore previous levels of development assistance targeted to catalyzing positive environmental change abroad. Multilateral policies that encourage private corporations to participate as engines of sustainability and ensure the integrity of corporate environmental performance should be adopted. In addition, average citizens can and should participate in this ambitious but achievable agenda by re-examining their patterns of consumption in response to international environmental challenges.

CHAPTER 11

DEMOCRACY DEMANDS DISCLOSURE

The American Tradition of Open Government

To advance progressive environmental goals, citizens must be adequately informed about the nature and extent of environmental problems, how private firms contribute to these problems, and what government is doing to address them. Without such information, citizens cannot make intelligent decisions or hold government and private polluters accountable for their actions.

The United States has a rich historical tradition that government must remain open to the people it serves. The Freedom of Information Act (FOIA) is perhaps the preeminent example of this tradition, establishing a presumption that government records are public documents, absent narrow exemptions. Similarly, the Administrative Procedure Act (APA) requires openness in rulemaking and promises a public right to participation in and comment on proposed agency rules. The Federal Advisory Committee Act (FACA) mandates government transparency in its interactions with outside, private-sector advisers to ensure that the government does not engage in secret consultations with biased groups. Other open government measures include the Presidential Records Act, the Sunshine Act, and the Privacy Act.

Environmental laws also embrace this traditional emphasis on transparent government. One of the most important, the National Environmental Policy Act (NEPA), requires federal agencies to analyze and publicly disclose the environmental effects of their proposed actions as well as alternatives to these actions. Although it lacks substantive mandates, the NEPA's disclosure requirements have opened to scrutiny many government projects and private projects requiring government approval. Opportunities for criticism and improvement come with that scrutiny.

Likewise, federal and state agencies write pollution permits under laws that require opportunities for review and comment by interested citizens. Facilities must keep compliance records publicly available. These laws also authorize "citizen suits" against government agencies that fail to fulfill their statutory mandates, as well as industrial facilities that violate the law. Any citizen or citizen group can bring such an action and, if they win, their attorneys are compensated for their time and litigation costs.

All of these provisions are based on a combination of healthy skepticism about government's ability to maintain its integrity in the absence of public scrutiny and a deep-seated idealism about the benefits of an open, democratic society. Early New Deal confidence that regulators who were granted broad authority would promptly address threats to public health has given way to recognition of the risks of regulatory dysfunction. The preeminent risk is that regulated industries will "capture" regulatory agencies, winning weak standards and broad exemptions. Conversely, regulatory targets fear overly zealous or imprudent regulatory actions resulting from what they perceive as the undue influence of public interest groups. Other concerns about poor government performance are based on a recognition that human beings are self-interested, which in this context means that regulators may drag their feet in the face of political pressure or because they are unwilling to work hard enough. Open government and citizen enforcement provide the best antidotes to this unacceptable state of affairs.

Openness and accountability requirements provide two further benefits. Because they are informed, citizens are more likely to have confidence in government, thereby strengthening democracy overall. In addition, courts charged with the ultimate responsibility to uphold the rule of law benefit because open and accountable procedures result in records that can later enhance the ability of courts to ensure that agencies adhere to legal requirements.

This chapter discusses the twin themes of promoting transparent government and disclosure of corporate activities that could harm the environment. In markets, law, and politics, creation of such an informed citizenry is among the most important preconditions for a healthy environment. Or, to express this idea from a different perspective, without disclosure and accurate information, neither markets nor democracy can flourish. As Supreme Court Justice Louis Brandeis observed more than 70 years ago, "Sunlight is said to be the best of disinfectants; electric light the most efficient policeman."[1]

---

1. Louis Brandeis, *Other People's Money* (National Home Library Foundation ed., 1933), 62.

Stealth Secrecy

In recent years, we have witnessed a steady stream of efforts to weaken the openness and accountability that have been the hallmarks of our political process and environmental laws. Many have occurred under the public's radar screen through complex, obscure regulatory or legislative changes. Frontal assaults on environmental laws and open-government requirements have failed repeatedly in the face of broad public support for such protections. Thwarted by public scrutiny, opponents of effective regulation have turned to stealth reform—piecemeal legislative exemptions and executive branch initiatives that make it harder for the public to follow what the government and regulated entities are doing.

For example, the Critical Infrastructure Information Act, a little noticed provision of the Homeland Security Act, passed in 2002, allows facilities to claim that information voluntarily submitted to the government is "critical infrastructure information" with national security consequences. This term is defined so broadly that it could be interpreted to encompass virtually *any* information about a facility's operations that might possibly prove useful to anyone trying to harm the facility; this definition includes information about health and safety performance, environmental releases, vulnerability to accidents, and so forth. Once this information is submitted, it becomes confidential and cannot be disclosed. Government officials who violate this prohibition face criminal sanctions. Most remarkably, critical infrastructure information cannot be used in any civil action, in any court, or by any person without the consent of the company that submitted the data.

As we discussed in Chapter 6, the Information Quality Act, an obscure but sweeping measure that was attached as a rider to a 2001 appropriations bill at the behest of an industry consultant, requires agencies to ensure the quality of information they disseminate and provides an administrative mechanism for people to correct inaccurate data. Despite its benign name, the statute will likely delay, and in some cases eliminate, public information provided by the EPA and other agencies. Industry groups already have used this measure to block the release of embarrassing or politically damaging data. Regulated industries have proposed erecting additional procedural hurdles to limit the flow of environmental information, such as giving industry the right to comment on and participate in EPA decisions about whether to release public data.

All of these provisions were supported by the Bush Administration, which has a well-earned reputation for being the administration most obsessed with secrecy in American history. Even before the terrorist attacks of Sept. 11, 2001, the Administration curtailed disclosures under the Freedom of Information Act dramatically. Rather than continuing the Clinton Administration's practice of making records available to the public except when doing so would cause "foreseeable harm," the Bush policy specifically encourages agencies to resist disclosure whenever possible. Regulated industries continue to press for further suppression of information, proposing, for example, that such routine information as basic emissions data from regulated facilities be exempted from FOIA requirements on the grounds that it might reveal "confidential trade secrets."

Another favored strategy is the so-called "streamlining" of regulatory proceedings in ways that cut out the assessment of environmental threats and opportunities for public participation. For example, the Bush Administration has proposed exempting various logging activities and forest-management plans from NEPA's requirements, including analyzing and disclosing project effects, alternatives, and mitigation measures. It has also called for speeding up the environmental review process for highway and airport construction projects and eliminating the public's right to file administrative appeals challenging certain forest-management decisions.

A particularly troubling example of this so-called streamlining trend is the military's attempt to exempt itself from public health and environmental requirements. Although military installations long have been among the worst polluters in the nation, the Pentagon seeks to exempt military bases from complying with the Clean Air Act, Superfund, the Endangered Species Act, the Marine Mammal Protection Act, the Resource Conservation and Recovery Act, and other laws. In 2003, the Bush Administration gained a statutory exemption from the Migratory Bird Treaty Act for the military. These proposals to sidestep review under our environmental laws are particularly imprudent given the military's shameful track record of environmental destruction resulting from past weapons testing, training, transportation, timber, and mining projects.

Undoubtedly encouraged by these bad government policies, regulated industries and their conservative political allies have repeatedly sought to pass a single "mega-statute" that would superimpose a host of cumbersome barriers to protective regulations. Such "regulatory reform" statutes would obligate agencies to assess costs and benefits of proposals, use peer reviewers to evaluate proposed regulations, and then modify regulatory choices in light of such analyses. A prime example is the regulatory reform bill that Congress narrowly defeated in 1995.

Although none of this legislation passed Congress in the immediate aftermath of the 1994 Republican electoral victories, regulated industries have succeeded in getting several of their proposals adopted administratively. Executive orders require the EPA and other agencies to prepare cost-benefit analyses of all major proposed rules and submit them to OMB before they are publicly released. The OMB's review of regulations can create significant internal pressures on agencies to weaken or alter proposals. These deliberations are subject only to partial disclosure after the fact. Moreover, these discussions are often highly technical and difficult for the public to follow.

Case Study: Campaign to Thwart Access to Information on Dangers of Asbestos Poses Risks to Workers

Asbestos is a naturally occurring fibrous material that has been used for many years in the United States in a variety of construction products. Perhaps less well known is that it has also been used by U.S. auto manufacturers in brake linings, and while most manufacturers no longer use asbestos, millions of older cars and replacement brakes still contain the material. In addition, it is estimated that asbestos materials for brakes worth over $124 million were imported into the United States last year from countries that heavily mine asbestos, including Mexico, China, Colombia, Brazil, and Canada, with imports of such materials increasing 300 percent in the last decade. Workers exposed to asbestos during brake repair and replacement can suffer severe and often fatal diseases, including mesothelioma, a fatal cancer of the lining of the lung and chest cavity, and asbestosis, a lung disease that can become so severe that the lungs cease to function. The serious risks of exposure to asbestos gained national attention after hundreds of residents of Libby, Montana, including mine workers, members of their families, and others exhibited symptoms of asbestos-related diseases. Some even died after inhalation of asbestos from a vermiculite mine.

In 1989, the EPA issued a final rule that would have instituted a phased prohibition on "the future manufacture, importation, processing, and distribution in commerce of asbestos in almost all products.... to reduce the unreasonable risks presented to human health by exposure to asbestos during activities involving these products." However, the part of the rule covering such existing asbestos products as brakes was struck down by the Fifth Circuit in the *Corrosion Proof Fittings* case discussed in Chapter 7. As a result of this decision and the near complete lack of inspections to ensure compliance with OSHA standards, hundreds of mechanics are regularly exposed to asbestos dust in violation of OSHA regulations, putting them at substantial risk of eventually dying from asbestos exposure.

If government, manufacturers, and employers will not protect workers, it is critical that workers protect themselves. Toward that end, the very least government can and should do is to provide workers with information about the danger. But, a Philadelphia law firm, on behalf of a client it has refused to identify, has attempted to use the Information Quality Act to deprive workers of asbestos information in a 1986 EPA guidance document specifically for brake workers. The "Gold Book," as the document is known, warns of the dangers of asbestos exposure during brake work, and provides guidelines for reducing exposure. The law firm claims that data in the Gold Book "were based on inadequate and inappropriate scientific data and literature," and that the book has been used to convey misperceptions about the hazards of brake-mechanic work and the risks of contracting asbestos-related illnesses. Members of Congress, environmental groups, attorneys representing brake workers with claims against

(Continued)

Case Study: *(Continued)*

asbestos brake manufacturers, doctors, scientists, and others urged the EPA not to withdraw the brake guidance, pointing to scientific data strongly supporting the conclusions in the Gold Book. In late November, 2003, EPA responded to the request by explaining that the Gold Book was being revised as part of an effort to update and revise materials available through its asbestos program. The document remains available through EPA's Asbestos Hotline, although EPA's website notes that the document is currently under agency review.

This is but one example of recent efforts to undermine openness and access to government information by way of the Information Quality Act. While the petitioner here was unsuccessful in removing the document from the public domain, the effort demonstrates the potential effect that such challenges can have on worker access to information critical to their health and safety.

Choosing Ignorance

Another major impediment to promoting greater government accountability is a lack of information about the condition of the environment. Even though environmental regulation has grown by leaps and bounds since the 1970s, we still lack adequate information about the quality of the air, water, and land of the United States; nor do we know if conditions are getting better or worse. As of 1998, states had assessed water quality for only 23 percent of the nation's rivers and streams; 42 percent of lakes, ponds, and reservoirs; and 32 percent of estuaries[2]—and only a portion of this data was collected using reliable methods. Air quality is monitored for only eight general pollutants, while the close to 200 toxic pollutants Congress identified in 1990 are not monitored regularly. In fact, air quality has never been measured in many areas.[3] As a result, we do not know when we are stressing ecosystems beyond the breaking point.

---

2. EPA, Office of Water, *The Quality of Our Nation's Water: A Summary of the National Water Quality Inventory: 1998 Report to Congress* [EPA841-S-0-001], June 2000, 5, http://www.epa.gov/305b/98report/98brochure.pdf.

3. Wendy Wagner, "Commons Ignorance: How the Environmental Laws Have Failed Us," *Duke Law Journal* 53 (forthcoming 2004) (citing Lynn Blais, et al., *Enforcement Against Toxic Air Hot Spots in Texas: A Report to the Texas Council on Environmental Quality* (draft December 2003); U.S. General Accounting Office, *Air Pollution, National Air Monitoring Network Is Inadequate,* GAO/RCED-90-15 (1989)).

Huge data gaps remain regarding the thousands of chemical substances that commercial interests have introduced into the environment in the past 50 years. As numerous expert panels have noted, we lack a strong theoretical understanding of how toxic chemicals affect health and the environment. While scientists have made progress in screening chemicals for their propensity to cause cancer, they have made far less headway in determining how to screen toxic chemicals for other harms, such as reproductive, neurological, hormonal, and developmental effects, or to account for variables in human susceptibility to these harms. Scientists also have woefully inadequate models for assessing and predicting harm to ecosystems as a result of toxic loading.

Often, we do not even measure levels of the relatively few chemicals for which toxicity tests have been developed. In 1984, the National Research Council found that no toxicity information had been gathered for 80 percent of the 45,000 toxic substances used in commerce.[4] In 1998, the EPA found that of the 3,000 so-called high-production volume chemicals (HPV), those produced or imported in quantities greater than one million pounds per year, 93 percent are missing some basic data necessary for a minimum understanding of a chemical's toxicity. The EPA found absolutely no basic toxicity data for 43 percent of HPV chemicals.[5]

Compounding these problems, corporations often refuse to disclose to the public the considerable information they have on the health and safety of their products and polluting activities. One way they shield information from public view is by claiming "trade secret" or "confidential business protections" exemptions for data that otherwise is covered by FOIA. While seeking to protect genuine trade secrets that could harm a competitive position is certainly a legitimate practice, studies by the EPA, the General Accounting Office, and others have found that many claims are made without basis. These confidentiality claims can be challenged, but the burden of doing so rests with the public. Overcoming them requires diligence, which greatly increases the time and effort the public must expend to obtain what should be publicly available data.

At the same time, existing disclosure laws are limited in scope. The Toxics Release Inventory (TRI) program, for instance, covers 654 substances—less than 1 percent of the more than 75,000 chemicals manufactured in the United States. It exempts small businesses and those below other production thresholds, generally

---

4. Steering Committee On Identification of Toxic and Potentially Toxic Chemicals for Consideration by the Nat'l Toxicology Program, Nat'l Research Council, *Toxicity Testing: Strategies to Determine Needs and Priorities,* 1984, 118, fig. 2.

5. EPA Website, Chemical Hazard Data Availability Study, 1998, http://www.epa .gov/oppt/chemtest/hazchem.htm.

facilities that manufacture less than 25,000 pounds of a TRI chemical or that use less than 10,000 pounds of a TRI chemical, and other releases from a variety of sources. Releases from sources that are not covered by TRI may very well exceed those that are. TRI also does not require reporting about chemical use.

Current rules governing securities disclosures require publicly traded firms to disclose to investors material financial issues, including legal proceedings involving a governmental authority with a probable penalty greater than $100,000. However, they do not mandate disclosure of other information about a firm's environmental, health, and safety record that may be as relevant to investors as a picture of the firm's financial well-being. A growing body of research shows that firms with superior environmental records perform better financially than those with weaker records, which demonstrates that environmental performance can serve as an important indicator of the risk of investing in a firm. But companies are not required to disclose indicators of such performance to investors. In fact, most companies ignore even the limited disclosures that Securities and Exchange Commission rules require. A 1998 EPA study found that, in the preceding two years, 74 percent of companies failed to disclose environmentally related legal proceedings likely to exceed the $100,000 threshold.[6]

We also lack data about how well federal and state environmental agencies are performing, and this problem is especially acute at the state level. State environmental agencies implement roughly 75 percent of the major federal environmental programs under the system of "cooperative federalism" established by most environmental laws. But the federal EPA does not systematically evaluate and disclose how well states are meeting their obligations under federal laws. Some states report on their progress in addressing environmental problems, but many do not, and the quality of the data varies greatly. In addition, there are major gaps in what states currently report. For example, few reliably measure the compliance rate of regulated facilities. All of this information is critical to assessing the effectiveness of our environmental programs.

The Progressive Perspective

Disclosure of corporate environmental effects has many important benefits. First, it can improve the efficient functioning of the market because it enables

---

6. EPA, Office of Enforcement and Compliance Assurance, *Memorandum, Guidance on Distributing the "Notice of SEC Registrants' Duty to Disclose Environmental Legal Proceedings" in EPA Administrative Enforcement Actions*, Jan. 19, 2001, 2, http://www.epa.gov/Compliance/resources/policies/incentives/programs/sec-guid-distributionofnotice.pdf.

consumers to make informed decisions and press for safer products when they are armed with better information. And better-informed workers can negotiate for less-toxic working conditions or demand wage premiums for hazardous jobs. Securities markets investors can act more knowledgeably. A growing movement toward socially responsible investment evaluates the environmental record of companies as a basis for investment in the stock market, so that firms with environmentally superior products or records of performance can be rewarded in the marketplace.

Disclosure promotes the power of ordinary citizens and encourages democratic decision-making. Equipped with better information, citizens can participate on more of an equal footing with regulated entities in the permit process, land use determinations, and other political decisions. The public can exert pressure on firms to reduce risky activities or eliminate unnecessary toxic exposures. Disclosure also enables the public to bring enforcement actions when environmental standards are violated.

Disclosure also serves fundamental liberty and autonomy interests. It provides the public with knowledge about the risks involved in their choices and allows citizens to decide whether to encounter such risks. For example, as the result of a recent lawsuit under Proposition 65, a California right-to-know initiative, signs in California grocery stores and restaurants warn consumers about the dangers of eating certain fish with high levels of mercury contamination. These signs allow pregnant women and nursing mothers to avoid such fish and reduce their risk level. In the United States, an estimated 630,000 children are born each year with an increased risk of brain damage because of their mothers' elevated mercury level,[7] so when disclosure leads to healthy consumer decisions, it can create large public health benefits.

Disclosure also can improve health and safety by facilitating emergency planning, avoiding accidents, and helping the government identify areas that need additional regulation. It also provides strong incentives for firms to self-regulate and reduce risky activities. For example, when companies face a choice between disclosing harmful substances in their products and reformulating the products to eliminate the harmful substances, they often choose to eliminate the substances. Unfortunately, relatively few environmental laws require businesses to disclose information about the adverse effects of their products and activities but those that do have been among the most successful.

---

7. Guy Gugliotta, "Mercury Threat to Fetus Raised, EPA Revises Risk Estimates," *Washington Post*, Feb. 6, 2004, A3.

The Emergency Planning and Community Right-to-Know Act, passed in 1986, requires industrial facilities to report their annual releases and transfers of 654 specified toxic chemicals under the Toxic Release Inventory program. The information is provided on standardized reporting forms that are submitted to the EPA and state officials and made available to the public. From 1988 to 2001, releases of chemicals subject to TRI reporting dropped by a remarkable 54.5 percent.[8]

Two other examples also come from states. California's Proposition 65, which was adopted by voters in 1986, requires businesses to provide warnings prior to exposing individuals to listed carcinogens and reproductive toxins. Proposition 65 has led to the reduction or elimination of toxics in numerous consumer products, such as ceramics, arsenic-treated wood used in playground equipment, nail polish removers, diaper rash creams, water filters, foil caps on wine bottles, submersible well pumps, brass faucets, calcium supplements, antidiarrheal medications, electrical tape, galvanized pipes and hair dyes. It also has reduced air emissions of certain toxic chemicals by approximately 85 percent.[9] The Massachusetts Toxic Use Reduction Act, passed in 1989, requires companies to analyze their use of toxic chemicals and undergo a detailed planning process aimed at identifying options for reducing chemical use. Companies are required to measure their progress annually and make this information available to the public. Firms are not required to take any specific action, but from 1990 to 1995, companies dramatically reduced their toxic chemical emissions by more than 66 percent, total chemical waste by 34 percent, and total toxic chemical usage by 24 percent.[10]

The Progressive Agenda

Keep Government Open and Transparent

To ensure that government continues to advance progressive environmental goals and remains accountable to the public, the business of government

---

8. EPA, *2001 Toxic Release Inventory Public Data Release, Executive Summary,* (EPA 260-S-03-001), July 2003, ES-24, http://www.epa.gov/tri/tridata/tri01/press/executivesummarystandalone.pdf.

9. David Roe, "Toxic Chemical Control Policy: Three Unabsorbed Facts," *Environmental Law Reporter* 32 (Envtl. L. Inst.) (2002): 10232.

10. Mary O'Brien, *Making Better Environmental Decisions: An Alternative to Risk Assessment* (2000), 155–160.

must remain open to the public. As federal appeals court Judge Damon Keith eloquently wrote in a recent case, "democracy dies behind closed doors."[11]

FOIA and other open-government laws, as implemented in the past three decades, contain ample protection for sensitive information that could compromise national security or harm commercial interests. These laws should continue to be implemented with an eye toward releasing information whenever possible, not seeking creative ways to shield it from public view. Likewise, the EPA and other agencies should take a very narrow view of the IQA and reject other efforts to impose new procedural hurdles before environmental data can be publicly released. Otherwise, data that is controversial, still evolving, or simply embarrassing to industry may be hidden from public view.

Congress should drastically narrow the "critical infrastructure information" provisions of the Homeland Security Act. Not only is the law too broad, but its premise that secrecy leads to greater safety from terrorism or other risks is highly debatable. When we suppress information about risky or vulnerable industrial facilities, we remove powerful incentives for industry to take steps to address the problems. We also shield from view information that the general public, local responders, and elected officials need to make sound decisions. A more effective and democratic deterrent to the inappropriate disclosure of sensitive information would be a process that compels the government to make thoughtful decisions about whether so-called critical infrastructure information qualifies for the legal protections already developed for "classified" material. Among other things, existing law does not allow agencies and departments to classify information that is already available to the public.

Stop Stealth 'Reform'

Stealth reform through meta-statutes, legislative riders, and hidden regulatory processes undermines democratic decision-making and makes it easier for opponents of environmental protection to roll back progressive regulation without honest public debate and deliberation. On a bipartisan basis, members of Congress should take a pledge to reject these subversive approaches.

---

11. *Detroit Free Press v. Ashcroft*, 303 F.3d 681, 683 (6th Cir. 2002) (Damon Keith, Judge).

Develop and Gather Knowledge

More public resources must be devoted to monitoring environmental conditions and trends in a consistent and comprehensive manner. In particular, we recommend that Congress establish an independent and truly impartial Bureau of Environmental Statistics, analogous to the federal Bureau of Labor Statistics, and that it provide this new agency with ample authority and resources to work effectively. This new bureau should be charged with assessing environmental data needs, creating guidelines for collecting environmental data, collecting and analyzing comprehensive statistics on environmental quality, and disseminating the data it gathers to the public. This action would raise the profile of environmental data and make it more likely to be used in public policy debates. Comparable data about economic conditions—such as joblessness, consumer spending, and consumer confidence—are widely disseminated in the media and help inform countless public and private decisions.

Publish Annual State Environmental Indicator Reports

We recommend that each state publish a comprehensive annual report regarding the quality of its environment. A substantial number of states have begun publishing such reports or similar environmental-indicator reports. These reports should present and discuss environmental data gathered according to guidelines prepared by the Bureau of Environmental Statistics. Reports should cover conditions and trends in all environmental media as well as all major natural resource systems in each state. They should be prepared in consistent formats to facilitate comparing information across states and over time.

Score State Performance

EPA should shine a spotlight on state environmental agency performance by means of regular and public evaluations of how well state agencies are meeting their obligations, based on a uniform set of criteria. Just as comparison shopping by informed consumers drives companies to offer better products, public disclosure and comparisons of agency performance would have great power to motivate state environmental agencies to improve.

Strengthen SEC Disclosure Requirements

To promote greater corporate accountability, we recommend a number of ways to expand what corporations currently disclose to the public. Noncompliance with the SEC's environmental disclosure rules is widespread. The SEC should systematically review the record of compliance with these requirements and take vigorous enforcement actions against violators. EPA should routinely provide the SEC with information about its enforcement actions, cleanup orders, and settlements in order to facilitate SEC monitoring of compliance with disclosure rules.

The rules also should be expanded to require disclosure of other significant information about a firm's environmental, health, and safety record, including data about TRI emissions, warnings provided about company products pursuant to environmental disclosure requirements, and criminal enforcement actions stemming from environmental, health, or safety violations. Additionally, the SEC should change the standard for data considered "material" under its rules to require disclosure when cumulative environmental liabilities, penalties, settlements, fines, and violations exceed regulatory thresholds. Finally, the SEC should require firms to follow a uniform set of guidelines for estimating costs and liabilities for environmental matters.

Expand Corporate Chemical Use Reporting

The TRI program marks a watershed in effective environmental regulation. EPA officials, environmentalists, and regulated entities regularly tout it as one of the nation's most effective environmental laws. Nonetheless, the scope of the program is unduly narrow and should be expanded in several ways.

First, TRI should be extended to require reporting of industrial firms' toxic chemical generation and use, in addition to environmental releases. The program should not be limited to its current 654 toxic chemicals, which represent a small fraction of the ecological footprint left by industrial activities. Corporations should be required to disclose the extent to which their facilities and activities generate and release solid waste, conventional air and water pollutants, and carbon dioxide—a major contributor to global warming. TRI should be extended to cover important categories of exempt facilities, including sewage treatment plants, hospitals, dry cleaners, automobile service stations, and airports.

Require Corporate Environmental Assessments

Federal and state laws do not require that firms undertaking private projects evaluate and publicly disclose the environmental implications of such activities on ecosystems, environmentally sensitive lands and resources, and threatened and endangered species. As we explained in Chapter 9, firms proposing major projects should conduct comprehensive assessments of their impacts, as the government does now under the National Environmental Policy Act. These reports should include accurate, scientifically sound assessments of any and all non-trivial environmental impacts of ongoing and planned corporate activities and projects, including the use and development of land and whether the corporate conduct in question is subject to any governmental regulation. They should be made available to interested members of the public and governmental agencies well before potentially harmful corporate activities or projects are authorized.

Tell Companies to Inform and Warn the Public

California's Proposition 65 has proven to be an effective tool for triggering product reformulations, as well as reductions in unnecessary toxic exposures. It also provides the public with the necessary information to make informed choices and avoid unnecessary risks. A similar requirement should be applied on a broader scale, requiring companies to provide clear and reasonable warnings prior to exposing people to toxic chemicals. Exposures that are below a level of significant risk should be exempt.

Expand Toxic Chemical Testing

Virtually every prominent expert panel convened to consider the effects of industrial activities on health and the environment has noticed the sorely deficient information base on chemical toxicity. Much of the blame for this data gap can be attributed to industry's vigorous resistance to producing information about the damage their chemicals may be causing to public health and the environment. Rather than presenting the opportunity for private profit, industry argues that developing this information generally will only have negative effects on them and lead to unwelcome additional attention or provide a basis for governmental regulation.

One way to remedy this data shortfall is to create incentives for firms to gather sufficient toxicity data on their products and emissions. Congress might accomplish that by requiring companies to publicly disclose the absence of toxicity data until testing is completed. For example, Congress could require producers to disclose the absence of a full suite of toxicity information for any "high production volume" chemical.

Public funding for disinterested government researchers and academic scientists to conduct basic and applied research in the effects of toxic chemicals must be expanded dramatically. To help support this research, a flat or graduated tax or other fee on manufacturers to support a portion of the necessary research is appropriate. For example, the tax could be based on a flat fee assessed on a chemical-by-chemical basis, or it could be based on the cumulative volume or weight of all chemicals produced by a company. The resulting revenues could then support federal development of improved screening tests and assessment methods as well as finance basic environmental research.

Enact a Corporate Freedom of Information Act

Claims of trade secrets or confidential business practices are often made without justification. While such assertions hinder public access to relevant data, no sanctions for making unjustifiably broad claims are on the books. One simple reform that could deter nonmeritorious claims is to require firms to substantiate their information and empower federal agencies to assess fines for claims found to be baseless according to an agency review following a FOIA request.

Even if such a reform were implemented, a great deal of what corporations do to affect environmental quality, as well as the health and safety of their employees and the public, remains shrouded in secrecy. In order to promote corporate openness and accountability, we recommend that Congress enact a Freedom of Information Act for corporations. This legislation should require that corporations disclose promptly, accurately, and fully the nature, extent, and impact of any corporate activity or practice that affects the environment or public health to any person who requests it. Disclosure would be subject to appropriate and very narrowly defined exceptions to protect proprietary information.

Conclusion

From public schools to investment firms to police departments, the public is demanding more information and greater accountability from society's institutions. We should demand and expect no less from government agencies and private firms whose decisions profoundly affect our public health and environment. Such openness and disclosure will enhance accountability and lead to greater environmental protection for our citizens.

CHAPTER 12

MAKE GOVERNMENT WORK

The Choice of Tools

In virtually any area of regulation, gaps between aspirations and actual implementation efforts are inevitable. Environmental, health, and safety laws often present particularly stark examples of disparities between high aspirations and meager or unexpected implementation results. As described in Chapter 2, much has been achieved since these laws were enacted in the 1970s. Now that some of the most obvious challenges from the first generation of laws have been conquered, attention has shifted to implementation and enforcement challenges. Preserving early successes and confronting new challenges requires close attention to questions of how the government can best achieve regulatory goals, especially in an era when federal and state health and safety agencies are suffering debilitating gaps in funding and mandates.

The issue of which regulatory tools will best address specific threats to human health and the environment is a major battleground where regulated industries, public interest groups, and government officials routinely clash. Increasingly, such disputes are resolved below the radar screen of public attention. Regulated industries and their conservative allies advocate regulatory tools they believe will discourage and forestall excessive regulation and, therefore, unnecessary cost.

The premier tool of deregulators is cost-benefit analysis, used by the Bush Administration as a gauntlet for proactive regulatory proposals. Special interests also have succeeded in persuading regulatory agencies to move away from traditional regulation in favor of so-called "market-based mechanisms" designed to minimize regulated industries' costs. The prominent manifestation of market-based approaches is "emissions trading," which allocates credits to polluters, giving them the right to continue operations so long as they have enough credits to cover the quantity of pollution they emit. If the polluter has excess credits, it may auction them to other firms. A third approach is to invoke so-called "performance-based regulation," which sets a broad standard for cleaning up the air or water and leaves the choice of methods by which to achieve those goals up to the polluter. A fourth approach is to use "information disclosure" to leverage pollution reduction and prevention rather than imposing more stringent facility-specific control requirements.

Progressives reject cost-benefit analysis as the litmus test for regulation on ethical, theoretical, and practical grounds. In response to proposals involving market-based and performance-based approaches, progressives have distinguished between the appeal of such ideas on paper and the missteps that occur when implemented. Progressives do not support unnecessarily rigid regulations that make industry spend money for no good reason. On the other hand, progressives are concerned that lack of political will, inadequate resources, undue influence by regulated industries in program design, and lax enforcement can doom market-based approaches to failure.

Federal environmental laws have not yet embraced market-based approaches, with one notable exception: the acid rain trading program in the 1990 amendments to the Clean Air Act (CAA). Rather, the laws address concerns about funding gaps, the "capture" of government agencies by the industries they regulate, and lax enforcement by adopting devices that force agencies to act, such as statutory deadlines and "hammer" provisions that impose a specific standard unless an agency acts to override it, and by specifying how and when agencies are to craft implementing regulation in great detail. The laws adopt technology-based standards to replace risk or ambient quality-based standards in some crucial areas, particularly the CAA, when experience has indicated that basing regulation on safe levels of exposure is not working. They impose stringent liability on practices, such as improper waste disposal, that cause great harm to the environment, giving industries that engage in such practices a strong incentive to eliminate or drastically moderate them. Before progressives agree to replace these powerful mechanisms with market-based approaches, we must be convinced that the alternatives conservatives favor do not serve as a Trojan horse for unrestricted deregulation. Progressives do not summarily reject innovative approaches, but we remain committed to opposing rampant and ill-conceived versions of such approaches.

For example, progressives and regulated industries agree, in theory, that carefully designed trading regimes, such as the acid rain trading program, can save money while protecting the environment. However, progressives strongly disagree with proposals to extend this approach to trading of toxics like mercury. Progressives are wary of performance-based regulation that does not establish enforceable interim targets for corporations striving to achieve an overall goal. Both sides support information disclosure in debates over regulatory tools. But regulated industries and their conservative allies often push information disclosure as a substitute for regulation while progressives view it primarily as a supplement to more direct controls.

This chapter explains why we must pay close attention to the details of regulatory tools proposed to solve outstanding problems, evaluating which approaches actually work and resisting the reflexive embrace of market-based remedies. No single regulatory instrument or tool will be effective everywhere. In general, progressives believe that transparency, efficacy, justice, and the need to stimulate innovative technology are the benchmarks of a sound process for selecting regulatory tools. The most popular regulatory tools—and the progressive view of their pros and cons—follow.

Before we embark on an evaluation of the pros and cons of the most important regulatory tools, we set the stage with a discussion of the growing problem of "hollow government"—severe underfunding of regulators at both the federal and state level—that undermines the implementation of existing regulation and must constrain the design of new approaches.

Condition Precedent: Hollow Government

Many of the problems administrative agencies have implementing environmental goals cannot fairly be attributed to flaws or inconsistencies in regulatory design. Rather, those failures are the direct and inevitable result of unrealistic limitations imposed on the resources available to such agencies. Funding gaps have put a great strain on agency staffs, tarnishing their reputations as effective guardians of the public interest. Regulatory critics have exploited these failures to argue for more flexibility for industry.

After accounting for inflation, the EPA is funded at the same level that it was in the mid-1980s—before the enactment of a number of ambitious statutory mandates, such as the 1990 Clean Air Act Amendments, as well as reauthorizations of the Clean Water Act; the Safe Drinking Water Act; the Federal Insecticide, Fungicide, and Rodenticide Act; Superfund; and the Resource Conservation and Recovery Act. The 1986 Superfund Amendments alone quadrupled the number of pages assigning mandates to the agencies, and the 1990 Clean Air Act Amendments are by far the most ambitious environmental law ever passed. The Bush Administration has dramatically compounded these intolerable funding gaps by proposing to cut EPA funding by 7.2 percent in fiscal year 2005.[1] Unfortunately, the states bear the burden of imple-

---

1. Spencer S. Hsu, et. al., "Locally, Bay Cleanup, Salaries are Targeted," *Washington Post*, February 3, 2004, A5.

menting many of these programs, and many struggle with funding gaps at least as bad as those at the EPA.

This chronic underfunding has often forced agencies to make Hobson's choices among important programs and goals. It may push them to choose ineffective instruments of pollution control, such as self-regulation, because they are less costly—not because they are a better way to regulate. Recent federal tax cuts and a burgeoning federal deficit threaten to exacerbate this already serious problem. Moreover, state budgetary shortfalls, as well as other kinds of problems and considerations, tend to preclude the devolution of federal regulatory responsibility to the states as a workable and effective solution to the problem.

The final nail in the coffin of government dysfunction is the fact that there is no parity—and most often a huge gap—between private and public sector pay scales at the federal and state levels. The result is a devastating "brain drain" that leaves government agencies hobbled by the constant loss of qualified staff. The executive and legislative branches have quite literally responded to budget deficits by refusing to address this problem, which is reaching catastrophic proportions. The result is that only the most idealistic people remain in the ranks of federal and state regulators for any significant period of time. And the demeaning of government service by regulated industries and conservatives sometimes drives even the idealistic public servants out the door.

Consulted privately, many corporate officials acknowledge these problems and agree that civil service reform would save their companies time and money. But any agreement to make civil service reform a priority is drowned out by the debate over regulatory goals and design. Elevating this issue to a top priority is crucial to the long-term success of the Progressive agenda.

With the essential, threshold understanding that restoring the human and financial strength of government is the foundation of effective reform, we turn now to three categories of regulatory tools: (1) generally useful and appropriate approaches; (2) tools we categorize as neutral because their effectiveness is so dependent on the details of their design and implementation; and (3) approaches that in practice have proved extremely destructive to the overall goal of protecting public health and the environment.

Useful Tools

Technology and Design Standards

As discussed in Chapter 5, technology-based regulation has produced some of the most outstanding successes of modern environmental law. Such approaches begin with a government survey of available pollution-control technologies. The government selects the most effective equipment available to an industrial sector and extrapolates the remaining levels of pollution after the equipment is installed. These standards, known as emissions limits under the CAA and effluent guidelines under the Clean Water Act (CWA), are then required for all new plants—and some existing plants—within the sector. A regulated entity also is free to install an alternative technology that will achieve the same level of reduction.

Technology-based standards are relatively easy for regulators to promulgate. They avoid the impossible task of accurately quantifying "safe" levels of pollution, a process that is more art than science in many cases, and one that leaves much room for error. At the same time, technology-based controls normally do not impose unreasonable costs on an industry because they are based on available technologies or technologies that are reasonably foreseeable. Statutes that require the use of technology-based performance standards permit regulators to make adjustments in light of unusual costs or other problems that would make compliance unreasonable.

Despite this high level of success, regulatory opponents are quick to criticize technology-based standards as a "command-and-control" approach. They claim these standards command corporations to use a particular technology in order to comply with regulatory standards, which prevents industry from adopting more cost-effective means of compliance. This criticism is entirely misplaced. As explained earlier, technology-based regulations set performance standards. Regulated entities are required to meet the level of protection achievable by the model technology, but these entities can use any equally effective method to meet this requirement. While companies often do adopt the model technology, they are not required to do so and they presumably will not do so when cheaper methods of meeting the regulatory requirement are available.

In order to enforce these standards, regulators must measure the pollution and compare it with the maximum permissible level under the regulation. In some circumstances, however, it is very difficult to take accurate measurements. In those cases, the only way to ensure compliance is to designate the use of a particular technology and have inspectors verify that regulated entities have installed and are using that technology. For example, the Resource Conservation and Recovery Act requires operators of hazardous waste landfills to install liners that meet elaborate specifications. They must also install monitoring equipment to verify that the landfill is not leaking, but the first line of defense is design specifications for the landfill's construction.

Regulators also mandate the use of design standards in circumstances where the risks of noncompliance can lead to catastrophic consequences. The Nuclear Regulatory Commission, for example, may mandate the use of a specific technology because it is seeking to prevent a catastrophic release of radioactive materials and because the commission may view the expense of verifying the reliability of the other technologies as excessive. Since the agency depends on computer projections and modeling to assess the reliability of safety technologies, the use of multiple technologies would require expensive and redundant assessments.

Substance Bans

Banning the use of specific hazardous substances is the most effective regulatory approach to controlling pollution. The phase-outs of ozone depleting chemicals and the use of lead in gasoline stimulated significant innovations, as did strict early health standards under the Occupational Safety and Health Act. These actions also resulted in dramatic reductions in the levels of pre-existing health and environmental risks. Emissions of lead into the ambient air, for example, fell by 98 percent between 1970 and 2001[2] as the EPA phased out its use as a fuel additive and Congress eventually banned its use altogether. Similarly, U.S. consumption of chlorofluorocarbons (CFCs) fell dramatically after Congress phased out their use. While it can be very difficult to achieve political support in cases where the substances serve a vital purpose and there are no reasonable alternatives, this tool should remain a first choice in appropriate cases.

Liability Provisions

Another extremely effective regulatory tool is the imposition of stringent liability for the consequences of industrial activity. On one hand, this tool is applied only after hazardous activities have threatened the environment and public health, as in the quarter-century old Superfund statute that imposes strict, joint and several liability on companies and other entities (including government) whose past practices led to the creation of abandoned toxic waste sites. On the other hand, even when such stringent liability lies dormant, it provides an extraordinarily powerful incentive for firms to engage in more re-

---

2. EPA, *Latest Findings on National Air Quality: 2002 Status & Trends,* August 2003, 2, http://www.epa.gov/airtrends/2002_airtrends_final.pdf.

sponsible behavior in an effort to avoid triggering what some regard as draconian, potentially ruinous lawsuits.

The use of liability as a deterrent has the further advantage of allowing regulated industry members complete freedom to develop their own methods for avoiding such suits. Companies that generate hazardous waste, for example, have developed highly creative and sophisticated programs for auditing the third parties that dispose of such materials, arguably doing an even more efficient job than the government in eliminating irresponsible actors from the market.

Although it is almost never mentioned by conservatives, probably for fear of alienating their industry allies, liability is effective precisely because it eliminates the draining, threshold debate between government and industry regarding the details of how—and how much—to reduce potentially harmful practices.

Neutral Tools

Information Disclosure

Corporate entities and their conservative allies frequently tout information disclosure as a low-cost method of reducing harms to people and the environment. They note that disclosure requirements are easily implemented by the government and leave it up to regulated industries to decide whether to shoulder the burden of public embarrassment or work to remove the conditions that trigger disclosure. They urge the government to use information disclosure to address hazards that are new or that have not been adequately addressed by existing approaches.

Although information disclosure has considerable merit as a regulatory tool, it cannot achieve the goals of protecting health and the environment by itself. Information disclosure works best as a supplement to other forms of regulation because it does not mandate any specific level of risk reduction. Indeed, the information accumulated by agencies such as the EPA as a result of mandatory disclosure programs can assist agencies in assessing the need for other requirements.

Emissions Trading

Trading programs are built on the concept that some sources can reduce pollution more cheaply than others. Rather than requiring all sources to install the same technology, trading programs effectively allow polluters with lower compliance costs to clean up for others. The central mechanism for this approach is the government's allocation of credits, which are typically measured in terms of the quantity of pollution a source is permitted to emit during a specific period (e.g., one ton annually). Sources are free to keep their credits to cover their emissions, or they can reduce emissions and sell their excess credits to firms that choose not to install pollution controls.

The primary example of a successful use of this premier market-based approach is Congress' 1990 decision to establish a trading system for sulfur dioxide. For power plant operators, the costs associated with installing pollution controls such as scrubbers or of limiting pollution by switching from high- to low-sulfur coal depend on where a plant is located, when it was built, and how it was designed. Owners of new plants find it relatively easy to install new technologies because they can design with such equipment in mind. Similarly, utilities located in the Southwestern part of the country have easy access to low-sulfur coal. Conversely, it is significantly more expensive to retrofit a 30-year-old plant built long before the control technology at issue was invented. For utilities located in the Midwest, it is far cheaper to buy high-sulfur coal from mines in West Virginia.

All utilities received initial allocations of baseline credits to emit a ton of sulfur dioxide in a given year. Plants with lower retrofit and fuel-switching costs would install pollution-control technologies and buy low-sulfur coal, in effect cleaning up for plants with higher retrofit and fuel-switching costs. By selling their extra credits, such owners could more evenly spread the total cost of reducing emissions. The entire system functioned under a national cap on sulfur dioxide emissions, improving the environment in the most economically efficient way.

The nation's experience with acid rain suggests that several threshold design issues determine the effectiveness of any trading system. First, the initial distribution of credits is the focus of intense jockeying among participants. Baseline allocations to existing sources can create barriers to market entry for new sources. Inevitably, covered sources attempt to negotiate exceptions to the baseline number and increase their initial allocations. This process can be politically useful, giving legislators and regulators currency to buy support for the overall scheme. The opportunity to encourage regulated entities to fight over how to cut up the pie, so to speak, rather than decide whether to bake it in the first place allowed Congress to break a decade-long political deadlock on how best to combat acid rain.

Another related issue is whether credits should be allocated on the basis of actual emissions or discharges produced in a given period or the allowable emissions or discharges authorized in the facility's permit. If offered an opportunity to either add a trading scheme to their compliance options or substitute trading for regulatory requirements, regulated entities are likely to argue that permit limits represent acceptable levels of pollution and that baselines should be set on the basis of allowable rather than actual emissions or discharges. Allowable permit levels are often much higher than what sources actually have achieved in practice because state air and water permitting systems are underfunded and erratic, and apply requirements that are often outdated and overly lenient. Basing allocations on allowable permit levels or on levels of emissions or discharges that are several years out of date or that were fixed during a time of extraordinarily high production can result in allocations that drive significant increases in overall and localized emissions.

A final threshold issue for designers of new trading schemes is whether traditional regulatory requirements remain in effect, providing a safety net for such regimes. The acid rain system took a conservative approach to this issue and retained existing permit requirements while seeking even greater reductions. However, cap-and-trade systems may be used as a substitute for traditional regulation that is already in place or, in lieu of traditional regulation, be applied to pollution problems that are not yet regulated.

The overall success of the acid rain trading system has provoked extravagant claims about the desirability of cap-and-trade systems as a more efficient alternative to traditional regulation. Industry critics and conservative reformers argue that trading saves money and accomplishes better environmental results. But other experiments with cap-and-trade systems have been considerably less successful than the acid rain system, provoking many to question whether trading without restrictions does more harm than good.

For example, some industry representatives and state regulators have advocated so-called "open-market" trading systems that do not impose a cap on total emissions but instead authorize unrestricted trading of already-accomplished emission reductions. Progressives have called for a moratorium on such programs and strenuously opposed EPA proposals to approve open-market programs in Illinois, Michigan, New Hampshire, and New Jersey. The New Jersey open-market trading program never received EPA approval and was cancelled by the state's top-ranking environmental officials after a Justice Department investigation revealed fraud in its implementation.

The establishment of a cap on total emissions is an essential ingredient for any trading system. Or, to put it another way, emissions trading without a cap is a market phenomenon that should not be regarded as a form of regulation, pollution control, or even an approach that has any beneficial implications for public health and the environment.

Several methods for establishing total caps are available. The acid rain program based its cap on actual emissions, as opposed to emissions that units were theoretically allowed to emit under their permits, for reasons we have already discussed. Alternatively, caps could be established on the basis of the total level of emissions that would result if every source installed a specific piece of pollution-control technology, creating an incentive for entrepreneurs to develop technologies that would do even better, thereby generating excess allowances for sale. Lastly, caps could be set on the basis of an analysis of ambient levels of pollution, and how much we need to reduce the load on a waterbody or an airshed to achieve better protection.

Even where caps on total emissions are employed, trading systems have failed when: (1) caps are set too high to motivate pollution reductions; (2) there are no effective mechanisms to count credits, track trades, and prevent fraud; and (3) trading is applied to toxic substances without effective limits on localized concentrations of emissions or "hot spots." Two efforts by California's South Coast Air Quality Management District (SCAQMD) to reduce smog in Los Angeles are examples of such fiascos.

In the mid-1990s, SCAQMD launched the RECLAIM program, which allowed utilities and other major stationary sources to trade sulfur dioxide and nitrogen oxide credits under a cap on total emissions. The cap was set too high, in part, because planners based initial allocations of credits on historically higher levels of pollution for covered sources as opposed to the lower levels of actual emissions at the time the program began. Compounding this error, the program supplanted rather than supplemented existing technology-based requirements, leaving no safety net to prevent excessive emissions from individual sources. As a result of these threshold mistakes, decreases in actual emissions were very small in the first three years of operation. Because the initial cap did not create a sufficient scarcity of credits to motivate covered plants to install pollution controls, few installed controls that would enable them to generate additional credits as the cap declined. Apparently, most owners and operators concluded that they could later purchase credits as the cap declined. In fact, at one point, nitrogen oxide credits were so plentiful that sources gave them away. In spring 2001, the ultimate calamity for the system came when a short supply of credits pushed the price of nitrogen oxide credits up to tens of thousands of dollars. Amid the hysteria provoked by California's energy crisis, SCAQMD hastily pulled utilities from the system and gave them a three-year grace period to return to compliance with traditional regulatory requirements.

The SCAQMD's other effort—the Rule 1610 Car Scrapping program—allowed operators of large stationary sources to buy their way out of compliance with CAA controls by paying owners of old, dirty cars to take them off the road. The program, which had fundamental design flaws similar to the RECLAIM program, placed no limits on the amount of credits stationary sources were able to purchase and failed to supervise the retirement of the cars that supposedly generated emissions reductions. The predictable result was the creation of extreme toxic hot spots that contained intolerably high levels of pollution in the neighborhoods located near four marine terminals. Exposure to these hot spots resulted in an intolerable cancer risk for people living in those neighborhoods, the vast majority of whom were Hispanic. Compounding these problems, SCAQMD auditors found rampant fraud in the program. Owners of old vehicles were paid to retire their vehicles and the bodies were scrapped, but the engines were transferred to other vehicles and put back on the road. In addition, stationary sources appear to have significantly underreported their emissions in order to save money by purchasing fewer credits.

The SCAQMD experience suggests that trading regimes involving toxics have unacceptable consequences for public health and the environment. Progressives believe that these pitfalls should rule out trading as a pollution control tool for toxics. Unfortunately, the Bush Administration has proposed using trading to address the severe public health threats posed by mercury emissions from power plants, as explained in Chapter 5.

Performance-based Regulation

Corporate reformers and their allies tout the benefits of government supervised "performance-based" regulation. These approaches differ from the voluntary approaches we discuss further below because they involve government requirements that regulated entities reduce environmental threats, but regulators delegate to industry some or even most of the responsibility for deciding how to meet those broad goals.

Performance-based regulation can take one of two forms. In some industries, the government requires industry to write its own plans concerning regulatory protections. In food-safety programs, for example, the government requires each food producer to establish food-safety procedures; regulators then monitor whether the firm is complying with the established procedures. OSHA and the EPA have similar approaches to addressing the problem of accidents at chemical plants that can endanger workers and people who live near a plant. Chemical plants are allowed to develop and implement safety procedures.

Proponents of this approach stress that it can be more effective than technology or design standards. Regulators can employ this approach if it is difficult to measure regulatory outputs and the government cannot effectively rely on design standards to overcome this defect. In the context of food safety, for example, the government lacks the resources to test all meat, poultry, or fish before it is sold, although there is spot-checking of these foods. Moreover, proponents contend that there is too much variability in how food producers operate to implement one or more design standards.

The success of this approach, however, depends on several factors. First, it works well only when the government sets clear and unambiguous goals that firms must meet in writing their plans. Otherwise, the government is not able to hold individual firms accountable for protecting the public. Second, unless proposed plans are subject to government preapproval, the public may be exposed to substantial risks. Regulators also must have the necessary expertise to determine the adequacy of proposed plans, and there must be enough reviewers to ensure timely processing. Finally, as with other forms of regulation, this approach only works to the extent that it is actively enforced. Otherwise, regulated entities will exploit lax government enforcement to cut corners and save money.

In other cases, the government relies on some industries to establish regulatory standards and enforce them. In this situation, Congress usually authorizes an agency to regulate an industry, but the agency also has the authority to rely on self-regulation as an alternative, although it is supposed to verify that the self-regulation adopted and implemented by an industry is adequate to protect the public. The two major stock exchanges, smaller regional exchanges, and over-the-counter securities markets, for example, all self-regulate under the supervision of the Securities and Exchange Commission (SEC). By relying on industry self-regulation, the SEC avoids the costs associated with writing and enforcing its own regulatory standards.

Proponents of self-regulation contend that a regulated industry is in a better position to determine cost-effective ways of protecting the public and enforcing those protections. These aspects of self-regulation, however, are risky for the public. Unless the government closely monitors an industry's performance, regulated firms can take advantage of the lack of government supervision to serve their own goals rather than protect the public. For example, in reaction to the Enron and other recent financial scandals, Congress restricted the extent to which the SEC can rely on trade associations in the accounting industry to produce generally accepted accounting and auditing principles and established a new oversight board to vet any such standards. However, if the government closely monitors industry self-regulation, then the approach may not save the government very much money when compared with traditional forms of regulation. In such circumstances, the costliness of such approaches makes self-regulation a dubious alternative to traditional forms of regulation.

Harmful Tools

Pre-decisional Analysis

Florida State University law professor Mark Seidenfeld has calculated that the typical federal health and safety agency engaged in rulemaking may have to run a gauntlet of as many as 120 different procedural or analytical steps.[3] Each overlaps with the others and, cumulatively, such requirements present multiple opportunities for confusion and delay. And the courts have not helped to rescue agencies from "paralysis by analysis." Conservatives and their supporters in regulated industries present their preference for extensive analytical requirements as methods to make regulation work better by avoiding excessive and irrational regulation. These techniques, however, constitute a sophisticated sabotage of the fundamental goals of the country's environmental, health, and safety laws.

As discussed earlier, existing laws commit the country to doing the best we can to protect people and the environment. These same laws put safety first in terms of resolving issues about the degree of risk posed by dangerous chemicals, products, and other hazards. These commitments respect the fundamental value of human life and our connections to the environment while taking into account regulatory costs and other impediments to achieving our aspirations. It is no accident that Congress has steadfastly refused to adopt cost-benefit analysis and other analytical requirements as the litmus test for whether a regulation goes forward. Popularly elected legislators are reluctant to construct a regime that will force them to explain to their constituents that they are not entitled to be protected from injury and death because their lives are not worth enough money.

In the face of multiple failures to codify their preferred approaches, regulated industries and their conservative allies have not abandoned their crusade. Instead, they have moved it underground. Agencies are now required to undertake cost-benefit analysis and other related analyses of proposed and

---

3. Mark Seidenfeld, "A Table of Requirements for Federal Administrative Rulemaking," *Florida State Law Review* 27 (2000): 533, 536.

final regulations. Acting through executive order, the White House Office of Management and Budget's Office of Information and Regulatory Affairs (OIRA) maintains a stranglehold on agency efforts to implement health and safety laws, requiring extensive cost-benefit calculations to support affirmative proposals but neglecting such requirements when decisions are made to roll back existing standards.

Regulatory critics have argued for the use of these techniques as ways of making existing regulations work better. This argument ignores the fundamental value conflict between reviewing proposed regulations under a cost-benefit test and then basing regulations on statutory standards that expressly reject this approach. The use of these techniques invites regulators to smuggle into the deliberations economic considerations that are not permitted under the agency's statutory mandates. And, since this behavior is difficult to police, it invites regulators and their White House overseers to sabotage legislative goals without public knowledge or accountability.

Voluntary Programs

Love of the free market has increasingly led to efforts that rely on "voluntary" or "self-regulatory" programs for environmental protection. By definition, a voluntary system lacks the threat of sanctions for those firms that do not honor the commitments they have made. In theory, good corporate citizenship or a desire to garner favorable publicity as a socially concerned business can prompt corporations to engage in socially useful behavior. In practice, however, this theory has been consistently refuted.

For example, the Bush Administration's reliance on voluntary reductions in greenhouse gas emissions has proven to be a feeble and ineffective substitute for the imposition of mandatory limits on those responsible for the emissions. Relatively few firms have made commitments to reduce their emissions. Conservative claims regarding the efficacy of another voluntary program— the so-called "33/50" program, which involved corporate offers to decrease harmful hazardous air pollutants—are consistently refuted by evidence that reductions either did not occur or would have occurred anyway as a result of inevitable trends in manufacturing practices.

Voluntary programs of this sort must be distinguished from reductions produced by mandatory disclosure as a result of such programs as the Toxic Release Inventory (TRI). As we discussed in Chapter 11, TRI's track record shows that using public disclosure to give companies an incentive to control pollution, when combined with appropriate mandatory requirements, can achieve powerful results.

The Progressive Perspective

Regulatory effectiveness depends upon choosing the most effective tools for each program. Critics are quick to challenge traditional methods of regulation, but a close look at many of the alternatives they propose indicates that they will lower compliance costs by weakening regulatory protections rather than improving regulatory implementation.

In this arena, progressives focus first and foremost on when government failure is due to lack of resources rather than the erroneous choice of a regulatory method. The Bush Administration has established a type of catch-22 regarding agency resources. Starving agencies of needed funding guarantees that agencies fall short, often woefully short, of achieving the goals Congress has set for them. The Administration then contends that the government should adopt new, less-intrusive techniques to address the same problems without even considering closing the funding gap that undermined agency efforts in the first place. The inevitable result is weak government oversight of essentially voluntary programs, an outcome that financially rewards firms that do not make a concerted effort to fulfill their obligations.

Progressives support technology-based regulation because it has a proven track record of protecting people and the environment at a reasonable cost. Regulatory critics seek to deflect public attention from this record by advocating various forms of voluntary, or self-regulation. Progressives agree that alternatives to technology-based regulations may be more efficient in some circumstances, but we do not share the widespread enthusiasm that regulated entities and their political allies have for these voluntary methods.

With respect to those alternatives, progressives support substance bans, stringent liability, and, as a supplement to well-designed regulatory systems, information disclosure requirements. The track record of all these approaches shows that they can produce extensive success when implemented aggressively.

As for the premier market-based mechanism advocated by conservatives—allowing firms to trade allowances to pollute among themselves—progressives believe that, from an ethical perspective, there is a difference between having the government award polluters a legally sanctioned opportunity to pollute and having the government use its authority to impose limits on pollution. Trading conflicts with the moral precept that environmental quality belongs to the public and that it should not be for sale. Trading credits for money is premised on the notion that the government is not only entitled to place an economic value on the public interest in natural resources but that it remains free to sanction the buying and selling of those resources.

For the same reasons, trading contradicts the idea that we hold the Earth in trust for our children. Activists, particularly those attuned to the environmental-justice implications of trading, often protest such schemes on moral grounds and assert that trading marks a significantly worse approach to controlling pollution than traditional regulation. From this perspective, the government controlled by today's adults has no moral authority to sanction economic transactions involving compromises in environmental quality beyond our expected life span.

These ideas also apply to more traditional approaches of controlling pollution. In that context, we tolerate the degradation of nature, which appropriates our children's interest in environmental quality, either because we do not wish to pay to reduce pollution or because we have not been able to find a way to clean up our own mess. Still, the government's active participation in facilitating the buying and selling of such compromises can be viewed as a significant ethical departure from traditional regulation, which at least recognizes that pollution should be controlled rather than traded like any other commodity. For all of these reasons, progressives support emissions trading— but only if it is carefully tailored to meet ambitious pollution-reduction goals, avoid hot spots, and is subject to monitoring and reporting requirements that prevent abuses.

As for other market-based mechanisms progressives support information disclosure as a supplement to pollution controls and as a method of achieving government and corporate accountability. Progressives are skeptical about self-regulation unless the government closely supervises it. Government-mandated planning programs may be appropriate in circumstances where neither technology-based nor design standards are sufficiently effective to protect people and the environment, but this approach must be designed to ensure compliance, which requires prior approval of proposed plans and careful regulatory monitoring.

The Progressive Agenda

Resuscitate Government

The chronic underfunding of regulatory agencies at the federal, state, and local level has done more to undermine the progress we have made in cleaning up the environment than any other policy—and arguably more than the cumulative total of the deregulatory ideas criticized throughout this book. Just as police and firefighters are often immune from budget cuts at the local level, regulators charged with responsibility for protecting public health and the environment should be immune at the national level. If we are to consolidate the gains we have made and meet new challenges, the funding levels for regulatory functions at such agencies must increase exponentially, by at least two orders of magnitude.

Federal and state governments should start work immediately on achieving parity between the compensation offered technical experts in the public and private sectors. Only by stopping the devastating brain drain of qualified personnel can we hope to prepare the government to meet the substantial challenges still before us.

When compared to massive defense spending, the deep tax cuts sponsored by the Bush Administration, highway spending, and the inordinate subsidies provided to those who consume natural resources on public land, these increases are minor and well within reach for a country as wealthy as the United States.

Fund the Restoration of Government through Emissions Fees and Fee-for-Service Provisions

Pollution charges create better incentives for innovation than emissions-trading programs that give away credits to pollute. They also serve the purpose of funding the resuscitation of government. Federal and state legislatures should increase the use of emissions fees as supplements to more traditional forms of regulation.

Past experiments with this powerful tool have been very successful. For example, Congress imposed an escalating tax on CFCs and other ozone-depleting chemicals at the same time it adopted a phase-out of their production and use. The effect was immediately apparent. CFC production fell so fast that the tax raised only half of the $6 billion it had been expected to raise between 1990 and the end of 1995.[4] The desire to avoid the tax clearly provided incentives for the development of environmentally safer alternatives. There is no reason why Congress cannot replicate this approach in other areas.

To produce significant innovation by themselves, however, charges would have to be high. Such charges could play a role in restoring the fiscal solvency of a government damaged by tax cuts, mounting defense expenditures, and

---

4. Robert V. Percival, Christopher H. Schroeder, Alan S. Miller, and James P. Leape, *Environmental Regulation: Law, Science, and Policy* (New York: Aspen Publishers, 4th ed. 2003), 1053.

looming problems in funding Social Security and Medicare, although there would eventually be reduced funding if the fees created a significant incentive to reduce pollution or other undesirable behavior.

A variant on a pollution charge, the "feebate"[5] can maximize innovation. Under this approach, fees imposed on dirty technologies could subsidize new, clean technologies. For example, a person who purchases a high-polluting vehicle might pay fees, but a person who buys a "clean" vehicle would receive a rebate. It is possible to structure such schemes to produce a continuous race to improve environmental quality—something emissions trading is unable to do.

Finally, many states have experimented with "pay as you go" or "fee for service" provisions. These programs fund expansion of government staff by asking industry to pay more to support those who review and act upon such documents as permit applications and plans to clean up abandoned waste sites, making government operations at regulatory agencies self-supporting, rather than dependent on a share of general tax revenues.

Make Technology-based Requirements the Default Regulatory Approach

Technology-based regulation is the single, most effective approach to the control of pollution and other harmful activities that we have ever used, and should become the default for future efforts to address the unfinished agenda of remaining problems.

Impose Liability in the Right Circumstances

When effective environmental protection depends on the modification of behavior by thousands, and even millions of entities (e.g., everyone who generates and manages more than small quantities of hazardous waste), the imposition of stringent liability can create a powerful, highly effective incentive for such firms to police their own conduct. When appropriately structured, such programs also relieve government of the obligation to micromanage such activities, instead imposing that burden, along with the freedom to develop the best ways to shoulder it, on the industrial actors with direct control.

---

5. David M. Driesen, *The Economic Dynamics of Environmental Law* (2003), 151–61.

Streamline Pre-decisional Requirements

The executive branch, especially the White House Office of Management and Budget (OMB), must be held accountable for its use of pre-decisional techniques. Without adequate accountability, its reviews subvert legislative mandates without public awareness and inevitably lead to less protection than the agency's mandate justifies. In particular, OMB overseers should be required to provide a written justification whenever they block an agency's issuance of a proposed or final rule, and agencies should be required to include in regulatory preambles a description of any significant changes that resulted from executive branch oversight.

Agencies should not be burdened with so many duplicative obligations to analyze proposed and final regulations that the rulemaking process virtually grinds to a halt. The executive branch must streamline the number of analytical hurdles agencies are asked to overcome by systematically combing the essential elements of the most important requirements and eliminating all the others.

Abandon Cost-Benefit Analysis as a Regulatory Litmus Test

Cost-benefit analysis as it is practiced now must be abandoned immediately. The president should issue a new executive order to guide its oversight of regulatory proposals to make the oversight process completely transparent and accountable to the public.

Regulators and their executive branch overseers should rely on a qualitative process for evaluating the costs and benefits of regulation and reject dubious and immoral estimations of the value of saving lives and preserving the environment. Under existing approaches, many regulatory benefits are ignored because of the difficulty of quantifying them. A qualitative process would be appropriate given the difficulty of measuring regulatory benefits and the undesirable moral implications of doing so.

Congress should facilitate such review by eliminating the current multiple, overlapping requirements and substituting a review process similar to that required by the National Environmental Policy Act (NEPA). Before taking actions that could harm the environment, NEPA requires agencies to identify and disclose such potential impacts. Unlike current regulatory analysis requirements, however, NEPA requires multidisciplinary input, does not require cost-benefit analysis, and discourages monetization, even if a cost-benefit analysis has been prepared in which there are important qualitative considerations. Moreover, agencies are required to identify and disclose what information is incomplete or lacking.

Only Trade Fair

At the threshold, trading systems should do no harm to the overall condition of the ambient environment or to localized concentrations of pollution. In order to verify the absence of harm, we must understand—and continue to monitor—the conditions of the ambient environment that trading will affect. Trading should never be used as a method for addressing toxic pollutants.

All trading systems must be based on continuously declining caps on overall pollution, which produces added environmental and public health benefits. Regulators should not sanction so-called open-market trading without caps.

Schemes that allow trading must employ comprehensive ambient monitoring to ensure that pollution is not pooling around specific facilities located near population centers, especially when no underlying health-based standard is incorporated into a current site-specific permit. If monitoring detects a problem, regulators must have the authority to stop trading immediately until the hot spot is eliminated.

So-called "cross-pollutant" (one chemical for another) and "cross-media" (air emissions for water discharges) trades should not occur in the absence of reliable scientific evidence that they will not worsen environmental conditions or cause and exacerbate hot spot problems. These expansions of traditional trading can result in exchanges of markedly more benign chemicals for their far more toxic cousins as well as the substitution of poorly characterized pollution in one medium for pollution in a medium in which the effects are better understood.

Trading regimes must prohibit and punish sham trading, which deprives the public of the immediate benefits such programs promise. If credits are worth significant sums of money—and this outcome is a threshold premise of trading schemes—the failure to verify allocations and track trades not only discredits trading but directly rewards those guilty of the fraud.

Conclusion

Few issues are more important to the successful implementation of regulatory programs than the choice of which tool will most effectively reach the overall environmental protection goals mandated by Congress. While regulatory innovation is a useful goal, many market-based approaches, when poorly implemented, amount to deregulation.

CHAPTER 13

EMPOWER PEOPLE

Complexification and Democracy

As noted in Chapter 11, federal and state environmental laws provide ample opportunities for public involvement in regulatory decision-making, allowing ordinary citizens to make their views known from the earliest stages of the rulemaking process through the years it takes to accomplish judicial review. The states, given the responsibility for implementing these rules, have similar processes. But like so many other aspects of the law discussed here, the impression given by these statutory provisions is a far cry from the reality of their implementation. In all but a few instances, it is very difficult for the average citizen to penetrate the extraordinarily detailed theoretical and factual morass that surrounds the vast majority of regulatory decisions. Decisions typically grow more complex in direct proportion to the decision's importance from regulated industries' financial point of view.

Just as the complexity of the public policy-making process leaves citizens feeling bewildered and ineffectual, consumers also face a marketplace in which their choices have far-reaching but often poorly understood environmental and social implications. Maintaining personal standards of ethical consumption is a difficult, if not impossible task. Unfortunately, corporations and the government too often respond to rapidly increasing consumer demand for products made without pesticides or genetic engineering by companies that do not engage in unsustainable harvesting, animal cruelty, or sweatshop labor with efforts to suppress information about just such practices and just such companies.

Progressives believe that it is vitally important for the government to work to overcome these barriers to citizen investment in the protection of human health and the environment. This chapter will first consider impediments to citizen efforts to influence government decision-making and will then turn to the role consumers can play in motivating corporations to reduce the activities that threaten environmental harm.

Citizens and Their Government

Effective participation in regulatory decision-making requires extensive expertise in the scientific, technical, legal, and economic aspects of the matter as well as the time to master the copious information mustered by prospective targets of the decision. It can be a full-time job to sit in on meetings, hearings, and other fora where decisions are being made. While the country has a well-developed network of national, state, and local groups organized to represent the public interest during such proceedings, the demand drastically exceeds the supply of paid advocates, especially those with the requisite expertise.

In response, some stakeholders and political scientists have called for a return to "civic environmentalism," a term that means moving decision-making authority to the local level, where grassroots groups would collaborate to develop creative, consensus-based solutions to the problems that have stymied government.[1] Civic environmentalists are often aligned with local government officials who object to the so-called "one-size-fits-all" and "unfunded mandate" requirements imposed by the federal government. These distinct interests are supported, too often behind the scenes, by regulated industries seeking to lighten the financial burden of federal regulation. The unfortunate result of such opportunistic alliances is the further obfuscation of what is really at stake in redesigning the existing system to make it more democratic.

Correcting the grassroots imbalance to the point where the ideals of civic environmentalism can be realized will require two major achievements. First, we must simplify rules and the regulatory process. Second, we must provide sufficient resources to enable average citizens to participate meaningfully, with the understanding that people have many pressing demands on their lives that make it practically impossible for them to find the time and energy to participate in the lengthy proceedings designed to accommodate the demands of stakeholders who can afford to pay professional advocates. While we are optimistic that improvements can be made on both of these fronts, we are unlikely to ever see the day when regulatory decisions are sufficiently simple and

---

1. Three representative samples of this literature are DeWitt John, *Civic Environmentalism, Alternatives to Regulation in States and Communities* (1994); Charles Sabel et al., "Beyond Backyard Environmentalism, How Communities Are Quietly Refashioning Environmental Regulation," *Boston Review,* Oct./Nov. 1999; and Debra S. Knopman et al., "Civic Environmentalism: Tackling Tough Land-Use Problems with Innovative Governance," *Environment* 42 (1999): 24.

transparent that direct forms of citizen participation can supplant the government's role in protecting the public interest.

If the ideas put forward by civic environmentalists are taken to their logical conclusion and citizen participation is not heavily subsidized, the inevitable result will be drastically weakened environmental protection that places ill-equipped, underfunded state and local governments at the mercy of well-supported industry experts. Some problems—most notably, "transboundary" pollution that crosses state lines—would never be solved. Worst of all, it would take years for people to grasp what was really going on because populist rhetoric would continue to disguise the implications of such changes.

These issues raise three discrete questions: (1) What is government's role in protecting the environment? (2) Which level of government is best suited to make these decisions? (3) How should citizens be further empowered to ensure that decisions are made in the public interest?

The Government's Role

Robert Putnam's widely read book, *Bowling Alone: The Collapse and Revival of American Community*, renewed the national angst about the alienation of the common citizen from government.[2] We agree that, at an extreme, alienation in the form of failure to vote or join civic associations, could prove disastrous for democracy. However, while we appreciate Putnam's concern about rips in the social fabric, we also believe that his conclusions overlook hopeful evidence that civic engagement is as intense as ever and has merely changed form. More to the point, we reject the tendency in Putnam's book to blame most of government's failure to protect public health and common resources on citizen apathy and moral decay. Even when couched in the euphemistic rhetoric of civic environmentalism, this analysis is another manifestation of the blame-the-victim mentality discussed in Chapter 4.

While an allegedly apathetic citizenry may play some role in eroding environmental protection, there are far more important causes of government dysfunction. William Ruckelshaus, a Republican who twice served as administrator of the EPA—both times at especially perilous moments in its history—has described the agency as a victim in its own right, suffering from "battered agency" syndrome and slowly starving to death because its mandates

---

2. Robert Putnam, *Bowling Alone: The Collapse and Revival of American Community* (2000).

far exceed the resources provided by Congress.[3] Two decades of conservative assault on the value and integrity of government, constant battles with powerful regulated industries, and chronic budgetary shortfalls have come close to crippling the EPA's ability to aggressively protect the public interest; and its state counterparts are in a similarly compromised condition. Rather than delegating its remaining power and responsibilities to the states in a pseudo-populist fervor, we must restore government's role as the final arbiter of pollution controls.

Federal regulatory agencies are best viewed as the civil analogue of the police and law enforcement agencies that protect us from criminals at home and abroad, as opposed to neutral facilitators of battles between private-sector groups. In the past decade, as part of the conservative movement to degrade government's role in people's lives, the concept of customer service has been used to criticize federal agencies whose primary mission is regulatory. Customer service is an important emphasis for agencies such as the Social Security Administration, but in the regulatory context, it frequently takes on the insidious interpretation that agencies should mollify their most vociferous constituencies, particularly the entities whose activities are subject to their supervision. Instead, as we do with more traditional law enforcement, regulators must get the clear message from elected officials at all levels of government that their independence and integrity will be protected when they make tough, necessary choices to serve the public interest.

Environmental Federalism

One of the strongest and healthiest tensions in the U.S. Constitution is the compromise between those who wished to preserve the states' individual autonomy and those convinced that a strong central government was the best way to navigate an increasingly complex world. Political scientist Daniel Elazar points out that the word federalism is derived from the Latin *foedus,* meaning covenant, to emphasize the partnership between different levels of government, cooperative relationships that make the partnership real, and negotiations among the partners as the basis for sharing power.[4]

The Civil War settled the issue of whether the states had enough autonomy to desert the Union and reaffirmed Washington's importance as a centralizing

---

3. William D. Ruckelshaus, "Stopping the Pendulum," *Environmental Forum* (Nov./Dec. 1995): 25.

4. Daniel J. Elazar, "Cooperative Federalism," in *Competition among States and Local Governments, Efficiency and Equity in American Federalism* (Daphne A. Kenyon & John Kincaid eds., 1991), 69.

influence. But, until the New Deal, political scientists characterized the relationship between national, state, and local government as "dual federalism," meaning the three levels of government essentially ran their affairs on separate tracks with clearly delineated areas of responsibility. State and local government played a dominant role in this duality, shouldering exclusive responsibility for primary and secondary education, public higher education, public welfare, public hospitals, police, fire protection, and sanitation, while the federal government's domestic role was confined to areas such as antitrust, fair-trade practices, and the regulation of railroads and radio.

From the Great Depression through to the Great Society, the balance of power and resources gradually shifted 180 degrees. National institutions were created to govern everything from farm policy to higher education, from inner-city housing to social welfare programs, and from interstate highway systems to environmental protection. By the late 1950s, the federal government was spending more on domestic programs than state and local governments combined. The result—federal standard-setting supported by congressional largesse—was labeled "cooperative federalism." National programs addressed complex and intractable problems, and state officials were willing to share authority with the federal government, so long as the states received support for federal initiatives and federal politicians and bureaucrats took the flak for unpopular decisions.

In 1980, President Reagan came to Washington pledging to change government as we knew it. Reagan's "new federalist" agenda, which has been amplified and refined by the subsequent generation of conservatives, cut the size of the federal bureaucracy, lowered levels of federal aid to state and local governments, devolved responsibility for social programs to the states, and rolled back regulatory protections, especially in the environmental arena. By claiming to have the states' interest in gaining more authority at heart and by promising to dismantle the federal bureaucracies that had stolen that authority, new federalists achieve political cover for withdrawing large amounts of federal funding from state and local government and for rolling back regulations offensive to major industrial supporters.

The rhetoric of the new federalism continues to be attractive in policy-making circles. Unfortunately, many states have been unable to carry out the responsibilities the federal government has sent their way. Others have met these challenges, shouldering their new responsibilities with competence, even enthusiasm. The fact remains, however, that no one would seriously debate the fact that state performance is uneven—adequate, even excellent, in some cases but abysmal in others. Can we live with this result or should we return to a stronger role for the national government?

Five principles justify a stronger role for the federal government in environmental protection. The first is the difficult problem of trans-boundary pollution, for example, nitrogen oxide pollution in the Northeast caused by Midwestern power plants and water pollution in multi-jurisdictional waters such as the Great Lakes and Chesapeake Bay. Only a strong federal government can seize control of such situations and develop effective, enforceable strategies for resolving them.

The second, closely related justification for a strong federal role is the possibility that the states, especially in troubled economic times, will compete with each other for economic development and remove the regulatory burdens industry finds onerous. A nationally uniform regulatory framework forestalls the bartering over environmental protection that quickly erodes the public interest.

Conversely, uniform regulatory requirements make it far easier for national and multinational corporations to do business in many states. Industry discerns this self-interest in the context of rules such as product-labeling requirements, but it can become opportunistic and endorse devolution when a patchwork of regulatory programs really means far fewer regulatory controls.

In areas as complex and scientifically demanding as health and safety regulation, a strong national role in standard-setting and rulemaking is justified by the need to assemble the best and brightest experts the nation has available to undertake such work. It simply makes no sense from either a public interest or economic perspective to reinvent the rulemaking wheel 50 times.

Last but by no means least, federalism ensures the important value of affording Americans an equal and stable base of public health protection. In this, as in so many other areas of our daily lives, a drive across state lines should not mean a descent into substandard environmental conditions that place public health at risk.

Once the federal government designs the standards and requirements that control trans-boundary pollution, reduces risks to equivalent levels, and uses the best information and expertise available to find these elusive solutions, the states are left with the unenviable responsibility of implementing and enforcing these rules. They derive their authority to do this job from the EPA's delegation of federal authority, as defined by each major federal statute. In theory, the EPA oversees their efforts and stands ready to withdraw authority if a state's performance is below par. In practice, the agency has withdrawn, or threatened to withdraw, authority only a handful of times. In recent years, the underfunding of state agencies has become such a significant problem that states have actually begun to threaten to hand authority back.

While some of the states' complaints about unfunded mandates emanating from Washington are justified, these arguments break down quickly when one considers the substance of the mandate. Regardless of whether Congress funds a mandate that states provide safe drinking water to their citizens, the water must be clean. States that disagree with the federal government's approach to such work have ample opportunities, both formal and informal, to affect such decisions. Too often, conservatives who protest big government overlook such fundamental distinctions, arguing that any mandate that is not funded at the national level is by definition illegitimate.

The Organized Citizen

As noted earlier, federal environmental statutes provide citizens many opportunities for involvement in the rulemaking process, even if only organized public interest groups have the capacity to take full advantage of these statutory rights and procedures. Nevertheless, the contribution of citizen activists to the evolution of the law should not be underestimated. In the past 40 years, many landmark legal decisions were based on cases brought by public interest groups who stepped into the breach left by federal agencies that lacked the will to resist assaults by regulated industries. At the local level, citizen activists have played an equally important role by pursuing corporate violators and imposing penalties when government prosecutors did not do their job.

Recognizing the importance of these aspects of the current system, regulated industries and their conservative allies have sought to discredit citizen activists both inside and outside the judicial system. In a broader political context, they claim that national environmental and labor organizations are corrupt, pursuing the effete concerns of their liberal memberships in a manner that not only fails to represent the true public interest but that thwarts government's efforts to make economically sound decisions.

This assault on environmentalists and labor unions carries over to the courts in the form of challenges to public interest organizations' standing to bring lawsuits. At the risk of oversimplifying a complex area of legal doctrine, "standing" means that a person has a sufficient, concrete interest in the case before the court and, therefore, has the right to a hearing and a court decision on the merits of one's claim. Regulated industries, their conservative allies, and sympathetic government officials argue that private sector public interest organizations do not meet this threshold requirement, raising the bar to participation so high that such groups would routinely be thrown out of court. In one particularly extreme opinion by the 4th U.S. Circuit Court of Appeals, the nonprofit environmental group Friends of the Earth was thrown out of court because it could not show that specific chemicals discharged by a chronic violator of the Clean Water Act had actually infiltrated the water supply and caused harm to its members.[5] Meeting this high burden of proof would have required an extensive network of monitoring equipment beyond the ability of most citizen groups, much less the government, to provide. Fortunately, recent Supreme Court decisions have constrained the worst of these trends.

The Average Citizen

Many civic environmentalists envision a system where decisions about solving water-pollution problems would be delegated to a group of volunteers, loosely supervised by regulators, who were drawn from communities in a given watershed. The regulatory infrastructure would remain in place nominally, but such grassroots committees would have discretion to negotiate deals regarding the application of legal requirements. In their enthusiasm for this democratic renaissance, civic environmentalists rarely consider details such as the ground rules for running the committees, the government's role in ratifying their decisions, compensation of volunteers, or procuring independent technical support.

Many things are wrong with this picture, and they should all be obvious to even a casual student of political science. In the absence of ground rules establishing a balanced committee, paid participants from industry and government will tend to dominate the membership, proceedings, and outcomes of committees. Even if a certain number of seats are reserved for average citizens, they will inevitably be very difficult to fill given the lack of compensation for a citizen's time, the complexity of the issues at stake, and the likelihood that paid experts will overwhelm non-experts who disagree with them. Finally, unless panels are comprised of equal numbers representing the public interest and regulated industry or the government plays an active role in steering compliance with the law, a simple majority vote is likely to nullify proposals advocated by public interest representatives.

We certainly are not opposed to further grassroots involvement of citizens in government decisions that affect public health and environmental quality. To make such involvement anything other than a fruitless and disillusioning exercise, however, the inequities in expertise and compensation for time must be addressed. Such groups should not be expected to supplant the government's role in protecting the public interest and should only be tasked with

---

5. *Friends of the Earth v. Gaston Copper Recycling Corp.*, 179 F.3d 107 (4th Cir. 1999), *reversed* 204 F.3d 149 (4th Cir. 2000) (en banc).

making certain kinds of decisions against a backdrop of strong federal standard-setting.

More to the point, we question the civic environmentalists' implicit premise that the solution to the problems plaguing the existing system is to replace failing government with eclectic, ad hoc grassroots committees. This approach recalls Putnam's intense but myopic diagnosis that America is in trouble because we have allowed the social fabric to fray and that the solution to these ills is re-engagement of citizens from the bottom up.

In his book, *The Good Citizen: A History of American Civic Life*, political scientist Michael Schudson argues that it is both misleading and inappropriate to blame citizen apathy for the government's failures.[6] Schudson notes the trends toward internationalism in business, remarkable technological improvements that allow people to live and work longer and communicate faster than previous generations dreamed possible, and the challenges these developments pose to democracies, especially our own. These changes have inspired a rapid proliferation of specialization in human activity. Schudson invokes journalist Walter Lippmann's warning that if democracy requires "omnicompetence and omniscience from its citizens, it is a lost cause."[7] Rather than expecting people to be capable of mastering all the nuances of every policy that affects them, Schudson urges us to embrace the model of a "monitorial citizen," who is well-informed and watchful, expressing disagreement as necessary but relying on government to do the heavy lifting of protecting the public interest on a daily basis.[8]

Citizens as Consumers

Public participation in government decision-making holds government accountable and deters decisions biased in favor of regulated industries. In their role as consumers, citizens can have a similarly strong effect on motivating better corporate behavior. Before we explain the potential for change as a result of consumer behavior in the context of growing efforts to stymie such results, we need to put this idea in context with all the other reforms we advocate.

6. Michael Schudson, *The Good Citizen, A History of American Civic Life* (Third Printing, 2002).

7. Ibid., 310.

8. Ibid., 311.

The Limitations of a Consumers' Republic

Any doubts about the perceived importance of consumption in American life were laid to rest shortly after the terrorist attacks of Sept. 11, 2001, when Commerce Secretary Don Evans was quoted as saying, "People ask all the time, 'What can I do, what sacrifices can I make for my country?'" His answer: "Go back to the stores."[9] Although long present in political and popular discourse, the act of equating patriotism with consumption and public life with market life became unmistakably apparent in the wake of the World Trade Center and Pentagon disasters. At a time when many Americans were seeking a deeper understanding of their newly vulnerable world and most were longing for meaningful contact with their family, friends, or community, citizens were urged to resume the national pastime of shopping. On the airwaves and in the newspapers, consumer spending was presented as the primary, if not the exclusive, avenue for citizen participation in the nation's effort to recover from 9/11.

As we explained in Chapter 4, similar conflation of citizen values and market values appears in the work of would-be regulatory reformers who contend that the government, when setting environmental, health, and safety standards, should heed only the preferences individuals reveal when acting as consumers, laborers, or other private-market actors, as opposed to the values people express through speaking, lobbying, or other public activity. In a particularly dramatic illustration of this stance, the head of the Office of Information and Regulatory Affairs in the White House Office of Management and Budget suggested that even the value of liberty could be derived through revealed preference methodologies.[10] Thus, along with sneakers, swordfish, and the name of a newly discovered star, apparently even the Bill of Rights has a price in our current era of market fundamentalism.

Secretary Evans' effort to reduce public engagement to a duty of private consumption threatens to quell the very wellspring of ideas and beliefs upon which democracy depends. Equating public involvement with private consumption not only reflects a bankrupt vision of human nature and democratic governance, it also fails to measure up from the standpoint of effective public policy design. Put simply, we cannot buy our way into a better world, no matter how ethically or environmentally conscious we become as shoppers. Many, if not most, of the problems that plague our environment and our communities occur across a social dimension that, in turn, requires a deliberately social response.

---

9. Brandon Loomis, "Commerce Secretary Urges Shopping," *AP Online*, Nov. 19, 2001.

10. Edmund L. Andrews, "New Scale for Toting Up Lost Freedom vs. Security Would Measure in Dollars," *New York Times*, March 11, 2003, A13.

Despite the unavoidable limitations of a consumers' republic,[11] progressivism has strong historical connections to political activism within the private consumer marketplace. Indeed, according to Harvard University historian Lizabeth Cohen, the golden age of Progressivism in the United States during the early 20th century was ushered in by the demands of female consumers who had been excluded from conventional avenues of political influence.[12] Most prominently, the Consumers' White Label campaign, which the female-led National Consumers' League (NCL) employed to assure consumers that garments bearing its mark were "made under clean and healthful conditions" without the use of overtime or child labor, proved instrumental to the emerging labor-rights movement in the early 1900s.[13] By encouraging previously nonpolitical individuals to regard their behavior as both relevant and significant to issues of public policy, the campaign helped to generate a foundation of support for the NCL that ultimately enabled it to play a key role in the Progressive Era labor movement.

Sit-ins, boycotts, affirmative purchasing campaigns—so-called "buycotts"—and other episodes of commercial activism proved essential to the success of the civil rights movement throughout the 20th century. For instance, black leaders in Lynchburg, Virginia spearheaded an early boycott of segregated trolley cars by urging consumers to "touch the quick of the white man's pocket" by not riding, for "'[t]is there his conscience lies."[14] Indeed, Cohen explains, by the time President Kennedy introduced the legislation that became the Civil Rights Act of 1964, consumers in local communities from Newark to Birmingham had been waging a grassroots struggle in the consumer marketplace for two decades.[15]

Impediments to Progressive Consumerism

In light of market dominance of efforts to understand public policy formation and individual self-actualization, it is perhaps not surprising that two of the most galvanizing democratic events of the past decade concerned issues

---

11. Lizabeth Cohen, *A Consumers' Republic: The Politics of Mass Consumption in Postwar America* (2003).

12. Ibid.

13. Kathryn Kish Sklar, "The Consumers' White Label Campaign of the National Consumers' League, 1898–1918," in *Getting and Spending: European and American Consumer Societies in the Twentieth Century* (Susan Strasser et. al., eds., 1998), 18.

14. Cohen, *A Consumer's Republic,* 42.

15. Ibid., 188.

that touched individuals as consumers. The first was the Food and Drug Administration's (FDA) refusal to require mandatory labeling of food products containing genetically engineered ingredients. More than 500,000 people signed a letter of protest demanding that the agency reverse its position.[16] The second occurred when the U.S. Department of Agriculture (USDA) issued a proposed standard for labeling organic food that permitted genetically modified ingredients, sewage sludge fertilization, irradiation, and a host of other practices that have long been prohibited under established understandings of organic agriculture. The public outcry was swift and passionate: the USDA received more public comments on the proposed organic standard than on any rulemaking procedure in its history, more than one for every minute of the public comment period.[17] To the extent that any event qualifies as a "republican moment" in an era of mass cynicism regarding politics, these two examples are leading candidates.

Of course, these episodes also seem to illustrate a disturbing failure by the federal government to comprehend and respect the altruistic preferences of its citizens. On any fair assessment, the originally proposed federal organic standards were both an insult to organic food consumers and a transparent attempt to confer undeserved market advantages on biotechnology companies and other agribusiness interests whose products and practices could not reasonably be regarded as organic. Apparently not content with a mere failure to require mandatory labeling, the FDA also has issued a guidance document on voluntary labeling of nongenetically modified foods that seems specifically designed to discourage producers from engaging in any effort to inform consumers about their production processes. This latter action closely resembles an earlier effort by the FDA to discourage dairy producers from identifying milk products produced without the use of Monsanto Company's synthetic bovine growth hormone, despite strong consumer demand for such information (see case study, p. 190).

Compounding the impact of these administrative decisions, federal courts have crafted constitutional commercial-speech doctrine in a way that narrows the circumstances under which states may mandate or otherwise regulate corporate disclosure of "process information," such as the techniques used during a product's manufacture. And these efforts to discourage consumers from using the social or environmental consequences of production as a basis for

16. Lisa A. Tracy, "Does a GM Rose Still Smell as Sweet? Labeling of GM Organisms Under the Biosafety Protocol," *Buffalo Environmental Law Journal* 6 (1999): 129, 156.

17. USDA Secretary Dan Glickman, *Remarks on the Release of the Final National Organic Standards* (Dec. 20, 2000), http://www.ams.usda.gov/oldnop/glickremarks.htm.

purchasing decisions are not limited to U.S. courts and regulators. In the past decade, WTO member nations have debated a legal concept known as the "process-product distinction," which does not allow member nations to restrict importation of products based on the manner in which they were made, as opposed to the presence of some safety or physical characteristic of the end products themselves. This process-product distinction became well-known outside trade circles during the "tuna-dolphin dispute" that involved a U.S. ban on the importation of tuna harvested without the use of U.S.-prescribed dolphin-mortality reduction techniques. The ban was rejected as illegal under GATT, although the dispute panel simultaneously upheld a voluntary dolphin-safe tuna labeling program.

Free Speech or Deceptive Advertising?

Beyond limiting the information that is available to guide consumer purchasing decisions, manufacturers have also insisted that they have the right to refute charges made against them in the popular media regarding their use of unpopular, even immoral practices such as sweatshop employment. Confronted by reports of deplorable working conditions for young women in its factories in Southeast Asia, Nike, Inc. launched a well-funded public relations campaign that relied heavily on paid advertisements. A consumer activist brought suit under a California law allowing citizens to challenge deceptive advertising, charging that Nike's defense was riddled with false statements. Nike and its supporters, which included the National Association of Manufacturers and the U.S. Chamber of Commerce, argued that information concerning the social or environmental implications of production processes should be regarded as "free speech" entitled to the full protections of the First Amendment rather than commercial speech subject to federal and state prohibitions on unfair and deceptive advertising. Although the U.S. Supreme Court decided the case without deciding this question, these constitutional arguments are likely to be repeated by product manufacturers trying to avoid state regulation ensuring the accuracy of claims regarding the social and environmental effects of production.

In sharp contrast to this protection from regulation sought by product manufacturers but with the same ultimate goal, several states have adopted "food disparagement" statutes, also known as "veggie libel" laws, that subject people to liability for raising doubts about the safety of food products and agricultural production practices unless such doubts are supported by rigorous scientific evidence. These statutes, which were adopted in the 1990s at the behest of the agriculture industry after consumer concern regarding pesticide

The Battle over Consumer Access to Product-Related Information: A Case Study

In 1993, Monsanto Corporation began marketing a synthetic bovine growth hormone designed to boost the milk production of cows by mimicking the effects of natural bovine hormones. Posilac®, known generically as recombinant bovine somatotropin (rbST), is the first widely marketed agricultural product to be developed using genetic engineering technology, and the United States is the only industrialized nation in the world to have approved rbST for general commercial use. Despite congressional investigations, intense public criticism, and substantial internal dissent, the Food and Drug Administration (FDA) concluded that milk from rbST treated cows is essentially the same as milk from untreated cows. In addition, the FDA issued labeling guidelines that not only failed to require milk from rbST-treated cows to be labeled as such, but that cast doubt on the ability of other retailers to label their milk as being derived from non-treated cows. Producers choosing to so label their milk were told by the FDA to comply with strict record-keeping requirements and to include on all product packages a contextual disclaimer such as a statement that "no significant difference has been shown between milk derived from rbST-treated cows and non-rbST-treated cows."[18]

Shortly after FDA approval of rbST, the state of Vermont initiated a mandatory labeling program requiring that all state retailers disclose whether their dairy products were derived from rbST-treated cows. In accordance with the FDA interim guidelines, the Vermont regulations required inclusion of a disclaimer that "the [FDA] has determined that there is no significant difference between milk from treated and untreated cows."[19] In addition, however, the regulations also required notice that "[i]t is the law of Vermont that products made from the milk of rbST-treated cows be labeled to help consumers make informed shopping decisions."[20]

A consortium of dairy manufacturers and food retailers challenged the Vermont program, arguing that the labeling plan should be stopped immediately because a full trial would likely demonstrate that it violated the First Amendment.[21] The federal appeals court agreed, reasoning that because FDA believed

(Continued)

18. Department of Health and Human Services, Food and Drug Administration, *Notice, Interim Guidance on the Voluntary Labeling of Milk and Milk Products from Cows That Have Not Been Treated with Recombinant Bovine Somatotropin,* 59 Fed. Reg. 6279 (Feb. 10, 1994).

19. Vt. Stat. Ann. Tit. 6, § 2754(c) (repealed 1998); Adopted Rules: rBST Notification and Labeling Regulations Relating to Milk and Milk Products, Vt. Gov't Reg. § 3.1b (1995).

20. Ibid.

21. *International Dairy Foods Ass'n v. Amestoy,* 92 F.3d 67 (2d Cir. 1996).

The Battle over Consumer Access to Product-Related Information: *(Continued)*

that "neither consumers nor scientists can distinguish rbST-derived milk from milk produced by an untreated cow," the only remaining reason for the Vermont labeling rule was "mere consumer concern" about "production methods."[22] In the court's view, that interest was not sufficient to justify Vermont compelling dairy producers to speak against their will: "[C]onsumer curiosity alone is not a strong enough state interest to sustain the compulsion of even an accurate, factual statement."[23] The dissenting judge noted that Vermont consumers had supported the labeling statute out of concern for the implications of rbST for animal welfare, human health and safety, the economic viability of rural communities, and the role of biotechnology in the food supply. In the eyes of the majority, though, FDA's approval of rbST eliminated these areas as legitimate bases of concern for consumers.

Monsanto has also aggressively challenged even voluntary labeling of milk by individual producers who do not use rbST, claiming that any representation that milk is non-rbST is misleading to consumers unless accompanied by a statement that "[s]cientific studies conclude that the use of rbST to improve milk production does not change the nutrition, taste, quality, or any other health or safety characteristics of milk."[24] For instance, the state of Maine offers a Quality Trademark for Milk and Milk Products on a voluntary basis to Maine dairy producers that do not use rbST. Monsanto has claimed that this program constitutes misleading advertising and an unlawful restriction on market access, and is suing a leading Maine dairy over its failure to stop using the state labels, which read simply, "Our Farmers' Pledge: No Artificial Growth Hormones."

Despite this vigorous, ongoing campaign to prevent consumer awareness of rbST-treatment, sales of organically produced dairy items, which cannot be derived from rbST-treated cows under certification guidelines, grew by more than 500 percent during the 1990s, reaching a total of $600 million in the year 2000.[25] "Mere consumer concern" apparently is stronger than the federal appeals court was willing to acknowledge.

22. Ibid., 73, and n. 1.

23. Ibid., 74.

24. Monsanto Statement Regarding Oakhurst Dairy Inc. Filing, http://www.monsantodairy.com/updates/OakhurstDairyInc.Filing.html.

25. U.S. Department of Agriculture, Carolyn Dimitri & Catherine Greene, *Recent Growth Patterns in the U.S. Organic Foods Market,* Agriculture Information Bulletin Number 777, Sept. 2002, 2, http://www.ers.usda.gov/publications/aib777/aib777.pdf.

use in commercial apple production led to a decline in sales, impose no corresponding liability for people whose assurances of safety lack compelling evidentiary support. In combination, attempts to expand the constitutional rights of corporate advertisers and adoption of so-called veggie libel laws suggest a marketplace for products in which information regarding the social and environmental consequences of production is becoming comparatively prejudiced against disclosure, scrutiny, and criticism.

The Progressive Perspective

Progressives believe that we must put government regulatory agencies, as authorized by Congress, back in the driver's seat of prescribing rules to protect public health and safety. This fundamental goal can only be accomplished by restoring government's credibility and closing the yawning gap between public- and private-sector compensation so that the best experts available are once again drawn to government service.

Progressives reject the anemic conception of civic life underlying the view that consumption equals patriotism or that one's willingness to pay determines the value of liberty. These viewpoints ignore the fact that individuals fulfill multiple social roles with different accompanying values and priorities and that the diversity of these roles is critical to a well-functioning democracy. Individuals espouse different attitudes and beliefs depending on whether they are acting as citizens or as consumers. In the voting booth, individuals assume a more altruistic outlook, assessing choices and outcomes based on their significance to society as a whole, while in the marketplace individuals may act purely in their own self-interest. Consistent with that framework, our proposals to improve public input in the policy-making process are premised on a hope and belief that such improvements will provide a stronger voice for interests such as environmental preservation or improvements in public health—interests that are insufficiently protected by market dynamics alone.

The Progressive Agenda

Put Government Back in the Driver's Seat

Polling consistently shows that Americans want a strong, proactive system of public health and safety regulation, especially with regard to toxic chemicals and environmental quality. But the government, not regulated industries or average citizens, must shoulder the burden of figuring out how to get us there.

Resuscitate Environmental Federalism

With all its flaws and difficulties, the basic framework of dividing responsibilities among federal and state government is sound and, with sufficient funding and the right conception of government's role in safeguarding the public interest, the best approach we are likely to develop to get this important work done. However, in addition to all the other reforms we recommend throughout this text, the one change that is critical to restoring credibility to this federalist system is to put federal agencies in a position where they can exert effective oversight over underperforming states. This outcome will require a combination of increased funding for effective oversight and the political will to withdraw a state's authority to enforce federal law when the state's performance falls below par.

Increase Federal and State Budgets for Environmental Protection

As we explained in Chapter 12, the restoration of the EPA and its state sisters will require major staffing increases. Not only must the size of their professional staff increase, their breadth and depth of staff expertise must be strengthened. Fundamental reform of the civil service system to close the disgraceful gap between public- and private-sector pay scales is essential. Lastly, rather than being characterized as a necessary evil by the executive branch and elected officials, government service and government's role in protecting the public interest must once again be viewed as honorable and important.

Encourage Progressive Consumerism through Disclosure

Given the importance of information regarding the social and environmental consequences of production, federal and state governments must reverse the traditional presumption against mandatory disclosure of such information. Because process information is a *quid pro quo* for progressive consumerism, government has a crucial role to play in enabling citizens to satisfy preferences for ethical and sustainable production methods by requiring manufacturers to disclose such information.

Enforce Deceptive Advertising Laws

Given the vehemence with which they oppose mandatory disclosure of process information, it is not surprising that corporations have sought every avenue available to combat circulation of such information in the marketplace, even going so far as to assert their constitutional rights as "persons" to escape their longstanding obligation to remain truthful in their advertising. The prohibition on deceptive and unfair advertising is a cornerstone of American capitalism. Corporate claims that the First Amendment shields them from compliance with these provisions must be rejected by the courts.

Conclusion

Whether they act as citizens or as consumers, Americans have consistently supported protection of public health and the environment. Rather than moderating those concerns at the behest of corporate entities, government must instead renew its own commitment to act as chief caretaker for the public interest. Harnessing market forces should mean requiring the disclosure of information that allows consumers to act on their preferences, as opposed to leaving companies free to thwart those preferences by either keeping information secret or drowning it out in a barrage of false claims.

CHAPTER 14

VISION FOR A PROGRESSIVE FUTURE

The Government's Moral Role

Americans have always had a love-hate relationship with their government. We resent paying for it, we often demean it, and we unfailingly criticize it. However, we also rely on it. From road construction to providing for the common defense, we depend on our local, state, and federal government. We value our freedom and individual rights, and sometimes we see the government as a threat to that liberty—for reasons real and imagined. But most of us recognize that our world would be a far harsher place if government did not keep police on the beat, provide a safety net for the destitute, and work to eradicate disease.

In his seminal book, *Moral Politics: What Conservatives Know That Liberals Don't*, University of California at Berkeley linguistics professor George Lakoff wrote that the fundamental political differences between the right and the left stem from their polar views of government and what they hope it will accomplish.[1] Lakoff posits that the political right wing views government as a patriarchal father figure whose job it is to help citizens develop into self-reliant, upright people. The greatest threat to citizens is not the unmitigated harshness of economic forces but the decay induced by decades of reliance on the misguided and corrosive welfare state. Conversely, progressives believe that government's job is to serve as a nurturing and protective parent, shielding its citizens from the worst the economy and hostile social forces have to offer.

We agree with Lakoff that these fundamental fault lines are extraordinarily important to the development of public policy, especially with respect to issues that, at their roots, concern the government's appropriate role. We also

---

1. George Lakoff, *Moral Politics: What Conservatives Know That Liberals Don't* (Chicago: Univ of Chicago Press, 2nd ed, 2002).

agree that the foundation of these differences in diametrically opposed moral worldviews remains obscure in the increasingly agitated debate between conservatives and progressives. The failure to understand each other's beliefs as deriving from fundamentally different moral perspectives hastens the slide into *ad hominem* attack, spurious posturing, and a dangerous emphasis on public relations as the determinant of our most important political contests.

Accordingly, the primary goal of this book is to articulate a progressive vision of how government should act to protect human health and the environment. We do not flinch from advocating as much "big government" as necessary to protect the public's interest in life, liberty, and the pursuit of happiness and to mitigate the effects of an unbridled marketplace.

Environmental protection has undoubtedly remained a bedrock value for most Americans because environmental problems are an instance of people hurting other people as the inevitable byproduct of other socially useful activities. For the antiregulatory movement to survive, it must obscure this powerful image of the consequences of environmental problems. Regulated industries and their conservative allies have done so by attempting to shift responsibility for pollution from polluters to the victims of pollution. Our environmental laws do not sanction this shift; instead, they are built on the premise that polluters should be the ones to address the consequences of pollution. Those laws remain on the books, despite energetic efforts by special interests to undermine them.

Rather than balancing the supposed imperative of industrial activity and economic development against the option of protecting pollution victims, progressives believe that government must begin with the assumption that those who cause harm to others must be held responsible. In this moral vision, which pervades most other aspects of the nation's religious, cultural, and social affairs, industries that produce pollution or harvest natural resources must do whatever they reasonably can to avoid and prevent harm to public health and the environment. Progressives consider the costs of protection and our goal is to make sensible, pragmatic decisions, but we reject the morally unacceptable concept of suspending protection until the monetized value of human lives saved exceeds industry estimates of compliance costs.

Shifting responsibility from the victims of pollution back to the corporate actors that create such conditions will require fundamental changes in the way we conceive of environmental protection. Instead of putting the free market first, we must begin with the idea that risks must be prevented or reduced by those who cause the harm whenever possible.

Each preceding chapter encompasses the progressive view of government in the context of some of the most important environmental, health, and safety issues of the day. Whether the issue is industrial emissions of invisible but deadly chemicals or the private destruction of what should be public land, the warming of the planet or the systematic weakening of enforcement against the worst polluters, we have drawn a forward-looking picture of a government that steps between citizens and the worst effects of industrial activities. We repudiate the right-wing arguments that the free market will provide such protection and that people should have only as much protection as they are willing or able to purchase.

This chapter summarizes our most important recommendations on how to achieve the progressive vision, where government is not the enemy or a necessary evil but a powerful protector of public health and natural resources. These recommendations are designed to transform the role of government, beginning with federal agencies and departments such as the EPA, and the Departments of Interior, Energy, Justice, as well as their state and local counterparts. How would government look in the wake of these changes?

Independence and Autonomy

First and foremost, the federal agencies and departments must recover their orientation toward making public protection their paramount value. Rather than being subject to overbearing supervision by the White House at the behest of regulated industries, they would enjoy sufficient respect that their policy recommendations would be presumed valid, especially when such determinations are developed in the context of the extensive rulemaking procedures now required by the courts.

Adequate funding for EPA and other regulatory agencies is critical. They need sufficient resources to be able to resist industry's inevitable threat to challenge regulatory and enforcement decisions in court, if the agency does not succumb to lobbying pressure. At the moment, federal and state agencies are so underfunded that, even in the absence of political pressure from the executive branch, minor industry resistance sends them scurrying to find a compromise lest the entire enterprise fail. The commitment of full funding, which would cost a few billion dollars as opposed to the tens of billions or even hundreds of billions we spend on other, less important endeavors, is essential to stop the backsliding that undercuts protections in virtually every context.

One important purpose of restoring resources to environmental, health, and safety agencies should be to achieve parity between career regulators and their counterparts in the private sector. The constant revolving door between government and industry, especially with respect to mid-level technical experts, is enormously destructive to the government's independence.

Another crucial component of restoring this independence and autonomy is to defeat the campaign that undermines environmental mandates by charging that the agencies do not use "sound" science. This allegation, which has brought the regulatory process to its knees in far too many contexts, is little more than an effort to disguise regulated industries' self-serving resistance to effective regulation as the search for scientific truth. Waiting until all scientists are in absolute agreement regarding the source, mechanism, and cause of environmental illness and ecosystem disruption can only result in unprecedented and irrevocable loss of life, health, and natural resources.

Finally, we reject the insidious idea that regulatory agencies such as the EPA exist to serve their "customers." This approach is like saying that the police must be considerate of their criminal constituencies. Too often, this definition of government's role as provider of customer service is also cast in moral terms: Conservatives argue that corporations are the backbone of the American way of life. Casting them as polluters impugns their integrity and will weaken the economy. We do not agree that wanting environmental cops on the beat is equivalent to an attack on all corporations. As we have seen in the recent wave of corporate scandals involving Enron, Tyco, and WorldCom, we cannot achieve a sound economy without regulators to ensure open and fair competition. Neither can we achieve a society that respects the health and safety of citizens and the environment without supervision of the free market.

Setting an Affirmative Agenda for Action

Rather than engaging in a zero-sum game that grapples with statutory mandates only in response to court orders and compels every affirmative proposal to run the gauntlet of a withering array of analytical requirements, government should systematically evaluate the raft of environmental threats that remain unaddressed. Such problems include:

- Global climate change, produced by industrial activity, that threatens the viability of life on Earth within the next century;
- Ambient air pollutants, especially ozone, sulfur dioxide, nitrogen oxide, and fine particulate matter, that threaten health in every major U.S. city, and the growing list of hazardous air pollutants, such as volatile organic compounds, butadiene, and mercury;
- Grandfathered old dirties, especially power plants and manufacturing facilities that use toxic substances such as mercury, that have long outlived their useful lives;

- Water pollution, including nutrient loading produced by nonpoint sources such as factory farms and harmful pollutants discharged by factories and sewage treatment plants that will soon need expensive upgrades to maintain their structural integrity;
- Ocean pollution, exacerbated by algal blooms, or "red tides", and oil spills;
- Asbestos, lead in paint, mercury in consumer products, and other similar legacies of our historical ignorance that pose threats not only to consumers but to workers forced to handle such substances;
- Overfishing and fishery contamination, which threaten an invaluable component of the human food chain as well as the soundness of natural ecosystems;
- Water shortages, which could produce drastic shortages and widespread famine as soon as 2025; and
- Government subsidies that convey unwarranted windfalls to large corporations while destroying natural resources that developed over millions of years.

Doing the Best We Can

Resolving these problems will not only take more resources, it will compel us to choose the most effective regulatory tools. Many of the greatest successes modern environmental law has achieved in the past 30 years were produced by enforceable requirements that polluting industries do the best they can to prevent or reduce pollution by installing state-of-the-art control technologies. Such regulations are relatively easy for agencies to write and enforcement of technology requirements is straightforward and fair.

Conservatives and their allies in regulated industries have waged a long campaign against technology-based controls, arguing that they are economically inefficient because they require every pollution source to clean up to the same level, regardless of compliance costs. These arguments distort how technology-based controls operate. Instead of calculating the precise amount of pollution that is safe—a hopeless task in many contexts—technology-based controls give industry a pollution-reduction target based on available equipment and then allow companies to select the means for achieving these levels on their own.

Because they dislike technology-based regulation but acknowledge that some pollution problems must still be resolved, conservatives tout the benefits of market-based approaches that allow companies to trade rights to pollute among themselves. The one national experiment with such a "cap and trade" system was largely successful, but only because the substance at issue—sulfur dioxide—is acutely toxic only at relatively high levels. Regional experiments with more toxic chemicals have created hot spots that pose an excessive risk to low-income and minority communities. While trading is a promising alternative in carefully limited circumstances, it can never replace technology-based controls as the bedrock upon which our regulatory system stands.

Putting Safety First

Both in defining an agenda of unfinished business and in developing effective regulatory programs to prevent such hazards, government must put public health and safety first. Because conservatives believe that government's primary role is to ensure that citizens take responsibility for their own problems without expecting a "free lunch," they typically isolate regulatory compliance costs by offsetting them against such essentials as food, clothing, and shelter. This myopic view of accounting contends that excessive regulation will harm the poorest and weakest among us by depriving them of such fundamental needs.

From this fatally flawed premise, conservatives make one further jump: The only way to avoid excessive regulation and its unacceptable social costs is to wait until we are certain that (1) there is a problem; (2) we know its source; and (3) we have developed a cost-effective solution. This search for absolute certainty has delayed government intervention for decades, despite the fact that one would be hard pressed to identify a single environmental problem targeted by the existing regulatory system that has turned out to be less serious than we initially thought.

Progressives believe it is government's job to take precautions and move to nip problems in the bud. Streamlining the regulatory process and restoring independence and integrity to regulatory science are essential to achieving this goal.

The Right Tools

Enforcement

In addition to restoring their commitment to technology-based controls and faithfully executing the statutory mandates Congress gave them, government agencies must make a far more aggressive effort to enforce the law. To supplement these efforts, citizens should have open access to the courts to bring enforcement actions as citizen activists when government regulators are unwilling or unable to do the job.

Performance-based Regulation

We agree with many conservatives that there is great promise in establishing standards of performance and leaving the means used to achieve those goals up to individual polluting firms. Indeed, this is how technology-based controls work. Firms are rarely required to install specific equipment. Instead, they are required to achieve at least the amount of pollution prevention achieved by the best equipment on the market, using whatever methods they choose. Performance-based regulation must never be voluntary; it must always impose enforceable, verifiable goals; and it must punish those who fail to make the grade.

Liability

Imposing stringent liability for harmful conduct after the fact can be one way to achieve these results. The Superfund toxic waste cleanup program is among the strongest examples of incentive-based regulation in the world and has led to dramatic improvements in managing industrial waste.

Information Disclosure

Another extraordinarily effective tool is public disclosure of private-firm performance. By spotlighting the amount and implications of industrial emissions and discharges, public opinion inspires firms responsible for damage to improve their performance. For these reasons, we advocate the expansion of the Toxic Release Inventory and the application of the Freedom of Information Act to private-sector behavior that has a major adverse impact on the environment.

Government Freedom from Ossification

To select, design, implement, and enforce the right regulatory tools, the government must be liberated from the gauntlet of overlapping and onerous analytical requirements Congress passes in a futile and poorly understood effort to prevent excessive regulation.

Delivering Justice

In administering programs that, in essence, authorize polluters to cause harm, the government must establish as routine the consideration of whether the distribution of such burdens is even and fair. Too often, low-income and minority communities assume a grossly disproportionate share of environmental risk. And these risks too often escape recognition because we have only a fragile and tentative understanding of the cumulative and synergistic effects of common chemicals.

Ensuring justice requires more than just lip service to vague notions of equal distribution of the pollution burden. Since much regulation occurs plant-by-plant through the permitting system, government cannot hope to achieve a larger perspective on these issues unless it is compelled to ensure that state programs do not discriminate on the basis of race or income, without regard to whether such discrimination was intentional.

Burden-Shifting to Close the Information Gap

To close the wide gap between the little we know about toxic chemicals and their ever-increasing circulation in the environment, the government should take three steps: (1) increase public funding for research; (2) require toxic chemicals to be screened before they enter the marketplace; and (3) shift the burden on existing chemicals by presuming them to be harmful until or unless comprehensive testing exonerates them. As it copes with already existing hazards, government can only hope to get a grip on future hazards by shifting the burden to chemical producers to investigate the potential harm new products will cause.

Leading the International Community

The United States has become a rogue nation in the eyes of the world with respect to the global environment. Walking away from the Kyoto Protocol was a fateful mistake, as is our official opposition to including environmental protection provisions in trade agreements with other countries. It is now clear that global warming is a potentially catastrophic threat that we can no longer ignore; it threatens future generations, perhaps beginning with our own children. If we do not exercise global leadership, underdeveloped countries will not take steps to avert the disastrous course we are traveling.

Protecting Nature

In his recent book, *Plan B: Rescuing a Planet Under Stress and A Civilization in Trouble*, longtime environmental advocate Lester Brown reported that we began to consume more of the Earth's natural resources than we could possibly replenish at least two decades ago.[2] A major reason for this distressing state of affairs is the misguided insistence of conservatives that the plundering of public resources—forests, oceans, and other wild spaces—must be evaluated on the basis of the market value they supposedly would have if sold to the highest bidder. This approach cannot help but sabotage every effort we make to ensure sustainable development.

The United States has a long tradition of protecting public land and resources, and we must return to it. Some things are priceless and will never come back once they are gone, including ecosystem diversity, habitats, and the overall health of the planet.

The Good Citizen

Some have suggested that we return decision-making authority over environmental protection to the local level, where requirements can be tailored to the specific circumstances faced by individual communities. Such civic environmentalism is billed, paradoxically, as the best way to ensure that regulation does not waste money and as a long-overdue route to reviving grassroots democracy.

We share the average citizen's distaste for the overly complex, highly technical nature of modern environmental regulation. Complex problems can call for complex responses, however, and it is not possible to simplify many of the issues we face in a manner suitable for majority vote by citizens who now work harder, longer, and with much less leisure time than previous generations.

Our vision of what it takes to be a good citizen in a pluralistic, highly advanced society such as ours is that people must monitor government from some distance, intervening when it appears, as it does now, that government has gotten off track in carrying out the public's will. While we believe strongly in the power of citizens as consumers to act as a force for good, we also think that government must provide tools to make such choices in the first instance by, for example, requiring manufacturers to produce more-efficient cars and appliances.

Conclusion

Overall, the United States has the best and most ambitious system for protecting public health and the environment in the world. After three decades of intense effort, we know better now how to control pollution and preserve

---

2. Lester R. Brown, *Plan B: Rescuing a Planet Under Stress and a Civilization in Trouble* (New York: W.W. Norton & Company, 2003), 4, http://www.earth-policy.org/Books/PlanB_contents.htm.

natural resources. We have developed technologies capable of cleaning up past mistakes and preventing new ones. Scientific breakthroughs in our understanding of how to improve the quality of life and restore fragile ecosystems continue at an unprecedented pace. In addition, our citizens, especially young people, are conscious of an environmental ethic that provides strong support for the commitment to keep our countryside free, clean, and even wild.

Yet, as we have explained throughout this book, the government entities that preside over all this progress are weaker than they have ever been, and their energy for the challenges ahead, much less for the difficult task of maintaining past victories, is draining. Slowly but surely, these protections are eroding, with government shrinking to the point that the entire regulatory system is threatened with collapse. The debate has shifted from how we can do more to a rigid and misleading trade-off between a clean environment and a healthy economy. As they have for many years, the same special interests oppose government efforts to protect the environment. But they have grown far more adept at portraying these disputes as marginal, discrediting those who advocate tougher protections as environmental extremists, and using the leverage of campaign contributions and an endless supply of ostensibly qualified experts to stop regulators in their tracks.

This right-wing campaign now has unprecedented traction, largely because it is conducted out of the public view. It may be years until visible pollution returns to a degree that the average American notices it. Even where the results of government failure are painfully obvious—such as when cities issue boil-water warnings to the elderly, families with young children, and the chronically ill—the public has great difficulty discerning the root cause. The efforts to obscure what is happening by making the debate mind-numbingly technical and pushing controversy below the public consciousness have also discouraged public interest groups, which are increasingly at a loss to reverse what seems to be the irrevocable subversion of the regulatory state.

Battles against further erosion of our country's commitment to the environment, health and safety must continue every day, and must always be fought on the battleground of what is politically feasible. At the same time, it is essential to be reminded of what our progressive goals are. We firmly believe that the vision we have constructed in the preceding pages will itself regain a firm hold on the politically feasible before we lose too much more precious ground.

The progress that we have made under the landmark health and environmental laws of the 1970s is a reassuring reminder of the capacity of this nation to accomplish great things, despite intense resistance by entrenched economic interests, when we set ourselves firmly to the task. It is time for a renewed commitment to our children, our country and our world to do the best we can with existing tools and fresh progressive approaches to preserve and protect our precious natural resources and our priceless public health.

Sources and Suggestions for Further Reading from CPR Member Scholars

Frank Ackerman

Frank Ackerman and Lisa Heinzerling, Priceless: On Knowing the Price of Everything and the Value of Nothing (2004).

Frank Ackerman & Alejandro Nadal, The Flawed Foundations of General Equilibrium: Critical Essays on Economic Theory (forthcoming late 2004).

Frank Ackerman, Why Do We Recycle? Markets, Values, and Public Policy (1997).

Frank Ackerman & Lisa Heinzerling, *Pricing the Priceless: Cost-Benefit Analysis of Environmental Protection,* 150 U. Pa. L. Rev. 1553 (2002), *reprinted in* Land Use & Envtl. L. Rev. (2003).

Frank Ackerman & Lisa Heinzerling, *The Humbugs of the Anti-Regulatory Movement,* 87 Cornell L. Rev. 648 (2002).

David E. Adelman

David E. Adelman, *Lost in Transcience: The Promise of the Genomics Revolution for Environmental Law* (forthcoming).

David E. Adelman, *Scientific Activism and Restraint: The Interplay of Statistics, Judgment, and Procedure in Environmental Law,* 79 Notre Dame L. Rev. 101 (2004).

David E. Adelman, *Harmonizing Methods of Scientific Interference with the Precautionary Principle: Opportunities and Constraints,* 34 Envtl. L. Rptr. 10131 (2004).

David E. Adelman & John H. Barton, *Environmental Regulation for Agriculture*, 21 Stan. Envtl. L.J. 3 (2002).

Robert W. Adler

Robert W. Adler, *The Supreme Court and Ecosystems: Environmental Science in Environmental Law*, 27 Vt. L. Rev. 249 (2003).

Robert W. Adler, *The Two Lost Books in the Water Quality Trilogy: The Elusive Objectives of Physical and Biological Integrity*, 33 Envtl. L. 29 (2003).

Robert W. Adler & Michele Straube, *Watersheds and the Integration of U.S. Water Law and Policy: Bridging the Great Divides*, 25 Wm. & Mary Envtl. L. & Pol'y Rev. 1 (2000).

Robert W. Adler, *Integrated Approaches to the Water Quality Problem: Lessons from the Clean Air Act*, 23 Harv. Envtl. L. Rev. 203 (1999).

Robert W. Adler & Charles Lord, *Environmental Crimes: Raising the Stakes*, 59 Geo. Wash. L. Rev. 781 (1991).

Richard N.L. Andrews

Richard N.L. Andrews, *NEPA in Practice: Environmental Policy or Administrative Reform?*, 6 Envtl. L. Rptr. 50001 (1976).

Richard N.L. Andrews, *Cost-Benefit Analysis as Regulatory Reform*, in Cost-Benefit Analysis and Environmental Regulations: Politics, Ethics, and Methods, (Daniel Swartzman, Richard Liroff, and Kenneth Croke, eds., Washington, DC: The Conservation Foundation, 1982).

Richard N.L. Andrews, *Environmental Regulation and Business "Self-Regulation,"* 31 Policy Sciences 177-97 (1998).

Richard N.L. Andrews, Managing the Environment, Managing Ourselves: A History of American Environmental Policy (New Haven: Yale University Press, 1999).

Richard N.L. Andrews, et al., *Environmental Management Systems: History, Theory, and Implementation Research*, in Regulating from the Inside: Can Environmental Management Systems Achieve Policy Goals?, (Cary Coglianese and Jennifer Nash, eds., Washington, DC: Resources for the Future Press, 2001).

John Applegate

The International Library of Essays in Environmental Law: Environmental Risk (John S. Applegate ed., Ashgate 2004).

John S. Applegate, *The Taming of the Precautionary Principle*, 27 Wm. & M. Envtl. L. & Policy Rev. 13 (2002).

John S. Applegate, *The Prometheus Principle: Using the Precautionary Principle to Harmonize the Regulation of Genetically Modified Organisms*, 9 Ind. J. Global Legal Studies 207 (2001).

John S. Applegate, *The Precautionary Preference: An American Perspective on the Precautionary Principle*, 6:3 Human & Ecological Risk Assessment 413 (2000).

John S. Applegate & Celia Campbell-Mohn, *Learning from NEPA: Some Guidelines for Responsible Federal Risk Legislation*, 23 Harv. Envtl. L. Rev. 93 (1999).

William W. Buzbee

Robert A. Schapiro & William W. Buzbee, *Unidimensional Federalism: Power and Perspective in Commerce Clause Litigation*, 88 Cornell L. Rev. 1199 (2003).

William W. Buzbee, *Recognizing the Regulatory Commons: A Theory of Regulatory Gaps*, 89 Iowa L. Rev. 1 (2003).

William W. Buzbee, *Standing and the Statutory Universe*, 11 Duke Envtl. L. & Pol'y F. 247 (2001).

William W. Buzbee, *Urban Sprawl, Federalism, and the Problem of Institutional Complexity*, 68 Fordham L. Rev. 57 (1999).

William W. Buzbee, *Regulatory Reform or Statutory Muddle: The "Legislative Mirage" of Single Statute Regulatory Reform*, 5 N.Y.U. Envtl. L. J. 298 (1996).

Holly Doremus

Holly Doremus, *The Purposes, Functions, and Future of the Endangered Species Act's Best Available Science Mandate*, Envtl. L. (forthcoming 2004).

Holly Doremus, *Shaping the Future: The Dialectic of Law and Environmental Values*, 37 U.C. Davis L. Rev. 233 (2003), 27 Environs Envtl. L. & Pol'y J. 233 (2003), *reprinted in* The Jurisdynamics of Environmental Protection: Change and the Pragmatic Voice in Environmental Law (Jim Chen ed., 2003).

Holly Doremus, *Constitutive Law and Environmental Policy*, 22 Stan. Envtl. L. J. 295 (2003).

Holly Doremus, *Adaptive Management, the Endangered Species Act, and the Institutional Challenges of "New Age" Environmental Protection*, 41 WASHBURN L. J. 50 (2001).

Holly Doremus, *Listing Decisions Under the Endangered Species Act: Why Better Science Isn't Always Better Policy*, 75 WASH. U. L.Q.1029 (1997), *reprinted in* 30 LAND USE & ENVT L. REV. [GGS1](1999).

David Driesen

DAVID DRIESEN, THE ECONOMIC DYNAMICS OF ENVIRONMENTAL LAW (2003).

David Driesen, *What is Free Trade?: The Real Issue Lurking Behind the Trade and Environment Debate*, 41 VA. J. INT'L L. 279 (2001).

David Driesen, *Getting Our Priorities Straight: One Strand of the Regulatory Reform Debate*, 31 ENVT'L L. REP. 10003 (2001).

David Driesen, *Is Emissions Trading an Economic Incentive Program?: Replacing the Command and Control/Economic Incentive Dichotomy*, 55 WASH. & LEE L. REV. 289 (1998).

David Driesen, *The Societal Cost of Environmental Regulation: Beyond Administrative Cost-Benefit Analysis*, 24 ECOLOGY L.Q. 545 (1997).

Alyson Flournoy

Alyson Flournoy, *In Search of an Environmental Ethic*, 28 COLUM J. ENVTL. L. 64 (2003).

Alyson Flournoy, *Restoration Rx: An Evaluation and Prescription*, 42 ARIZ. L. REV. 187 (2000).

Alyson Flournoy, *Preserving Dynamic Systems: Wetlands, Ecology and Law*, 7 DUKE ENVTL. L. & POL'Y F. 105 (1997).

Alyson Flournoy, *Coping with Complexity*, 27 LOY. L.A. L. REV. 809 (1994).

Alyson Flournoy, *Beyond the Spotted Owl Problem: Learning from the Old-Growth Controversy*, 17 HARV. ENVTL. L. REV. 261 (1993).

Sheila Foster

Sheila Foster, *From Harlem to Havana: Sustainable Urban Development*, 16 TUL. ENVTL. L.J. 783 (2003).

Ari Afilalo & Sheila Foster, *The World Trade Organization's Anti-Discrimination Jurisprudence: Free Trade, National Sovereignty and Environmental Health in the Balance* , 15 GEO. INT'L ENVTL. L. REV. 633 (2003).

Sheila Foster, *Environmental Justice in an Era of Devolved Collaboration*, 26 HARV. ENVTL. L. REV. 459 (2002).

SHEILA FOSTER & LUKE COLE, FROM THE GROUND UP: ENVIRONMENTAL RACISM AND THE RISE OF THE ENVIRONMENTAL JUSTICE MOVEMENT (2001).

Sheila Foster, *Justice From the Ground Up: Distributive Inequities, Grassroots Resistance and the Transformative Politics of the Environmental Justice Movement*, 86 CAL. L. REV. 775 (1998).

William Funk

William Funk, The *Court, the Clean Water Act, and the Constitution: SWANCC and Beyond*, 31 ENVTL. L. REP. 10741 (July 2001).

Eileen Gauna

EILEEN GAUNA & CLIFF RECHTSCHAFFEN, ENVIRONMENTAL JUSTICE: LAW, POLICY AND ENVIRONMENTAL PROTECTION (2002).

Eileen Gauna, *An Essay on Environmental Justice: The Past, the Present, and Back to the Future*, 42 NAT. RESOURCES J. 701 (2002).

Eileen Gauna, *EPA at Thirty: Fairness in Environmental Protection*, 31 ENVTL. L. REP. 10528 (2001).

Eileen Gauna, *The Environmental Justice Misfit: Public Participation and the Paradigm Paradox*, 17 STAN. ENVTL. L.J. 3 (1998).

Eileen Gauna, *Major Sources of Criteria Pollutants in Nonattainment Areas: Balancing the Goals of Clean Air, Industrial Development, and Environmental Justice*, 3 HASTINGS W.-Nw. J. ENVTL. L. & POL'Y 379 (1996).

Robert L. Glicksman

Christopher H. Schroeder & Robert L. Glicksman, *Chevron, State Farm, and the EPA in the Courts of Appeals During the 1990s*, 31 ENVTL. L. REP. 10371 (2001), *reprinted in* 32 LAND USE & ENV'T L. REV. 327 (2002).

Stephen R. McAllister & Robert L. Glicksman, *Federal Environmental Law in the "New" Federalism Era*, 30 ENVTL. L. REP. 11122 (2000).

Robert L. Glicksman & Stephen B. Chapman, *Regulatory Reform and (Breach of) the Contract With America: Improving Environmental Policy or Destroying Environmental Protection?*, 5 KAN. J. L. & PUB. POL'Y 9 (1996).

Robert L. Glicksman & Christopher H. Schroeder, *EPA and the Courts: Twenty Years of Law and Politics,* 54 LAW & CONTEMP. PROBS. 249 (1991), *reprinted in* 24 LAND USE & ENV'T L. REV. 289 (1993).

Sidney A. Shapiro & Robert L. Glicksman, *Congress, the Supreme Court, and the Quiet Revolution in Administrative Law,* 1988 DUKE L.J. 819 (1988).

Lisa Heinzerling

Lisa Heinzerling & Rena Steinzor, *A Perfect Storm: Mercury and the Bush Administration,* 34 ENVTL. L. REP. 10297 (2004) (Part I) and 34 ENVTL. L. REP. 10485 (2004) (Part II).

Lisa Heinzerling, *Five-Hundred Life-Saving Interventions and Their Misuse in the Debate Over Regulatory Reform,* 13 RISK 151 (2002).

Lisa Heinzerling, *The Rights of Statistical People,* 24 HARV. ENVTL. L. REV. 189 (2000).

Lisa Heinzerling, *Environmental Law and the Present Future,* 87 GEO. L.J. 2205 (1999).

Lisa Heinzerling, *Regulatory Costs of Mythic Proportions,* 107 YALE L.J. 1981 (1998).

Donald T. Hornstein

Donald T. Hornstein, *From Metaphor to Mechanism: Adaptive Governance, Complexity Theory, and the Evolution of Policy,* ___ DUKE L.J. ___ (forthcoming 2004).

Donald T. Hornstein, *Accounting for Science: The Independence of Public Research in the New Subterranean Administrative Law,* 66 LAW & CONTEMP. PROBS 227 (2003).

Donald T. Hornstein, *From Beef to Bove: Are Cultural Preferences in International Trade Legitimate?, in* GLOBAL VIEW (UNC University Center for International Studies ed., Spring 2001).

Douglas A. Kysar

Douglas A. Kysar, *The Expectations of Consumers,* 103 COLUM. L. REV. 1700 (2003).

Douglas A. Kysar, *Some Realism About Environmental Skepticism,* 30 ECOL. L.Q. 223 (2003).

Douglas A. Kysar, *Law, Environment, and Vision*, 97 Nw. U. L. Rev. 675 (2003).

Douglas A. Kysar, *Sustainability, Distribution, and the Macroeconomic Analysis of Law*, 43 B.C. L. Rev. 1 (2001).

Jon D. Hanson & Douglas A. Kysar, *Taking Behavioralism Seriously: Some Evidence of Market Manipulation*, 112 Harv. L. Rev. 1420 (1999).

Thomas O. McGarity

Thomas O. McGarity, *Some Thoughts on Deossifying the Rulemaking Process*, 41 Duke L. J. 1385 (1992).

Thomas O. McGarity, *A Cost-Benefit State*, 50 Admin. L. Rev. 7 (1998).

Sidney A. Shapiro & Thomas O. McGarity, *Not So Paradoxical: The Rationale for Technology-Based Regulation*, 1991 Duke L. J. 729 (1991).

Thomas O. McGarity, *Substantive and Procedural Discretion in Administrative Resolution of Science Policy Questions: Regulating Carcinogens in EPA and OSHA*, 67 Geo. L.J. 729 (1979).

Thomas O. McGarity, *Politics by Other Means: Law, Science, and Policy in EPA's Implementation of the Food Quality Protection Act*, 53 Admin. L. Rev. 103 (2001).

Joel Mintz

Joel Mintz, *Some Thoughts On the Merits of Pragmatism As A Guide for Environmental Protection*, 31 B.C. Envtl. Aff. L. Rev. 1 (2004).

Joel Mintz, *Enforcement Overfiling In the Federal Courts: Some Thoughts on the Post-Harmon Cases*, 21 Va. Envtl. L.J. 425 (2003).

Joel Mintz, *Time To Walk The Walk: U.S. Hazardous Waste Management and Sustainable Development*, 32 Envtl. L. Rpt. 10307 (2002).

Joel Mintz, *Two Cheers For Global POPs: A Summary and Assessment of the Stockholm Convention on Persistent Organic Pollutants*, 14 Geo. Int'l L. Rev. 319 (2001).

Joel Mintz, *Economic Reform of Environmental Protection: A Brief Comment on a Recent Debate*, 15 Harv. Envtl. L. Rev. 149 (1991).

Cliff Rechtschaffen

Cliff Rechtschaffen & Dave Markell, Reinventing Environmental Enforcement and the State/Federal Relationship (2003).

Cliff Rechtschaffen, *Deterrence vs. Cooperation and the Evolving Theory of Environmental Enforcement*, 71 S. CAL. L. REV. 1182 (1998).

Cliff Rechtschaffen, *The Warning Game: Evaluating Warnings Under California's Proposition 65*, 23 ECOLOGY L.Q. 303 (1996).

Christopher H. Schroeder

PERCIVAL, SCHROEDER, MILLER AND LEAPE, ENVIRONMENTAL REGULATION: LAW, SCIENCE AND POLICY (4th ed. 2003).

Christopher H. Schroeder, *Environmental Law, Congress and the Court's New Federalism Doctrine*, 78 IND. L. REV. 413 (2003).

Christopher H. Schroeder, *Lost in the Translation: What Environmental Regulation Does That Tort Cannot Duplicate*, 41 WASHBURN L.J. 583 (2002).

Christopher H. Schroeder, *Third Way Environmentalism*, 48 KAN. L. REV. 801 (2000).

Sidney Shapiro

DAVID BOLLIER, THOMAS McGARITY & SIDNEY SHAPIRO, SOPHISTICATED SABOTAGE: THE INTELLECTUAL GAMES THAT INDUSTRIES PLAY TO SUBVERT RESPONSIBLE REGULATION (2004).

Sidney Shapiro, *The Information Quality Act and Environmental Protection: The Perils of Reform By Appropriations Rider*, 28 WM. & MARY ENV. L. & POL'Y REV. 339 (2004).

SIDNEY SHAPIRO & ROBERT GLICKSMAN, RISK REGULATION AT RISK: RESTORING A PRAGMATIC APPROACH (2003).

Sidney Shapiro & Robert L. Glicksman, *Goals, Instruments, and Environmental Policy Choice*, 10 DUKE ENVTL. L. & POL'Y F. 297 (2001).

Sidney Shapiro, *Administrative Law After the Counter-Reformation: Restoring Faith in Pragmatic Government*, 48 KAN. L. REV. 689 (2000).

Rena Steinzor

Rena Steinzor, *"Democracy Dies Behind Close Doors:" The Homeland Security Act and Corporate Accountability*, 12 KAN. J. L. & PUB. POL'Y 641 (2003).

Rena Steinzor, *Toward Better Bubbles and Future Lives: A Progressive Response to the Conservative Agenda for Reforming Environmental Law*, 32 ENVTL. L. REP. 11421 (2002).

Rena Steinzor & Linda Greer, *Bad Science*, ENVTL. F. 28 (2002).

Rena Steinzor, *EPA and Its Sisters at Thirty: Devolution Revolution, or Reform?*, 31 ENVTL. L. REP. 11086 (2001).

Rena Steinzor, *Reinventing Environmental Regulation: The Dangerous Journey from Command to Self-control*, 22 HARV. ENVTL. L. REV. 103 (1998).

Robert Verchick

Robert Verchick, *Steinbeck's Holism: Science, Literature, and Environmental Law*, 22 STAN. ENVTL. L.J. 1 (2003).

Robert Verchick, *Feathers or Gold? A Civic Economics for Environmental Law*, 25 HARV. ENVTL. L. REV. 95 (2001).

Robert Verchick, *The Commerce Clause, Environmental Justice, and the Interstate Garbage Wars*, 70 S. CAL. L. REV. 1239 (1997).

Robert Verchick, *In a Greener Voice: Feminist Theory and Environmental Justice*, 19 HARV. WOMEN'S L.J. 23 (1996).

David Vladeck

David Vladeck, *Lessons From A Story Untold: Nike v. Kasky Reconsidered*, 54 CASE W. RES. L. REV. __ (forthcoming 2004).

David Vladeck & Alan B. Morrison, *The Roles, Rights and Responsibilities of the Executive Branch of the Federal Government under the Rehnquist Court*, in THE REHNQUIST COURT (Herman Schwartz ed., 2002).

David Vladeck, *Defending Courts: A Brief Rejoinder to Professors Rosenberg and Fried*, 31 SETON HALL L. REV. 631 (2001).

David Vladeck, *Hard Choices: Thoughts for New Lawyers*, 10 KAN. J.L. & PUB. POL'Y 349 (2001).

David Vladeck, *Devaluating Truth: Unverified Health Claims in the Aftermath of Pearson v. Shalala*, 54 FOOD DRUG L.J. 535 (1999).

Wendy Wagner

Wendy Wagner, *Commons Ignorance: How the Environmental Laws Have Failed Us*, 2004 DUKE L. REV. __ (forthcoming 2004).

Wendy Wagner & David Michaels, *Equal Treatment for Regulatory Science: Extending the Controls Governing the Quality of Public Research to Private Research*, __ AM. J. L. & MED. __ (forthcoming 2004).

Wendy Wagner, *Sabotaging Science: The Use of Adversarial and Political Processes to Determine Scientific Quality*, __ AM. J. PUB. HEALTH __ (forthcoming 2003).

Wendy Wagner, *The Triumph of Technology-Based Standards*, 2000 U. ILL. L. REV. 83 (2000).

Wendy Wagner, *The Science Charade in Toxic Risk Regulation*, 95 COLUM. L. REV. 1613 (1995).

David Wirth

David Wirth, *The President, the Environment, and Foreign Policy: The Globalization of Environmental Politics*, __ UTAH J. ENERGY, NAT'L RESOURCES & ENVTL. L. __ (forthcoming 2004).

David Wirth, *Precaution in International Environmental Policy and United States Law and Practice*, 10 N. AM. ENVTL. L. & POL'Y 219 (2003).

David Wirth, *Globalizing the Environment*, 22 WM. & MARY ENVTL. L. & POL'Y REV. 353 (1998), *reprinted in* BEYOND SOVEREIGNTY 198 (Maryann K. Cusimano ed., 2000).

David Wirth, *International Trade Agreements: Vehicles for Regulatory Reform?*, 1997 U. CHI. LEGAL F. 331 (1997).

David Wirth, *Public Participation in International Processes: Environmental Case Studies at the National and International Levels*, 7 COLO. J. INT'L ENVTL. L. & POL'Y 1 (1996).

INDEX